Object Oriented Design
Interview

Desmond Zhou | Fawaz Bokhari | Alex Xu

Object-Oriented Design Interview

Other Books By ByteByteGo

The following books are available in paperback on Amazon:

Acknowledgment

This book has been created with significant input and reviews from several dozen engineers and managers. Thank you all, so much: Victor Anya, Mouatassem Ben, Ashish Bhandari, Vineet Bhatkoti, Kundana C, Frank Chan, Kashish Chanana, Tony Chang, Parth Chaturvedi, Rajeev Das, Udy Dhansingh, Aman Gaur, Jason Guan, Ibrahim Elsawaf, Björn Holtvogt, Steve Huynh, Nate Kidwell, Kasturi Krishnamachari, Ajay Kumar, Công Pha Lê, Debanjan Mahata, Karthiek Naagaraj, Faidh Naife, Ben Nelson, Armin Norouzi, Parvathi Pai, Dhawal Patil, Qingchuan, Kapila Raghubanshi, Sakthignanavel Rajendran, Ali Ramazon, Sonam Ramchand, Sakthignanavel Rajendran, Sachin, Irina Saiz, Piyush Sharma, Gurpreet Singh, Kapila Raghubanshi, Saurabh Rai, Anurag Rao, Manoj C Rao, Varun Rawat, Dileep Reddy, Sahad S., Aayush Kumar Singha, Narasinga Rao Tamminana, Bharat Tiwary, Ibrahim Wynters, Ling Xie, Mingyang Zhang, Jintao Zhang, Chenyan Zhou, Quan Zhou, and Jingjing Zhu.

Contents

What is an Object-Oriented Design (OOD) Interview?

Object-oriented design interviews have become increasingly popular in technical hiring. This shift reflects companies' growing emphasis on skills that align with real-world software development. OOD interviews are important at companies like Amazon, Bloomberg, and Uber, serving as a practical coding exercise. These interviews test your ability to build logical, maintainable systems and gauge how effectively you apply object-oriented design principles and patterns.

Unlike algorithm interviews, which demand a single, optimal solution, OOD interviews leave space for creativity. There's no one-size-fits-all answer, as various approaches can produce a coherent and working design. For example, some questions focus on real-world systems like a Parking Lot or a Vending Machine, while others take a more abstract turn, such as a Unix File Search or a Tic-Tac-Toe game. Each question presents unique challenges to test your skills, but they all build on the same basic knowledge and follow a similar interview structure.

How is This Book Structured?

This brief chapter explains what OOD interview questions are. Next, we'll present a framework for approaching OOD interviews and guide you through a complete end-to-end example. Then, we'll cover common design principles and patterns used in OOD. After that, the rest of the book focuses on typical case study questions, tackling them one at a time.

Why Do Companies Use OOD Interviews?

Companies use OOD interviews to hire skilled developers who can write effective code fast. They look for candidates who can define the problem scope, clarify requirements and edge cases, create practical, low-level designs, and build software that is easy to understand, maintain, and extend.

OOD interviews, along with System Design and Behavioral Questions, help companies decide a candidate's level. Doing well in OOD often sets intermediate and senior engineers apart by showing deeper design skills.

Here's what interviewers are typically looking for:

Product Sense: Translate real-world needs into software by applying domain knowledge and making user-centered decisions.

Systems Thinking: Break down a complex system into subsystems and components. Set clear roles for each and define how they work together.

Decision Making: See beyond immediate requirements, anticipate future needs, and design with flexibility in mind. Strike the right balance between making designs too complicated and keeping them too basic.

Code Quality: Write clean, logical, and maintainable code to implement your design. That's why modern OOD questions focus on coding, not just diagrams.

OOP Knowledge: Use object-oriented techniques, SOLID principles, and design patterns to make software simple and production-ready.

Communication: Ask clear questions, guide the discussion, explain your ideas well, and stand by your solutions confidently.

How Are OOD Interviews Different From Coding Interviews?

OOD interviews and algorithm coding interviews both involve writing code, but they focus on different goals. If you're familiar with algorithm interviews, you'll need to shift your mindset for OOD. Here's how they differ:

Focus on quality, not speed

Algorithm interviews want the fastest solution, focusing on time and space efficiency. OOD interviews value clean, maintainable software. You'll use objects and create well-structured code with abstractions and decomposing logic, even if it takes a bit longer, which is fine in OOD interviews. Write clear, organized code with intuitive names so your ideas stand out without extra explanation.

Design with objects, not steps

Algorithm interviews often push you to solve problems fast, so you might write all the logic in one function. OOD interviews, on the other hand, focus on objects, what they are, what they do, and how they interact with each other. Instead of listing steps, think about each object's role and relationships.

Demonstrate OOP skills, not just answers

In algorithm interviews, solving the problem matters most. OOD interviews also test your OOP skills. Use ideas like encapsulation, inheritance, and design patterns to build your solution. Demonstrating a strong grasp of SOLID principles shows that you can design clean, maintainable systems. They value your thinking process, not just the result.

Plan extensible designs, not short-term fixes

Algorithm interviews keep you racing against the clock, leaving little time to plan for future changes. In OOD interviews, the best solution often requires less coding, and the pacing gives you time to discuss how your solution scales to future requirements. A good design adapts to updates with minimal rework.

How to Prepare for an OOD Interview?

This book helps you prepare with the most up-to-date view on OOD interviews. It covers the basics, a complete walkthrough, and examples of common OOD problems with solutions. You can also try other resources to build your skills.

Here are a few ways to prepare:

Learn OOP fundamentals: Read articles, tutorials, or books on OOP. This strengthens your interview skills and your job performance later. Start with simple ideas like encapsulation, inheritance, polymorphism, and abstraction. Then, explore SOLID principles and design patterns using online guides.

Practice high-frequency problems: This book includes examples of typical OOD problems. Some, like Parking Lot, show how to model real-world systems. Others, like Elevator System, test complex logic, while systems like the Linux File Search evaluate your abstraction skills. Code along with us, then try solving them on your own and review your work.

Mock interview and practice communication: OOD interviews value clear communication, not just coding. Our walkthrough chapter offers tips on key topics, but practice explaining your designs out loud. Work with a friend in a mock interview or record yourself when doing OOD and practice explaining your design decisions while you are coding.

Run the Code

All the code included in this book is executable. We encourage you to download the repository, run the code, and experiment with the solutions to deepen your understanding of OOD principles. Instructions for setting up and running the code are provided in the repository's README file.

GitHub repo link: github.com/ByteByteGoHq/ood-interview

A Framework for the OOD Interview

Having a clear framework for the OOD interview is more important than many realize. Without structure, the interview can feel disorganized and difficult for you and the interviewer to follow.

This chapter introduces a four-step framework to help you navigate open-ended OOD discussions with confidence. It guides you in transforming abstract requirements into concrete architecture or code, while showcasing your ability to make thoughtful trade-offs under real-world constraints.

Keep in mind that OOD interviews are highly versatile, and this framework is not foolproof. The structure and expectations can vary depending on the interviewer's preferences, so you'll need to be flexible and adapt accordingly.

Before we dive into the framework itself, let's first explore the common types of OOD interviews you might encounter.

Different Types of OOD Interviews

OOD interviews typically emphasize one of three areas, each with a preferred deliverable format. Early in the interview, gauge the interviewer's expectations by asking, "Are we focusing on high-level class diagram, code structure, or a full implementation?" This question helps you tailor your approach and ensures you deliver what's needed within the time constraints (usually 45–60 minutes). The three primary deliverable formats are:

UML diagrams: UML diagrams were once the standard and are still commonly used to visually represent system designs. A UML class diagram helps illustrate the relationships between classes, including their attributes, methods, and interactions.

Code skeleton: This approach has become increasingly popular in modern interviews, as it more closely resembles real-world software development. It allows interviewers to explore implementation details as needed. In this style, you define the structure of your design directly in code using appropriate class and method declarations, while leaving method bodies unimplemented.

Working code: With the renewed emphasis on OOD interviews, interviewers sometimes request fully functional, bug-free implementations. They may also ask for test cases. This approach offers the highest fidelity to real industry development.

The expected deliverable often depends on the interviewer's preference and the time constraints. If you're asked to produce working code, don't be intimidated. Interviewers typically simplify the problem to ensure it's manageable within the allotted time.

> 💡 **Tip:** In an OOD interview, the journey is just as important as the final deliverable. Coding in silence doesn't make a strong impression. Instead, share thoughtful insights throughout the process to demonstrate your design thinking and communication skills.

A Guiding Framework for the OOD Interview

Here are the four steps we recommend:

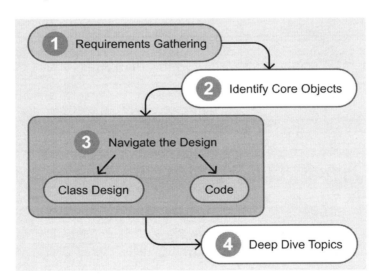

OOD Interview Framework

Step 1: Requirements Gathering (5-10 minutes): Begin by thoroughly analyzing the problem statement and identifying key functional and non-functional requirements. Ask targeted questions to resolve ambiguities, establish realistic constraints, and confirm any assumptions. This ensures that you and the interviewer share a clear understanding of the scope and priorities.

Step 2: Identify Core Objects (3-7 minutes): With requirements clarified, select a primary use case and walk through it step-by-step to identify core objects and their interactions. A practical approach is to map **nouns in the requirements to objects** (e.g., "parking lot," "vehicle," "ticket") and **verbs to methods** (e.g., "assign spot," "calculate fee"). This creates a naive but relevant initial design, serving as a foundation for refinement.

> _✎_ **Note:** While use case diagrams can help visualize workflows and clarify interactions between objects, they are optional for most OOD interviews.

Step 3: Design Class Diagram and Code (20-25 minutes): Now that the core objects and their roles are clear, it's time to develop the class diagram and demonstrate how it translates into code.

Start by designing the classes using either a top-down or bottom-up approach:

- **Top-down approach:** First, identify high-level components or parent classes, then refine their attributes and methods.
- **Bottom-up approach:** Define concrete classes first (attributes, methods) and build relationships from there.

Define how the objects will interact and assign responsibilities in a way that follows key design principles such as low coupling and high cohesion. This is the stage where you solidify your object model and flesh out the details of its attributes and methods.

Once the design is in place, implement the core classes to demonstrate how the structure translates into code. In some cases, a complete implementation isn't necessary. Focus on the essential parts unless the interviewer requests otherwise.

> _✎_ **Note:** The primary focus of an OOD interview is design and code quality. But you should not ignore time and space complexity and efficiency. Strong class and relationship modeling includes selecting appropriate data structures for performance. For example, choose between `List` and `Set` carefully based on access pattern and performance. Likewise, `HashSet` and `TreeSet` are also not interchangeable. Get familiar with more complex collections or nesting. During the actual interview, mention your thoughts and make the right choice, but do not go into exhaustive analysis or overly optimize by inventing your own.

Step 4: Deep Dive Topics (10-15 minutes, optional): After validating your design with key use cases, refine it to handle edge cases and resolve any inconsistencies. This is typically the point in the interview where the deep dive begins. Interviewers may ask follow-up questions to assess your understanding, challenge your design decisions, or explore more advanced aspects of your solution.

A Step-by-Step Example

To better understand how an OOD interview unfolds, let's walk through a realistic example from start to finish. This section shows how an interview might naturally unfold, from a vague problem description to a structured and thoughtful solution.

Step 1: Requirements Gathering

Anne, a software engineer, is interviewing for a backend role. The interviewer, Beth, asks her to design a parking lot system, giving her 45 minutes to present the design.

Anne starts by digesting the problem, asking a few clarification questions to create a shared understanding of the scope. She quickly learns that the parking lot needs to support different vehicle types, reserved spaces, and accurate fee calculation.

> **Sample dialogue:**
>
> **Anne:** What types of vehicles should the parking lot support? Are we considering cars and motorcycles?
> **Beth:** Yes, and also buses. Each bus takes up three spots.
>
> **Anne:** Should we design different types of parking spaces for the different types of vehicles?
> **Beth:** Yes, you can decide how to design that.

Anne continues to ask thoughtful questions to clearly define the scope and constraints. She avoids common mistakes such as:

- Asking overly obvious or excessively detailed questions.
- Repeating previously answered questions, which could signal inattentiveness.
- Introducing irrelevant or overly complex topics that distract from the main problem.

Tips for effective requirements gathering

The first few minutes of an OOD interview are critical. Here are a few tips for effective requirements gathering.

Focus on the most essential requirements

Start by focusing on the most essential requirements and confirming that both you and the interviewer are aligned on the problem's scope. Once Anne has a clear understanding of the task, she restates and lists down the core functionality to validate her interpretation:

> **Anne:** The system will support parking and unparking vehicles, track space availability, and calculate fees based on vehicle type and parking duration. It should also support three types of vehicles.

Use examples to clarify scope

Rather than relying solely on stating the requirements, Anne uses concrete examples to ground the discussion and expose edge cases. She presents one simple scenario and one more complex one to fully explore the system's expected behavior.

Simple case:

> **Anne:** Let's consider a basic scenario: a car enters the lot, finds an available space, parks, and leaves after two hours. The system should allocate a space, track the duration, and calculate the fee.

Complex case:

> **Anne:** Now, imagine a bus with a reservation entering the lot. Some spaces are too small or reserved for other types. The system needs to find the most suitable available space while optimizing future availability.

By walking through these contrasting examples, Anne clarifies ambiguities and ensures both the interviewer and she are on the same page.

With a solid grasp of the core problem and its constraints, she's now ready to move on to identifying the building blocks (classes, methods, and attributes), that will form the backbone of her design.

Step 2: Identify Core Objects

To kick off the design, Anne walks through a key use case: parking a car. As she steps through the process, she identifies relevant objects by paying attention to nouns and verbs in the requirements. This leads her to a simple but effective initial design.

> **Anne:** When a car enters, the system will find an available space of the appropriate size, assign it, generate a ticket, and mark the space as occupied.

By focusing on two or three representative use cases, Anne allows the requirements to naturally guide the design. She avoids trying to model everything up front, prioritizing clarity and relevance over completeness.

As she works through the use case, she keeps the design focused and minimal. For example:

> **Beth:** How would you handle edge cases like a full lot?
> **Anne:** Good question. If no spaces are available, the system should return an appropriate message. I'll refine this logic once I have the complete design.

When more complex topics arise, Anne acknowledges them without getting sidetracked:

> **Anne:** Let's finish the core use case first. If time permits, I'll extend the design to support configurable pricing, perhaps using a strategy pattern.

Anne's goal during this phase is to identify the core objects and define their responsibilities clearly.

Core Objects of Parking Lot

Optional use case diagram: If helpful, Anne could create a simple use case diagram to visualize workflows and clarify object interactions. While not required in most interviews, she can ask if the interviewer would like to see one.

Step 3: Class Design and Code

Once the core objects are identified, Anne begins defining classes, sketching relationships, and implementing a basic structure in code.

Defining the classes

She starts with foundational components that form the system's backbone. In the parking lot example, she focuses on: `ParkingLot`, `ParkingSpot`, `Vehicle`, and `Ticket`.

> **Anne:** The key entities are `ParkingLot`, `ParkingSpot`, `Vehicle`, and `Ticket`. Each space has attributes like size and availability, and each vehicle has a type. A `Ticket` will track the entry time and calculate the fee.

She then sketches a UML diagram to show relationships:

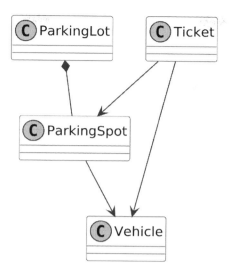

Class diagram of Parking Lot

- ParkingLot contains multiple ParkingSpots.
- Each ParkingSpot can hold one Vehicle.
- A Ticket links a Vehicle to a ParkingSpot and tracks the time.

Anne ensures that each class is well-defined and adheres to OOP principles like encapsulation, single responsibility, and inheritance:

> **Anne:** The ParkingLot manages the overall structure, including tracking spaces and handling vehicle flow. Each ParkingSpot handles its own availability status and the vehicle parked in it.
>
> **Anne:** We can define a base Vehicle class with subclasses like Car, Motorcycle, and Bus since their parking requirements and fee calculations differ.

She avoids overcomplicating the model and focuses only on objects that carry meaningful behavior.

Code implementation

With the design in place, Anne writes class definitions and adds relevant attributes and method signatures. For example:

- ParkingLot: manages a collection of spots and handles assignments.
- ParkingSpot: tracks size, availability, and assigned vehicle.
- Ticket: stores entry time and calculates the fee.

As she codes, Anne explains her rationale to the interviewer, ensuring her thought process remains transparent. She also validates the design as she progresses:

> **Anne:** This setup covers the main use cases we discussed. I'll check if it also holds up under edge conditions.

By staying focused and grounding her choices in solid OOD principles, Anne builds a practical and extensible design.

Step 4: Deep Dive Topics

At this point, Anne's design is nearly complete, whether in the form of a detailed UML diagram or a coherent code skeleton. The final step is refinement, taking a step back to examine the design from a high level, address edge cases, and consider improvements.

Addressing gaps

Anne revisits edge cases and refines the design:

> **Anne:** For edge cases, I'd add logic to handle full lots and group spaces for buses. I'd also include validation for invalid tickets during checkout.

She updates her diagram or code as needed to support grouped space handling or special logic for larger vehicles.

Summarizing the design

Anne then summarizes the system:

> **Anne:** This design supports key use cases, scales to different vehicle types, and includes logic for core edge cases. If time allows, I'd explore enhancements like dynamic pricing based on time of day.

This recap reinforces her understanding and gives the interviewer a complete picture of her thinking.

Making thoughtful trade-offs

Refinements often involve trade-offs in areas like inheritance vs. composition, data modeling, or design patterns. The goal isn't just to choose the "right" answer, but to clearly explain *why* the decision makes sense.

She also knows when to say "this is good enough" and move on. If her design already addresses the primary use cases, she avoids getting bogged down in hypotheticals or over-optimization.

What If the Interview Doesn't Go as Planned?

No matter how well you prepare, real interviews rarely follow a perfectly linear path. You might face curveballs such as shifting requirements, unexpected deep dives, or even a disengaged interviewer. The key is to stay adaptable, communicate clearly, and remain focused on delivering a thoughtful design.

This section explores common challenges during OOD interviews and how to handle them with confidence and grace.

1. Shifting requirements and expanding scope

In some interviews, the scope of the problem may expand as you go. You might be halfway through a design when the interviewer introduces new requirements or constraints. Don't panic. This is often intentional.

What to do:

- Acknowledge the new requirement and briefly assess its impact.
- Explain how your current design can accommodate the change, or what trade-offs might be required.
- Be flexible but strategic. Adapt your solution without overhauling it unnecessarily.
- If the interviewer keeps expanding on a specific area, it's likely that flexibility and scalability are part of what they're testing.
- In some cases, the shifting scope may be a subtle hint that your current design has a blind spot. Take a moment to re-evaluate and be one step ahead by recognizing potential design flaws.

2. Being pulled into a deep dive too early

Sometimes, the interviewer may want to dive into details before you've mapped out the broader structure. If you go too deep too soon, you risk losing sight of the big picture and running out of time.

What to do:

- Set expectations early: "I'll start with a high-level overview, then we can dive deeper where needed."
- Periodically check in on time and structure.
- If you're stuck in one area, say: "Here's the direction I'd take for now. Completing the rest of the system will give me the context to refine this."
- Don't forget to circle back to that part later. It shows follow-through.
- Avoid premature optimization or over-specificity early in the interview, as these can derail your momentum.

3. Struggling to communicate your thought process

Clear communication is as important as solid design. If your thoughts feel jumbled or hard to explain, it can weaken the impact of your solution.

What to do:

- Begin with a high-level summary of your system before diving into class-level details. "The system has three main components: A, B, and C. Here's how they interact."
- Use visuals. A class diagram or code skeleton can anchor the conversation.
- Focus on *why* you made design decisions rather than just describing what they are.
- Choose intuitive names for classes and methods. Good naming reduces the need for lengthy explanations and reinforces clarity.

4. Dealing with a disengaged interviewer

Not every interviewer will give active feedback. If they appear disinterested, confused, or silent, don't let it throw you off.

What to do:

- Politely ask for feedback to re-engage them: "Would it be helpful if I clarified anything or focused on a specific part of the design?"
- If that doesn't work, let your work speak for itself. Focus on delivering clean diagrams or runnable code.
- Especially in code-heavy interviews, executing working code can demonstrate your competence more effectively than conversation alone.

5. When your design decisions are challenged

It's common for interviewers to challenge your choices. This isn't a bad sign. It's a chance to demonstrate your reasoning and adaptability.

What to do:

- Stay calm and explain your thought process.
- Use concrete examples or real-world analogies to support your point.
- If relevant, reference trade-offs using terms like time complexity, extensibility, or maintainability.
- Offer alternatives: "I considered both inheritance and composition. I chose inheritance here because..."
- If you're unsure, it's okay to pause or ask for clarification: "Would you mind giving a specific case where you see this approach falling short?"

6. Encountering unfamiliar terminology

If the interviewer uses a term or concept you're not familiar with, it's better to clarify than to guess.

What to do:

- Ask politely: "Could you clarify what you mean by that term?"
- Or show partial understanding and align: "My understanding of this concept is X. Please let me know how it differs in your context."
- This approach shows humility and professionalism without undermining your credibility.

7. Struggling with the right level of abstraction

Not sure how much detail to go into? This is a common tension in OOD interviews. Going too broad can make your solution feel vague; going too deep too early wastes time.

What to do:

- Start with a general structure and layer in details as needed.
- Ask the interviewer what level of depth they'd like you to go into: "Would you prefer a high-level architecture here or a more detailed class breakdown?"
- Stay flexible, and be prepared to zoom in or out depending on the interviewer's cues.
- Each OOD problem has its own natural complexity, whether it's in abstraction, data modeling, or behavior logic. Over time, you'll develop a sense for what to emphasize.

8. Addressing concurrency in OOD interviews

Concurrency is an advanced topic that interviewers may bring up, often by asking how your system handles multiple users or processes accessing the same resources at the same time.

A classic example is a ticket booking system, where the key concern is preventing double bookings when multiple users attempt to select the same seat. This scenario is a great opportunity to demonstrate techniques like locking, optimistic locking, or using language-specific synchronization mechanisms and concurrent data structures.

Keep your explanation concise and your implementation simple. In most interviews, a high-level description of your concurrency strategy, along with a brief code snippet to illustrate how you prevent race conditions, is more than enough.

In some cases, your system itself may need to run concurrently. If you're coding in Java, understanding classes like Thread, Runnable, Callable, and ExecutorService is valuable, as it helps you avoid reinventing concurrency from low-level primitives.

Final Thoughts

The object-oriented design interview is about more than just technical skills. It's about thinking clearly under pressure, communicating effectively, and applying OOP principles to build maintainable, scalable solutions.

By breaking the process into manageable steps and learning how to navigate unexpected challenges, you'll be well-prepared to handle even the most unpredictable interviews. With practice and the right mindset, you can turn curveballs into opportunities and leave a lasting impression.

3

OOP Fundamentals

This chapter introduces OOP, a popular programming paradigm that organizes code and data into objects. These objects interact to perform tasks and model real-world entities, providing a structured approach to building flexible, maintainable software.

Why Learn OOP?

Understanding OOP fundamentals, including core principles such as encapsulation and advanced design guidelines like SOLID, is key to excelling in OOD interviews. OOP knowledge equips you with a clear mental model and foundational skills. It enables you to make design decisions aligned with widely accepted principles, articulate your reasoning to interviewers, and leverage established patterns to solve common problems efficiently.

OOP interviews often mirror real-world business applications and technical components. Understanding OOP concepts and SOLID guidelines not only prepares you for interviews but also makes you a stronger developer once hired. While functional programming and other paradigms are gaining traction, OOP remains the backbone of general software development. To deepen your expertise, supplement this chapter's essentials with additional resources on OOP principles.

Cornerstones of Object-Oriented Programming

Object-oriented programming is built on four fundamental principles: Encapsulation, Abstraction, Inheritance, and Polymorphism.

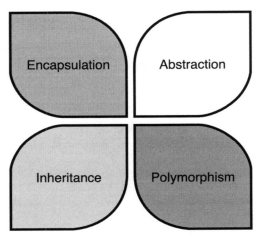

Cornerstones of OOP

These principles guide how we organize code and design software. The other techniques and design patterns stem from these principles, and they are important for evaluating solutions. Let's dive into each principle with practical examples.

Encapsulation

Encapsulation is the concept of bundling data as attributes and logic as methods, and then putting related attributes and methods within a single unit called an object. The object's internal state is hidden from the outside world, and access to the data or state is controlled through well-defined interfaces available as public methods. A description of a type of object is a class, while a specific object is called an instance.

To see how encapsulation works in practice, let's explore the Person class, which bundles data like name and age with methods to manage them while controlling access to that data.

How to work toward encapsulation?

To achieve encapsulation, follow these steps:

- **Define your classes:** Identify objects in your requirements, think about the data they hold, and the functionality they support. For the Person class, the data includes name and age, and the functionality includes accessing and modifying these attributes.
- **Enforce encapsulation:** Declare the class's data members (attributes) as private to restrict direct access from outside the class. Provide public methods (getters and setters) to access and modify those attributes.
- **Use access modifiers:** The private access modifier restricts direct access to the attributes outside the class. Only methods in the class have access to these private members. Public methods are the interface through which external code interacts with the object's attributes, hiding internal implementation details and maintaining the object's integrity.

Implementing encapsulation in Java

Let's demonstrate encapsulation in Java with a simple class representing a "Person":

```java
public class Person {
  // Private data members (attributes)
  private String name;
  private int age;

  // Public constructor
  public Person(String name, int age) {
    this.name = name;
    this.age = age;
  }

  // Public getter methods (accessors)
  public String getName() {
    return name;
  }

  public int getAge() {
    return age;
  }

  // Public setter methods (mutators)
  public void setName(String name) {
    this.name = name;
  }

  public void setAge(int age) {
    if (age >= 0) {
      this.age = age;
    }
  }
}
```

- The Person class has private attributes name and age, which cannot be accessed directly from outside the class.
- Public getter methods, `getName()` and `getAge()`, allow external code to read (access) the private attributes.
- The setter methods, `setName()` and `setAge()`, are also public, allowing external code to modify (mutate) the private attributes.

This implementation ensures that the `Person` object's internal state is protected, and external code interacts with it only through controlled methods.

When to use encapsulation?

Encapsulation is particularly useful in the following scenarios:

- **Protecting data integrity:** When you need to ensure an object's data remains consistent and valid. For example, in the Person class, encapsulation hides name and age as private attributes, allowing the `setAge()` method to enforce rules like non-negative values, preventing invalid modifications, and ensuring the object's state is reliable.
- **Controlling access and improving security:** Encapsulation restricts direct access to sensitive data. While attributes like name and age in a Person class are not highly sensitive, encapsulation becomes essential for classes handling critical information such as passwords. Although encapsulation alone does not guarantee full security, it acts as a foundational layer by limiting unwanted access.
- **Modularity and reusability:** When designing classes that can be reused across different applications. The Person class's clear interface makes it modular and reusable in contexts like school management or social networking systems.

Common pitfalls

While encapsulation is powerful, avoid these common mistakes:

- **Over-encapsulation:** Creating excessive getter and setter methods for every attribute can make code verbose and harder to maintain.
- **Under-encapsulation:** Failing to hide internal details can lead to tight coupling and reduced modularity. For instance, if name and age in the Person class were public, other parts of the code could modify them directly, leading to potential inconsistencies.

Abstraction

Abstraction can simplify complex systems by hiding unnecessary details. It separates the "what" an object does from the "how" it does it, enabling users to interact with objects through simplified interfaces. For example, the volume button on a television remote control provides a simple way to adjust sound without exposing the TV's internal circuitry. In programming, abstraction is achieved using mechanisms like abstract classes and interfaces.

To see how abstraction works in practice, let's explore a Shape class and a Drawable interface, which define simplified behaviors for shapes like circles.

How to work toward abstraction?

To achieve abstraction, use **abstract classes and interfaces**: Define abstract classes or interfaces with abstract methods, which are declared without implementation and must be implemented by subclasses. These allow users to call methods without needing to know their internal details.

Implementing Abstraction in Java

Let's demonstrate abstraction in Java with an abstract class representing a Shape and an interface representing a `Drawable` object:

```
// Abstract class
abstract class Shape {
  protected String color;
```

```java
  public Shape(String color) {
    this.color = color;
  }

  // Abstract method
  public abstract double area();

  // Concrete method
  public void displayColor() {
    System.out.println("This shape is " + color + ".");
  }
}

// Interface
interface Drawable {
  void draw();
}

// Concrete class implementing Shape and Drawable
class Circle extends Shape implements Drawable {
  private double radius;

  public Circle(String color, double radius) {
    super(color);
    this.radius = radius;
  }

  // Implementing abstract method from Shape
  @Override
  public double area() {
    return Math.PI * radius * radius;
  }

  // Implementing method from Drawable interface
  @Override
  public void draw() {
    System.out.println("Drawing a circle.");
  }
}
```

The implementation demonstrates abstraction through:

- The Shape abstract class defines an abstract `area()` method that subclasses must implement and a concrete `displayColor()` method, which provides a default behavior.
- The Drawable interface, which declares a `draw()` method that implementing classes must define.
- The Circle class extends Shape and implements Drawable, providing specific imple-

mentations for `area()` (calculating the circle's area) and `draw()` (describing the drawing action).

This structure allows users to interact with shapes using high-level methods like `area()` and `draw()` without needing to know the underlying drawing logic.

When to use abstraction?

Abstraction is particularly useful in the following scenarios:

- **Simplifying complex systems:** Abstraction helps provide a clean and consistent interface for complex functionality. For example, in the Shape class, abstraction allows users to call `area()` without understanding the mathematical calculations, making the system easier to use.
- **Promoting code flexibility:** When you anticipate that subclasses will provide specific implementations of generalized behavior, abstraction becomes essential. The Shape class's abstract `area()` method ensures that shapes like circles or rectangles implement their area calculations, allowing flexibility in design.
- **Supporting extensibility:** Abstraction makes it easier to extend systems without modifying existing code. For instance, adding a new shape like Triangle to the Shape hierarchy only requires implementing `area()`, without changing existing code that uses shapes.

Abstraction vs. Encapsulation

Abstraction and encapsulation are distinct but complementary OOP principles, often confused because both involve hiding details. Here's how they differ:

Characteristics	Abstraction	Encapsulation
Focus	Hiding complexity by exposing only what an object does through simplified interfaces, without revealing how it does it.	Bundling data and methods into a single unit (a class) and protecting data by restricting direct access.
Purpose	Simplifies user interaction and promotes flexibility by defining high-level behaviors.	Ensures data integrity and maintainability by controlling access to an object's data.
Implementation	Uses abstract classes and interfaces, e.g., the `Shape` abstract class with `area()` or the `Drawable` interface with `draw()`.	Uses access modifiers (e.g., `private`, `public`) and methods, e.g., private radius in `Circle` with public `getRadius()` and `setRadius()`.

By understanding these differences, you can apply abstraction to simplify interfaces and encapsulation to protect data, creating robust and user-friendly systems.

Inheritance

Inheritance allows a class (subclass or derived class) to inherit properties and behaviors from another class (superclass or base class). It promotes code reuse and creates a hierarchical relationship between classes. Think of inheritance like a family tree, where children inherit traits from their parents, and grandchildren inherit traits from both their parents and grandparents. The subclass can extend and specialize the functionality of its superclass, reducing code duplication.

Common patterns of class hierarchy

Building on the concept of inheritance, we now explore common patterns for structuring class hierarchies in Java.

Single inheritance

A subclass extends only one superclass. This is the standard type of inheritance supported in Java. Below is an example of single inheritance.

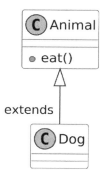

Single inheritance

In the above example, we demonstrate single inheritance by creating a Dog class that extends the Animal class. The Dog class inherits the `eat()` method from Animal.

Multilevel Inheritance

A subclass that inherits from another subclass, creating a chain of inheritance, is called multilevel inheritance. Consider a scenario with three classes: Animal, Mammal, and Dog, where Animal is the superclass of Mammal, and Mammal is the superclass of Dog.

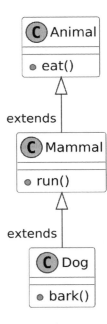

Multilevel inheritance

In the above example, the `Dog` class inherits behavior from the `Animal` and `Mammal` classes. Multilevel inheritance is useful when you have classes that exhibit a hierarchical relationship, with each subclass specializing and adding new behavior to the existing hierarchy.

Hierarchical Inheritance

In hierarchical inheritance, multiple subclasses inherit from the same superclass, forming a hierarchical structure. In the example below, you can see two subclasses, `Car` and `Motorcycle`, both inherit from the `Vehicle` class, forming a hierarchical inheritance relationship.

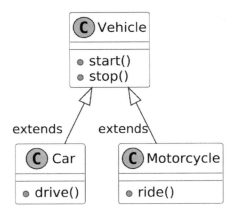

Hierarchical inheritance

Hierarchical inheritance is beneficial when multiple classes share common attributes or behaviors from a single superclass.

When to use inheritance?

Inheritance is particularly useful in the following scenarios:

- Whenever we encounter an 'is-a' relationship between objects, we can use inheritance.
- When multiple classes share common attributes or methods, a superclass can define them once, allowing all subclasses to inherit them and avoid duplication.
- When classes form a natural hierarchy, such as `Animal` being a parent to `Dog` and `Cat`, inheritance organizes the structure clearly.

Drawbacks of inheritance

While Inheritance promotes code reuse, its overuse can complicate designs. Here are the key drawbacks to consider:

- **Tight coupling:** Subclasses depend heavily on their superclass. Changes to the superclass, such as modifying the `Animal` class's `eat()` method, can break subclasses like `Dog` or `Cat`, making the code harder to maintain.
- **Inappropriate behavior inheritance:** Inheritance can force subclasses to inherit behaviors that don't apply. For example, adding a `fly()` method to the `Animal` superclass assumes all subclasses (e.g., `Penguin`) can fly, leading to errors or awkward workarounds like throwing exceptions.
- **Limited flexibility:** Inheritance locks in relationships at design time. If you later need a `RobotDog` that barks but doesn't eat, it can't inherit from `Animal` without inheriting irrelevant methods.

To address these issues, consider alternatives like composition (combining objects) or interfaces, which offer flexibility and loose coupling.

Inheritance vs. Composition

Given inheritance's limitations, it's helpful to compare it with composition, another way to structure classes. Inheritance creates an "is-a" relationship, where a subclass is a type of its superclass (e.g., `Dog` is an `Animal`). Composition creates a "has-a" relationship, where a class contains other objects to provide its behavior, such as installing apps on a phone for specific tasks.

Consider the Dog and `RobotDog` scenario. Using inheritance, `RobotDog` extends `Animal` to inherit `bark()`, but it also gets `eat()`, which doesn't apply, causing issues like exceptions. Using composition, you define a `BarkBehavior` interface with a `bark()` method. `Dog` and `RobotDog` each have a `BarkBehavior` object, implemented differently (e.g., `DogBark` for "Woof!" and `RobotBark` for "Beep!"). This lets `RobotDog` bark without inheriting `eat()`.

Here's a simple composition example in Java:

```java
interface BarkBehavior {
```

```
  void bark();
}

class DogBark implements BarkBehavior {
  public void bark() {
    System.out.println("Woof!");
  }
}

class RobotBark implements BarkBehavior {
  public void bark() {
    System.out.println("Beep!");
  }
}

class Dog {
  private BarkBehavior barkBehavior;

  public Dog(BarkBehavior barkBehavior) {
    this.barkBehavior = barkBehavior;
  }

  public void bark() {
    barkBehavior.bark();
  }
}

class RobotDog {
  private BarkBehavior barkBehavior;

  public RobotDog(BarkBehavior barkBehavior) {
    this.barkBehavior = barkBehavior;
  }

  public void bark() {
    barkBehavior.bark();
  }
}

public class Main {
  public static void main(String[] args) {
    Dog dog = new Dog(new DogBark());
    RobotDog robotDog = new RobotDog(new RobotBark());
    dog.bark();        // Output: Woof!
    robotDog.bark();   // Output: Beep!
  }
}
```

When to use composition?

To choose between inheritance and composition, follow these guidelines:

- **Design choice:** Use inheritance for clear "is-a" relationships with stable, shared behaviors. Choose composition for "has-a" relationships or when you need flexible, swappable behaviors, as it's easier to modify and maintain.
- **Interview strategy:** In OOD interviews, favor composition when flexibility or loose coupling is key, as it's preferred in modern design. For example, explain how `RobotDog` uses `BarkBehavior` to avoid inheritance's tight coupling. Highlight inheritance's use for simple hierarchies, but note its drawbacks.

These insights will help you design robust systems and justify your choices in interviews. With this comparison in mind, let's explore how Polymorphism builds on these ideas to create flexible behaviors.

Polymorphism

Polymorphism is the concept of implementing objects that can take on multiple forms or behave differently depending on their context, all within a common interface. It provides the flexibility to add new behaviors without modifying existing code.

Consider a media player as a real-world example. Different types of media, such as audio, video, and streaming content, would be played on the same rendering widget and controlled by the same "play" button. But they require different internal processing and rendering logic. The user only interacts with a uniform interface, while polymorphic behavior manages the varying objects.

Types of Polymorphism

Polymorphism in object-oriented programming is typically categorized into two main types: compile-time (static) and runtime (dynamic) polymorphism.

Compile-Time polymorphism via method overloading

Method overloading allows a class to have multiple methods with the same name but different parameters. The compiler determines the appropriate method to call based on the number and type of arguments passed during compile time. Method overloading enhances code readability by using the same method name for similar operations with different parameters.

Here's an example of method overloading in Java:

```java
class MathOperations {
  public int add(int a, int b) {
    return a + b;
  }

  public double add(double a, double b) {
    return a + b;
  }

  public String add(String str1, String str2) {
```

```
      return str1 + str2;
  }
}

public class Main {
  public static void main(String[] args) {
    MathOperations math = new MathOperations();

    int sum1 = math.add(5, 10);
    double sum2 = math.add(3.5, 7.2);
    String result = math.add("Hello, ", "World!");

    System.out.println("Sum of integers: " + sum1);
    System.out.println("Sum of doubles: " + sum2);
    System.out.println("Concatenated string: " + result);
  }
}
```

In this example:

- The MathOperations class defines multiple add methods with different parameter types or counts.
- The compiler selects the appropriate add method based on the arguments passed, enhancing code readability by using a single method name for related operations.

Runtime polymorphism via method overriding

Method overriding occurs when a subclass provides a specific implementation for a method already defined in its superclass. The method to be executed is determined at runtime based on the actual type of the object, not the reference type. This is often referred to as dynamic dispatch, a hallmark of runtime polymorphism.

Here's an example of method overriding in Java:

```
class Animal {
  public void sound() {
    System.out.println("Animal makes a sound.");
  }
}

class Dog extends Animal {
  @Override
  public void sound() {
    System.out.println("Dog barks: Woof!");
  }
}

class Cat extends Animal {
  @Override
  public void sound() {
```

```java
        System.out.println("Cat meows: Meow!");
    }
}

public class Main {
    public static void main(String[] args) {
        Animal animal1 = new Dog();
        Animal animal2 = new Cat();

        animal1.sound(); // Dog's sound() method is called
        animal2.sound(); // Cat's sound() method is called
    }
}
```

In this example:

- The `Animal` class defines a generic sound method.
- The `Dog` and `Cat` subclasses override sound to provide specific implementations.
- At runtime, the JVM determines the actual type of the object (`Dog` or `Cat`) and calls the appropriate sound method, even though the reference type is `Animal`.
- The loop demonstrates polymorphic behavior by treating different objects uniformly through the `Animal` type.

When to use polymorphism?

Polymorphism is particularly valuable in the following scenarios:

- **Shared interface:** When multiple classes need to perform the same action in different ways, such as a `play` method for various media types (e.g., audio, video). Interfaces or superclasses ensure a consistent contract across implementations.
- **Extensibility:** When designing systems that need to accommodate new classes without modifying existing code. For example, adding a new media type to a player only requires implementing the existing `play` interface, preserving system stability.
- **Customization:** When subclasses need to tailor the behavior of inherited methods. For instance, a `Dog` barking differently from a `Cat` uses method overriding to provide specific implementations while adhering to the `Animal` interface.

SOLID Principle of Good Design

Aside from the core OOP principles (encapsulation, abstraction, inheritance, and polymorphism), you should also be familiar with the SOLID principles. SOLID offers guidelines to create software that is easy to understand, modify, and extend. These principles are particularly valuable in OOD interviews, where articulating design decisions and their rationale can help you stand out.

The SOLID acronym stands for:

Single Responsibility Principle (SRP)

A class should have only one reason to change, meaning it should have a single, well-defined responsibility.

Open/Closed Principle (OCP)

Software entities (e.g., classes, modules) should be open for extension but closed for modification. This promotes the idea of extending functionality without altering existing code.

Liskov Substitution Principle (LSP)

Subtypes (derived classes) must be substitutable for their base types (parent classes) without altering the correctness of the program.

Interface Segregation Principle (ISP)

Clients should not be forced to depend on interfaces they don't use. This principle encourages the creation of smaller, focused interfaces.

Dependency Inversion Principle (DIP)

High-level modules should not depend on low-level modules; both should depend on abstractions. This promotes the decoupling of components through abstractions and interfaces.

SOLID Principles

This section explores each principle through practical examples.

Single Responsibility Principle (SRP)

The "S" in the SOLID principles stands for the Single Responsibility Principle (SRP), which states that a class should have only one reason to change or, in other words, it should have a single, well-defined responsibility or task within a software system.

Violation of SRP

Here's an example of a class that violates SRP by taking on multiple responsibilities:

```
class Employee {
  private String name;
  private double salary;

  public Employee(String name, double salary) {
    this.name = name;
    this.salary = salary;
  }

  public double calculateSalary() {
```

```
    return salary * 12; // Annual salary
  }

  public void generatePayrollReport() {
    System.out.println("Payroll Report for " + name + ": $" + salary *
    12);
  }
}
```

The `Employee` class above violates SRP because it has two responsibilities: calculating an employee's salary and generating a payroll report. This means the class could change for two unrelated reasons, i.e., updates to salary logic or changes to report formatting, making it harder to maintain.

Fixing the violation

To address the violation, let's refactor the code to separate concerns and ensure that each class has a single, well-defined responsibility. We'll create distinct classes for calculating an employee's salary and generating a payroll report:

- The `Employee` class manages employee data, such as name and salary, and calculates the annual salary based on the monthly salary.

- The `PayrollReportGenerator` class takes an employee's data and produces payroll reports.

This separation ensures that each class has a single task, and changes to salary calculations won't affect reporting, and updates to report formats won't impact employee data, making the system easier to maintain.

Here is the visual representation of the classes and implementation of the single responsibility principle (SRP).

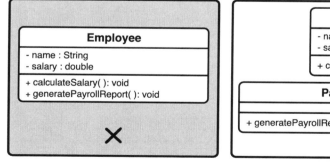
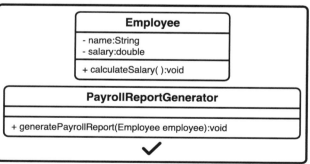

Single Responsibility Principle (SRP)

Best practices

To adhere to the SRP effectively, consider the following guidelines:

- Aim to define a clear role for each class, focusing on one specific task.
- If a class handles multiple tasks, refactor it into smaller, focused classes with single responsibilities.
- Design classes so that changes to one task don't impact others.

Open/Closed Principle (OCP)

The Open/Closed Principle (OCP) states that software entities, such as classes, should be open for extension but closed for modification. This means you can add new functionality without altering existing code.

Violation of OCP

Here's an example of a class that violates OCP by requiring changes to support new shapes:

```
class Rectangle {
  private double width;
  private double height;

  public Rectangle(double width, double height) {
    this.width = width;
    this.height = height;
  }

  public double calculateArea() {
    return width * height;
  }
}

class AreaCalculator {
  public double calculateArea(Rectangle rectangle) {
    return rectangle.calculateArea();
  }
}
```

In the above example, the `AreaCalculator` class works only with `Rectangle` objects. Adding support for new shapes, like circles or triangles, would require modifying its code. This makes the system harder to maintain and prone to errors, as each new shape requires altering the core logic.

Fixing the violation

- We can refactor this design to support new shapes without changes by introducing an abstract `Shape` class that defines a common behavior for all shapes: calculating their area.
- Specific shapes, like `Rectangle` and `Circle`, inherit from `Shape` and provide their area calculations.

This design allows new shapes, such as triangles, to be added by creating new classes that inherit from `Shape`, without modifying `AreaCalculator` or existing shape classes.

Below is the visual representation of the classes and implementation of OCP.

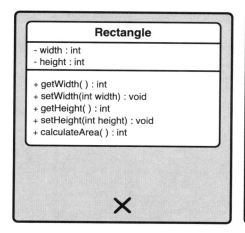 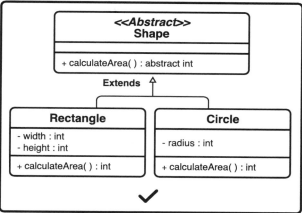

Open/Closed Principle (OCP)

Best practices

With this extensible design in place, here are guidelines to ensure OCP compliance:

- Consider introducing abstract classes or interfaces to create flexible blueprints that classes can extend with new functionality.
- Allow subclasses to override methods to provide specific behaviors, such as unique area calculations for different shapes.
- Use polymorphism to treat objects of different classes, like various shapes, uniformly through a common interface or base class.

Liskov Substitution Principle (LSP)

The Liskov Substitution Principle (LSP) states that objects of a derived class should be able to replace objects of the base class without affecting the correctness of the program. In other words, if class A is a subtype of class B, then instances of class B should be replaceable with instances of class A without causing issues.

Violation of LSP

Here's an example of a design that violates LSP by assuming all birds can fly:

```
class Bird {
  public void fly() {
    System.out.println("Flying in the sky.");
  }
}

class Ostrich extends Bird {
```

```
  @Override
  public void fly() {
    throw new UnsupportedOperationException("Ostriches cannot fly.");
  }
}

// Program calls bird.fly() to test bird behavior
```

In this code, the `Ostrich` class inherits from `Bird` but throws an exception for fly, as ostriches cannot fly. This breaks the expectation that any `Bird` can fly when a program tests this behavior. This violates the principle that derived classes should behave as expected when replacing their base class, making the design unreliable.

Fixing the violation

To align with LSP, we can refactor this hierarchy to ensure substitutability:

- Instead of assuming all birds can fly, we redefine the `Bird` class as an abstract class with a more general behavior, such as moving, that all birds can perform.

- The `Bird` class defines a move method, which each bird implements according to its abilities. For example, a `Sparrow` might implement move by describing flying in the sky, while an `Ostrich` implements move by describing running on land.

This design ensures that any derived class, like `Ostrich`, can replace `Bird` seamlessly, maintaining the program's correctness.

Here is the visual representation of the classes and implementation of LSP.

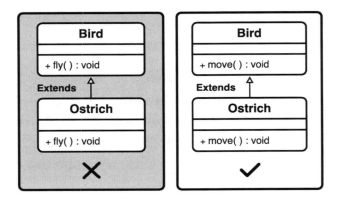

Liskov Substitution Principle (LSP)

Best practices

With this flexible design in place, here are the guidelines to ensure LSP compliance:

- Ensure that derived classes maintain the behavioral compatibility of their base classes. Methods in derived classes should follow the same contracts as the base class methods.

- When overriding methods, derived classes must respect the base class's method contracts. Specifically:
  - **Preconditions:** Derived class methods should require the same or weaker preconditions (e.g., input constraints) than the base class method. This ensures that the derived class does not impose stricter requirements that could break client expectations.
  - **Postconditions:** Derived class methods must provide the same or stronger postconditions (e.g., output guarantees) as the base class method, ensuring that the method's results meet or exceed the base class's promises.
  - **Invariants:** Derived classes must maintain all invariants defined by the base class, ensuring that the object's state remains valid according to the base class's rules.
- Use polymorphism to allow derived class objects to replace base class objects, often by overriding methods to provide specialized behavior while maintaining the core functionality of the base class.

Interface Segregation Principle (ISP)

The "I" in the SOLID acronym stands for the Interface Segregation Principle (ISP), which emphasizes that clients (classes or components that use interfaces) should not be forced to depend on interfaces they don't use. In other words, an interface should have a specific and focused set of methods that are relevant to the implementing classes.

Violation of ISP

Here's an example of a design that violates ISP by including methods that not all implementing classes need:

```java
interface Worker {
  void work();
  void eat();
  void sleep();
}

class Robot implements Worker {
  public void work() {
    System.out.println("Performing tasks like welding.");
  }
  public void eat() {
    throw new UnsupportedOperationException("Robots don't eat.");
  }
  public void sleep() {
    throw new UnsupportedOperationException("Robots don't sleep.");
  }
}

class Human implements Worker {
  public void work() {
    System.out.println("Performing tasks like coding.");
```

```
  }
  public void eat() {
    System.out.println("Eating a meal.");
  }
  public void sleep() {
    System.out.println("Sleeping for rest.");
  }
}
```

In this code, the `Worker` interface forces `Robot` to implement `eat` and `sleep`, which are irrelevant, leading to unsupported operations. This makes the code harder to maintain and prone to errors, as classes must handle methods that don't apply to them.

Fixing the violation

To align with ISP, we can refactor this interface to be more focused:

- Instead of a single `Worker` interface with unrelated methods, we split it into three smaller, tailored interfaces: `Workable`, `Eatable`, and `Sleepable`.
- The `Workable` interface includes only the work method, which all workers, like robots and humans, can implement.
- The `Eatable` interface includes the eat method, relevant to humans but not robots.
- The `Sleepable` interface includes the sleep method, which is also specific to humans.

This design ensures classes implement only the methods they need, making the code cleaner and more maintainable.

A visual representation of the refactored interfaces (`Workable`, `Eatable`, `Sleepable`) adhering to the ISP is shown below.

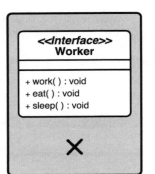
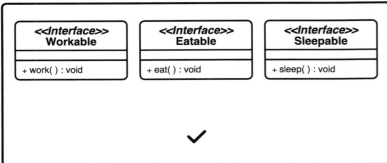

Interface Segregation Principle (ISP)

Best Practices

Here are guidelines to ensure ISP compliance:

- Aim to design interfaces with a specific purpose, including only methods directly related to that purpose.

- Consider creating multiple smaller interfaces that classes can choose to implement, rather than a single large interface with unrelated methods.
- Think from the perspective of the classes implementing the interface, providing only the methods they require.

Dependency Inversion Principle (DIP)

The Dependency Inversion Principle (DIP) states that high-level modules (or classes) should not depend on low-level modules; both should depend on abstractions, such as interfaces. In simpler terms, the principle encourages the use of abstract interfaces to decouple higher-level components from lower-level details.

Violation of DIP

Here's an example of a design that violates DIP by having a high-level class depend directly on a low-level class:

```
class LightBulb {
  public void turnOn() {
    System.out.println("LightBulb is on.");
  }
  public void turnOff() {
    System.out.println("LightBulb is off.");
  }
}

class Switch {
  private LightBulb bulb;

  public Switch(LightBulb bulb) {
    this.bulb = bulb;
  }

  public void operate() {
    bulb.turnOn();
  }
}
```

The Switch class above violates DIP because it depends directly on the low-level LightBulb class, rather than an abstraction. This tight coupling means that changing the LightBulb class, such as modifying its methods, or replacing it with another device, like a Fan, requires altering the Switch class's code. This makes the system less flexible and harder to maintain, as high-level modules should not be tied to low-level details.

Fixing the violation

To align with DIP, we can refactor this design to use abstractions:

- We introduce a `Switchable` interface that defines standard methods, such as `turnOn` and `turnOff`, which any switchable device can implement.
- The `Switch` class is modified to depend only on the `Switchable` interface, not on specific devices.
- The `LightBulb` class implements the `Switchable` interface, providing its `turnOn` and `turnOff` behavior.

Now, `Switch` can work with any device that implements `Switchable`, like a `Fan` or a `Heater`, without needing changes to its code. This design decouples `Switch` from low-level details, making the system more flexible and easier to extend.

A visual representation of the dependency inversion is shown below.

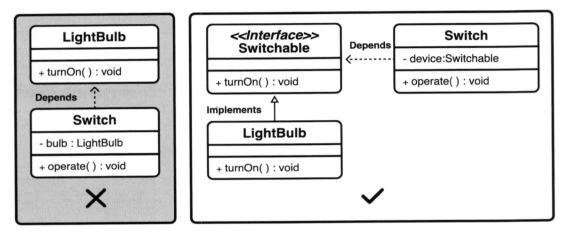

Dependency Inversion Principle (DIP)

Best Practices

With this decoupled design in place, here are guidelines to ensure DIP compliance:

- Introduce interfaces or abstract classes to represent dependencies, allowing high-level modules to depend on these abstractions.
- Use dependency injection to inject concrete implementations into high-level modules through their abstractions. This promotes loose coupling.

Wrap Up

This chapter has helped you understand how to use Encapsulation, Abstraction, Inheritance, Polymorphism, and the SOLID principles. These concepts form the backbone of robust software design, enabling you to create flexible, maintainable, and scalable systems. Applying these tools will help you articulate clear design decisions, justify your approach, and demonstrate adherence to industry-standard practices.

To further refine your skills and deepen your expertise, explore the following resources:

- *'Clean Code: A Handbook of Agile Software Craftsmanship'* by Robert C. Martin
- *'Design Patterns: Elements of Reusable Object-Oriented Software'* by Erich Gamma, Richard Helm, Ralph Johnson, and John Vlissides.
- *'Tidy First?: A Personal Exercise in Empirical Software Design'* by Kent Beck

-0

4

Parking Lot System

In this chapter, we explore the object-oriented design of a Parking Lot system, one of the most popular questions in technical interviews. This parking lot application aims to provide a comprehensive solution for efficiently managing a parking lot. It automates various processes, including vehicle entry, exit, and spot allocation, while also providing accurate information about parking lot occupancy and generating parking tickets.

To build this system, we first need to clarify its requirements.

Parking Lot

Requirements Gathering

The first step in designing the parking lot system is to clarify the requirements and define the scope. Here's an example of a typical prompt an interviewer might present:

"Imagine you're arriving at a busy parking lot, eager to park your car. At the entrance, you're issued a ticket. You then drive in, find a spot suited to your vehicle's size, and park. Later, when you prepare to leave, you present your ticket at the exit, the system calculates your fee, and the spot is freed up for the next vehicle. Behind the scenes, the parking lot is assigning spots based on vehicle size, recording entry and exit times, and updating availability for new arrivals. Now, let's design a parking lot system that handles all this."

Requirements clarification

In this step, we ask clarifying questions to narrow down the list of requirements, understand the constraints, and define the problem that can be solved in 30-45 minutes.

Here is an example of how a conversation between a candidate and an interviewer might unfold:

Candidate: What types of vehicles are supported by the parking lot?
Interviewer: Three types of vehicles should be supported: *motorcycles*, *cars*, and *trucks*.

Candidate: What parking spot types are available in the parking lot?
Interviewer: The parking lot supports three types of parking spots: compact, regular, and oversized.

Candidate: How does the system determine which spot a vehicle should park in?
Interviewer: The system assigns spots based on the size of the vehicle, ensuring an appropriate fit.

Candidate: Are parking tickets issued to vehicles upon entry and charged at the exit?
Interviewer: Yes, a ticket is issued with vehicle details and entry time when a vehicle enters. On exit, the system calculates the fee based on duration and vehicle size, then marks the spot as vacant.

Candidate: How are parking fees calculated?
Interviewer: Fees are based on parking duration and vehicle size, with rates varying depending on the time of day.

Requirements

As we ask clarifying questions, we should note down the key requirements for this problem. Putting the key requirements in writing will help us avoid ambiguity and contradictions, as there is nothing worse than realizing you are solving the wrong problem.

Here are the key functional requirements we've identified:

- The parking lot has multiple parking spots, including compact, regular, and oversized spots.
- The parking lot supports parking for motorcycles, cars, and trucks.
- Customers can park their vehicles in spots assigned based on vehicle size.
- Customers receive a parking ticket with vehicle details and entry time at the entry point and pay a fee based on duration, vehicle size, and time of day at the exit point.

Below are the non-functional requirements:

- The system must scale to support large parking lots with many spots and vehicles.
- The system must reliably track spot assignments and ticket details to ensure accurate operations.

With these requirements set, we now identify the core objects.

Identify Core Objects

Before diving into the design, it's important to enumerate the core objects.

- **Vehicle:** This object represents a vehicle that needs a spot. It encapsulates details like the license plate and size (small for motorcycles, medium for cars, large for trucks), serving as the foundation for spot assignment and fee calculation.
- **ParkingSpot:** This object models an individual parking spot in the parking lot. It's the physical space where a `Vehicle` parks, ensuring only appropriately sized vehicles can park based on its capacity.
- **Ticket:** This object represents a parking ticket issued when a `Vehicle` enters the parking lot. It stores critical details, including the ticket ID, the associated `Vehicle`, the assigned `ParkingSpot`, and entry time, which are later used to calculate fees and free up spots upon exit.
- **ParkingManager:** This object oversees the parking lot's spot allocation, managing the assignment, lookup, and release of `ParkingSpot` instances. It ensures a `Vehicle` gets the right spot by checking availability based on size, and updates the system when vehicles leave, keeping parking operations smooth and efficient.
- **ParkingLot:** This acts as a facade, providing a central interface to manage the system's key functionalities: vehicle entry, spot assignment, ticketing, and fee calculation. It keeps its logic lightweight by delegating tasks such as spot allocation to the `ParkingManager`, fee computation to a `FareCalculator` class, and coordinating the flow of vehicles in and out without handling the details.

> ✂ **Design choice:** We chose these five objects to separate concerns. `Vehicle` and `ParkingSpot` define the core physical entities, `Ticket` tracks sessions, `ParkingManager` handles allocation, and `ParkingLot` coordinates as a facade.

Note: To learn more about the Facade Pattern and its common use cases, refer to the **Further Reading** section at the end of this chapter.

Design Class Diagram

Now that we've identified the core objects and their responsibilities, the next step is to design the classes and methods that bring the parking lot system to life.

Vehicle

We have modeled the `Vehicle` as an interface to set a standard for all vehicle types. It defines two key methods:

- `getLicensePlate()`: Returns the vehicle's license plate number.
- `getSize()`: Returns a `VehicleSize` enum (`SMALL`, `MEDIUM`, `LARGE`), indicating the space it occupies.

Concrete classes like `Motorcycle`, `Car`, and `Truck` implement the `Vehicle` interface, each defining its size:

- `Motorcycle`: Small-sized.
- `Car`: Medium-sized.
- `Truck`: Large-sized.

Below is the representation of the Vehicle interface and its concrete classes.

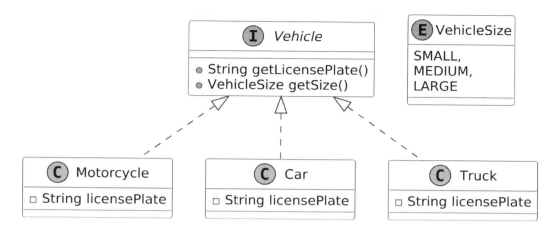

Vehicle and its concrete classes

> **✂ Design choice:** You might wonder: why use a `getSize()` method instead of a `getType()` method in the `Vehicle` class? Using `getType()` would tie us to specific vehicle names like "`Motorcycle`" or "`Car`", forcing updates to the system's logic every time a new type (say, "`Scooter`") comes along. For example, fee calculations or spot assignments would need new cases for each type.
>
> With `getSize()`, we abstract that away. The parking lot cares more about the size of a vehicle, such as small, medium, or large, than its exact type. A truck and a van might both be large, so they're treated the same for parking purposes. Adding an electric scooter? Just mark its size as small, and it fits in like a motorcycle. This keeps the system lean and adaptable, focusing on space over semantics.

ParkingSpot

The `ParkingSpot` interface represents a parking spot in the parking lot system. It captures spot-specific details, such as whether it's occupied and its size. Concrete parking spot types (`CompactSpot`, `RegularSpot`, and `OversizedSpot`) are implemented as classes that adhere to the `ParkingSpot` interface. These classes bring the interface to life, defining spots for small, medium, and large vehicles, respectively.

The UML diagram below illustrates this structure.

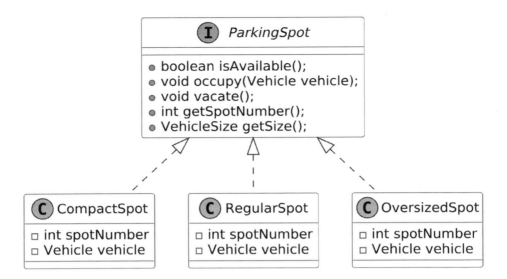

Parking Spot and its concrete classes

> **⚒ Design choice:** The `ParkingSpot` class is intentionally designed to be simple, only encompassing its state (e.g., availability and size). The `ParkingManager` class is responsible for more complex operations, such as locating available parking spots and monitoring parked vehicles. This design choice promotes adding new spot types without introducing unnecessary complexity.

ParkingManager

The `ParkingManager` is responsible for managing the allocation and tracking of parking spots within the parking lot system. Its primary functions include identifying available parking spaces, assigning the most suitable spot for each vehicle, and maintaining a record of parked vehicles and their locations. These tasks are accomplished through two key methods.

- `parkVehicle(Vehicle vehicle)`: Assigns a spot that matches the vehicle's size when it arrives.

- `unparkVehicle(Vehicle vehicle)`: Frees up the spot when the vehicle leaves, ensuring the system stays up-to-date.

Here is the representation of the `ParkingManager` class.

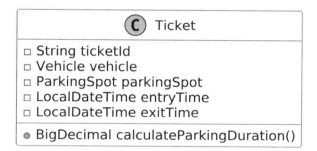

```
                    C   ParkingManager
  □ Map<VehicleSize, List<ParkingSpot>> availableSpots
  □ Map<Vehicle, ParkingSpot> vehicleToSpotMap
  ● ParkingSpot findSpotForVehicle(Vehicle vehicle)
  ● ParkingSpot parkVehicle(Vehicle vehicle)
  ● void unparkVehicle(Vehicle vehicle)
```

�֎ Design choice: The `ParkingManager` class is designed to encapsulate the logic for parking spot allocation, deallocation, and tracking within the parking lot system. This centralization ensures that the `ParkingLot` class operates as a lightweight facade, focusing solely on orchestrating high-level operations such as vehicle entry, ticketing, and exit processing. By delegating spot management to `ParkingManager`, the system maintains a clear separation of concerns, enhancing modularity and scalability.

Ticket

The `Ticket` class represents a parking ticket generated when a vehicle enters the parking lot. It keeps track of when a vehicle arrives and leaves, using these times to calculate duration, and links the vehicle to its assigned spot.

Below is the representation of the `Ticket` class.

```
                    C   Ticket
  □ String ticketId
  □ Vehicle vehicle
  □ ParkingSpot parkingSpot
  □ LocalDateTime entryTime
  □ LocalDateTime exitTime
  ● BigDecimal calculateParkingDuration()
```

✖ Design choice: The `Ticket` class is designed as a concise, immutable record of a parking event, capturing essential details such as the ticket ID, associated `Vehicle`, assigned `ParkingSpot`, entry time, and exit time. Its primary role is to serve as a data container, ensuring simplicity and focus by delegating complex logic, such as parking fee calculation, to the `FareCalculator` class.

FareStrategy and FareCalculator

We design the `FareStrategy` interface to establish a standard method for modifying the parking fee, allowing various pricing rules to fit into the system. Its concrete classes handle specific pricing rules:

- `BaseFareStrategy` establishes the base fee using the ticket's duration and vehicle size.
- `PeakHoursFareStrategy` modifies it based on the time of day.

Since a parking session often involves multiple pricing rules, like duration, size, and time, we design a `FareCalculator` class to coordinate these changes and calculate the final fee. It is designed to determine the cost for each ticket by combining the effects of all applicable strategies (`BaseFareStrategy`, `PeakHoursFareStrategy`), ensuring the system applies the right fee based on how long the vehicle stays, its size, and when it is parked.

This association between `FareStrategy` and `FareCalculator` maintains a structured pricing process, with `FareStrategy` defining the rules and `FareCalculator` pulling them together.

The pricing logic relies on the **Strategy Pattern**, which enables the system to dynamically select and swap between different rules for calculating parking fees.

Note: To learn more about the Strategy Pattern and its common use cases, refer to the Further Reading section at the end of this chapter.

The UML diagram below illustrates this structure.

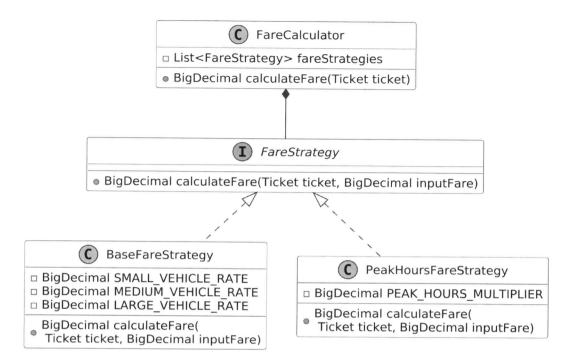

FareStrategy interface and FareCalculator class

> ✂ **Design choice:** The FareStrategy interface encapsulates pricing logic for the parking lot system, enabling modular and interchangeable rules for calculating parking fees. By defining a standard contract for pricing strategies (e.g., BaseFareStrategy, PeakHoursFareStrategy), it ensures that the ParkingLot facade remains lightweight, delegating fee calculations to the FareCalculator class, which orchestrates these strategies. This design, rooted in the Strategy Pattern, promotes flexibility, maintainability, and extensibility while keeping the system's core logic clean and focused.

ParkingLot

We design the ParkingLot class as the core component of the system to act as a facade, providing a simple interface for managing the parking lot's key operations. It manages vehicle entry and exit by generating tickets for arrivals, assigning spots through the ParkingManager, and calculating fares with the FareCalculator when vehicles leave, tying the system's main functions together.

Below is the representation of this class.

```
┌──────────────────────────────────────────────┐
│               Ⓒ  ParkingLot                    │
├──────────────────────────────────────────────┤
│  ▢ ParkingManager parkingManager               │
│  ▢ FareCalculator fareCalculator               │
├──────────────────────────────────────────────┤
│  ● Ticket enterVehicle(Vehicle vehicle)         │
│  ● void leaveVehicle(Ticket ticket)             │
└──────────────────────────────────────────────┘
```

Next, we'll connect these objects in a class diagram to visualize their relationships.

Complete Class Diagram

Take a moment to review the complete class structure and the relationships between them. This diagram demonstrates how a seemingly complex system can be constructed using simple, well-designed components working together cohesively.

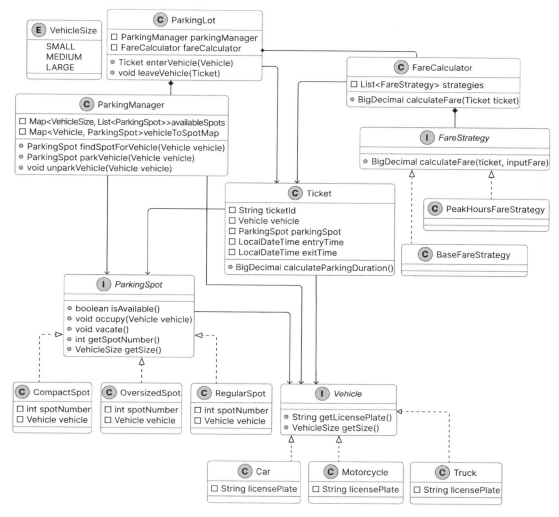

Class Diagram of Parking Lot

With this design in place, we move to implementation.

Code - Parking Lot

In this section, we'll implement the core functionalities of the parking lot system, focusing on key areas such as managing vehicle entry and exit, assigning parking spots efficiently, and calculating parking fees accurately.

Vehicle

We define the `Vehicle` interface, along with its supporting `VehicleSize` enum and concrete classes `Motorcycle`, `Car`, and `Truck`, to set up how vehicles are identified and sized in the parking lot system.

Here is the implementation of this interface and its concrete classes.

```java
public interface Vehicle {
  String getLicensePlate();
  VehicleSize getSize();
}

public class Car implements Vehicle {
  private String licensePlate;

  public Car(String licensePlate) {
    this.licensePlate = licensePlate;
  }

  @Override
  public String getLicensePlate() {
    return this.licensePlate;
  }

  @Override
  public VehicleSize getSize() {
    return VehicleSize.MEDIUM;
  }
}

public enum VehicleSize {
  SMALL,
  MEDIUM,
  LARGE
}
```

This interface ensures every vehicle provides two key attributes: a license plate for tracking and a size for managing parking spaces. This design ensures that every vehicle provides consistent, type-safe attributes critical for tracking, parking spot allocation, and fee calculation.

For the sake of brevity, we have not shown the code for the `Motorcycle` and `Truck` classes.

Implementation choice: The `VehicleSize` enum (`SMALL`, `MEDIUM`, `LARGE`) standardizes vehicle and parking spot sizes, ensuring type-safe, error-free size comparisons for efficient spot allocation and fee calculation.

Alternatives and trade-offs:

- **Strings:** Prone to typos and slower comparisons ($O(n)$), requiring validation. Rejected for fragility and performance issues.
- **Integers:** Ambiguous and error-prone, lacking type safety. Rejected for reduced clarity and reliability.

ParkingSpot

We define the `ParkingSpot` interface to represent individual parking spots in the parking lot system, along with its concrete classes `CompactSpot`, `RegularSpot`, and `OversizedSpot`.

Here's the code for the `ParkingSpot` interface:

```java
public interface ParkingSpot {
  boolean isAvailable();
  void occupy(Vehicle vehicle);
  void vacate();
  int getSpotNumber();
  VehicleSize getSize();
}
```

isAvailable(): Checks if the spot is free. Helps `ParkingManager` decide if the spot can be assigned.

occupy(Vehicle vehicle): Assigns a vehicle to the spot if it's available, setting vehicle to the provided instance.

vacate(): Clears the spot by setting the vehicle to null, making the spot free for reuse. Allows `ParkingManager` to reassign it to another vehicle.

getSize(): Returns the spot's fixed `VehicleSize` (e.g., `SMALL` for `CompactSpot`). Guides `ParkingManager` in matching vehicle sizes to parking spot capacities.

The concrete class `CompactSpot` implements this interface:

```java
public class CompactSpot implements ParkingSpot {
  private int spotNumber;
  private Vehicle vehicle;  // The vehicle currently occupying this spot

  public CompactSpot(int spotNumber) {
    this.spotNumber = spotNumber;
    this.vehicle = null;  // No vehicle occupying initially
  }

  @Override
  public int getSpotNumber() {
    return spotNumber;
  }

  @Override
  public boolean isAvailable() {
    return vehicle == null;
  }

  @Override
```

```java
  public void occupy(Vehicle vehicle) {
    if (isAvailable()) {
      this.vehicle = vehicle;
    } else {
      System.out.println("Spot is already occupied.");
    }
  }

  @Override
  public void vacate() {
    this.vehicle = null;   // Make the spot available
  }

  @Override
  public VehicleSize getSize() {
    return VehicleSize.SMALL;  // Compact spots fit small vehicles
  }
}
```

For brevity, we omit the full code of `RegularSpot` and `OversizedSpot`, but they follow a similar structure:

- `RegularSpot`: Returns `VehicleSize.MEDIUM`, suitable for medium-sized vehicles like cars.
- `OversizedSpot`: Returns `VehicleSize.LARGE`, designed for large vehicles like trucks.

This implementation keeps `ParkingSpot` lean and focused, managing its state while delegating allocation logic to `ParkingManager`.

ParkingManager

The `ParkingManager` class manages the allocation and tracking of parking spots in the parking lot system. It searches and assigns spots to vehicles, freeing them when vehicles leave and keeping an accurate record of which vehicles occupy which parking spots.

Here's the implementation of this class:

```java
public class ParkingManager {
  private final Map<VehicleSize, List<ParkingSpot>> availableSpots;
  private final Map<Vehicle, ParkingSpot> vehicleToSpotMap;

  // Create Parking Manager based on a given map of available spots
  public ParkingManager(Map<VehicleSize, List<ParkingSpot>>
    availableSpots) {
    this.availableSpots = availableSpots;
    this.vehicleToSpotMap = new HashMap<>();
  }

  public ParkingSpot findSpotForVehicle(Vehicle vehicle) {
```

```
      VehicleSize vehicleSize = vehicle.getSize();

      // Start looking for the smallest spot that can fit the vehicle
      for (VehicleSize size : VehicleSize.values()) {
        if (size.ordinal() >= vehicleSize.ordinal()) {
          List<ParkingSpot> spots = availableSpots.get(size);
          for (ParkingSpot spot : spots) {
            if (spot.isAvailable()) {
              return spot;  // Return the first available spot
            }
          }
        }
      }
      return null;  // No suitable spot found
    }

    public ParkingSpot parkVehicle(Vehicle vehicle) {
      ParkingSpot spot = findSpotForVehicle(vehicle);
      if (spot != null) {
        spot.occupy(vehicle);
        // Record the parking spot for the vehicle
        vehicleToSpotMap.put(vehicle, spot);
        // Remove the spot from the available list
        availableSpots.get(spot.getSize()).remove(spot);
        return spot;  // Parking successful
      }
      return null;  // No spot found for this vehicle
    }

    public void unparkVehicle(Vehicle vehicle) {
      ParkingSpot spot = vehicleToSpotMap.remove(vehicle);
      if (spot != null) {
        spot.vacate();
        availableSpots.get(spot.getSize()).add(spot);
      }
    }
  }
}
```

---

findSpotForVehicle(Vehicle vehicle):

- Searches for an available parking spot that fits the vehicle's size.

parkVehicle(Vehicle vehicle):

- Assigns a parking spot to the vehicle by calling findSpotForVehicle() and then marks it as occupied via occupy().
- Records the vehicle-spot pair and removes the spot from the available pool, ensuring accurate tracking and availability updates.

unparkVehicle(Vehicle vehicle):

- Retrieves the parking spot for the given vehicle, frees the spot via `vacate()`, and adds it back to the available pool.
- Removes the vehicle-spot mapping, keeping the system's state current for future allocations.

Implementation choice:

As shown in the code above, we used two `HashMaps`. Let's understand their purpose.

- The `availableSpots` map maintains a list of parking spots ready for use, organized by `VehicleSize`. It ensures that vehicles land in the best-fit parking spot. For instance, motorcycles fit into small spots like `CompactSpot`, while cars use medium spots like `RegularSpot`. This organization allows `ParkingManager` to quickly find the smallest, most suitable size available.
- The `vehicleToSpotMap` records which parking spot each vehicle occupies. It allows `ParkingManager` to locate and free up a parking spot when a vehicle leaves, keeping the system's state up to date.

Here's why these choices matter:

- **Performance:** Using `HashMaps` provides $O(1)$ time complexity for accessing parking spots by size or finding a vehicle's parking spot. However, checking availability within a specific size requires additional steps.
- **Best fit:** Organizing parking spots by `VehicleSize` ensures vehicles park in the smallest spot that fits them, optimizing space usage.

Ticket

The `Ticket` class acts as a record of a parking event, linking a vehicle to its parking spot and tracking the time spent in the parking lot.

Below is the implementation of this class.

```java
public class Ticket {
  private final String ticketId; // Unique ticket identifier
  private final Vehicle vehicle; // The vehicle associated with the
    ticket
  // The parking spot where the vehicle is parked
  private final ParkingSpot parkingSpot;
  // The time the vehicle entered the parking lot
  private final LocalDateTime entryTime;
  // The time the vehicle exited the parking lot
  private LocalDateTime exitTime;

  public Ticket(String ticketId, Vehicle vehicle, ParkingSpot parkingSpot
```

```java
    , LocalDateTime entryTime) {
    this.ticketId = ticketId;
    this.vehicle = vehicle;
    this.parkingSpot = parkingSpot;
    this.entryTime = entryTime;
    // Initially, exitTime is null because the vehicle is still parked
    this.exitTime = null;
  }

  public BigDecimal calculateParkingDuration() {
    return new BigDecimal(Duration.between(entryTime, Objects.
    requireNonNullElseGet(exitTime, LocalDateTime::now)).toMinutes());
  }

  // getter and setter methods are omitted for brevity
}
```

FareStrategy and FareCalculator

We implement the FareStrategy interface and its concrete classes, BaseFareStrategy and PeakHoursFareStrategy, along with the FareCalculator class. These components manage the parking fee calculation process in the parking lot system. Together, they determine the cost of each parking session.

Here's the code for the FareStrategy interface:

```java
public interface FareStrategy {
  BigDecimal calculateFare(Ticket ticket, BigDecimal inputFare);
}
```

Implementation choice: We define **FareStrategy** as an interface to support a flexible and extensible approach to pricing rules, allowing new strategies (e.g., a **WeekendDiscountStrategy**) to integrate without altering existing code.

The concrete class **BaseFareStrategy** implements this interface:

```java
public class BaseFareStrategy implements FareStrategy {
  private static final BigDecimal SMALL_VEHICLE_RATE = new BigDecimal("
    1.0");
  private static final BigDecimal MEDIUM_VEHICLE_RATE = new BigDecimal("
    2.0");
  private static final BigDecimal LARGE_VEHICLE_RATE = new BigDecimal("
    3.0");

  // Calculate fare based on the duration and add it to the input fare to
    return a new total
  @Override
  public BigDecimal calculateFare(Ticket ticket, BigDecimal inputFare) {
    BigDecimal fare = inputFare;
```

```
    BigDecimal rate;
    switch (ticket.getVehicle().getSize()) {
      case MEDIUM:
      rate = MEDIUM_VEHICLE_RATE;
      break;
      case LARGE:
      rate = LARGE_VEHICLE_RATE;
      break;
      default:
      rate = SMALL_VEHICLE_RATE;
    }
    fare = fare.add(rate.multiply(ticket.calculateParkingDuration()));
    return fare;
  }
}
```

calculateFare(Ticket ticket, BigDecimal inputFare): Provides the foundational cost for the parking session, reflecting size-based pricing.

The concrete class PeakHoursFareStrategy implements this interface:

```
public class PeakHoursFareStrategy implements FareStrategy {

  // 50% higher during peak hours
  private static final BigDecimal PEAK_HOURS_MULTIPLIER = new BigDecimal(
    "1.5");

  public PeakHoursFareStrategy() {

  }

  @Override
  public BigDecimal calculateFare(Ticket ticket, BigDecimal inputFare) {
    BigDecimal fare = inputFare;
    if (isPeakHours(ticket.getEntryTime())) {
      fare = fare.multiply(PEAK_HOURS_MULTIPLIER);
    }
    return fare;
  }

  private boolean isPeakHours(LocalDateTime time) {
    int hour = time.getHour();
    return (hour >= 7 && hour <= 10) || (hour >= 16 && hour <= 19);
  }
}
```

calculateFare(Ticket ticket, BigDecimal inputFare):

- Multiplies the input fare by 1.5 if the entry time falls within peak hours. Otherwise, it leaves it unchanged.

- Adjusts the fare for high-demand periods, increasing costs during busy times.

isPeakHours(LocalDateTime time): Checks if the given time's hour is within peak ranges.

The `FareCalculator` class uses these strategies:

```java
public class FareCalculator {
  private final List<FareStrategy> fareStrategies;

  public FareCalculator(List<FareStrategy> fareStrategies) {
    this.fareStrategies = fareStrategies;
  }
  public BigDecimal calculateFare(Ticket ticket) {
    BigDecimal fare = BigDecimal.ZERO;
    for (FareStrategy strategy : fareStrategies) {
      fare = strategy.calculateFare(ticket, fare);
    }
    return fare;
  }
}
```

FareCalculator(List<FareStrategy> fareStrategies): Initializes with a list of strategies, setting up the rules to apply during fare calculation.

calculateFare(Ticket ticket): Starts with a zero fare, iterates through each strategy in the list, and applies their rules in sequence to build the final fare.

Implementation choice: We implement `FareCalculator` using a `List<FareStrategy>` to hold strategies, enabling the sequential application of multiple rules (e.g., base fare followed by peak adjustment). We choose List over an array or Set because it preserves order. Strategies like `BaseFareStrategy` must be applied before `PeakHoursFareStrategy` for correct fare calculation. A Set can prevent duplicates but loses order, while an array maintains a fixed size, limiting flexibility.

ParkingLot Code

The `ParkingLot` class acts as a facade, providing a simple interface for clients to interact with the parking lot system while delegating complex tasks to `ParkingManager` and `FareCalculator`. It relies on `ParkingManager` for spot allocation and `FareCalculator` for pricing, managing the flow of vehicles through entry and exit operations.

Here's the implementation of the `ParkingLot` class:

```java
public class ParkingLot {

  // Manages parking spots and vehicle assignments
```

```java
private final ParkingManager parkingManager;
// Calculates fare for parking sessions
private final FareCalculator fareCalculator;

public ParkingLot(ParkingManager parkingManager, FareCalculator
  fareCalculator)
{
  this.parkingManager = parkingManager;
  this.fareCalculator = fareCalculator;
}

// Method to handle vehicle entry into the parking lot
public Ticket enterVehicle(Vehicle vehicle) {
  // Delegate parking logic to ParkingManager
  ParkingSpot spot = parkingManager.parkVehicle(vehicle);

  if (spot != null) {
    // Create ticket with entry time
    Ticket ticket = new Ticket(generateTicketId(), vehicle, spot,
  LocalDateTime.now());
    return ticket;
  } else {
    System.out.println("No available spots for vehicle: " + vehicle.
  getLicensePlate());
    return null;  // No spot available
  }
}

// Method to handle vehicle exit from the parking lot
public void leaveVehicle(Ticket ticket) {

  // Ensure the ticket is valid and the vehicle hasn't already left
  if (ticket != null && ticket.getExitTime() == null) {

    // Set exit time
    ticket.setExitTime(LocalDateTime.now());

    // Delegate unparking logic to ParkingManager
    parkingManager.unparkVehicle(ticket.getVehicle());

    // Calculate the fare
    BigDecimal fare = fareCalculator.calculateFare(ticket);
    System.out.println("Vehicle " + ticket.getVehicle().getLicensePlate
  () + " has left. Total fare: $" + fare);
  } else {
    System.out.println("Invalid ticket or vehicle already exited.");
  }
}
}
```

enterVehicle(Vehicle vehicle): Coordinates vehicle entry by requesting a parking spot from `ParkingManager`. It then generates a Ticket with a unique ID, vehicle, parking spot, and current entry time.

leaveVehicle(Ticket ticket): Manages vehicle exit by setting the exit time, frees the parking spot via `ParkingManager`, and calculates the fare with `FareCalculator`.

Deep Dive Topics

In this section, we'll cover common follow-up questions interviewers may ask about the parking lot system. These are important topics that interviewers might expect you to explore in detail.

Adding a New Parking Spot Type

The parking lot system is designed to support multiple parking spot types (e.g., `CompactSpot`, `RegularSpot`, `OversizedSpot`). However, there may be a need to introduce a new type, such as a handicapped parking spot, to accommodate specific requirements like accessibility. The challenge is to extend the system efficiently without modifying existing classes, adhering to the Open-Closed Principle (open for extension, closed for modification).

To achieve this, we can introduce a new `HandicappedSpot` class that implements the existing `ParkingSpot` interface. This approach ensures smooth integration with the system's spot allocation and management logic, as `ParkingManager` already relies on the `ParkingSpot` interface for handling spots.

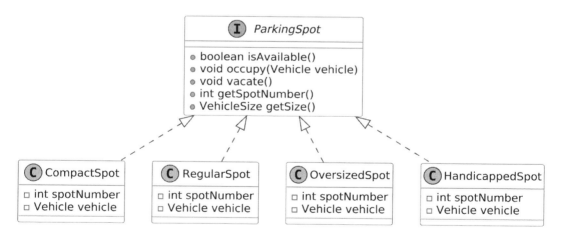

`ParkingSpot` with `HandicappedSpot` class

Below is the implementation of the `HandicappedSpot` class.

```
public class HandicappedSpot implements ParkingSpot {
    private int spotNumber;
    private Vehicle vehicle;
```

```java
  public HandicappedSpot(int spotNumber) {
    this.spotNumber = spotNumber;
    this.vehicle = null;
  }

  @Override
  public int getSpotNumber() {
    return spotNumber;
  }

  @Override
  public boolean isAvailable() {
    return vehicle == null;
  }

  @Override
  public void occupy(Vehicle vehicle) {
    if (isAvailable()) {
      this.vehicle = vehicle;
    } else {
      System.out.println("Spot is already occupied.");
    }
  }

  @Override
  public void vacate() {
    this.vehicle = null;
  }

  @Override
  public VehicleSize getSize() {
    return VehicleSize.MEDIUM;
  }
}
```

Faster Parking Spot Management

The mapping we currently have is one-way: from Vehicle to ParkingSpot. This allows us to quickly find the parking spot assigned to a specific vehicle. But what if we want to find which vehicle is parked in a specific spot? Without a reverse mapping, we would need to search through all parking spots, which isn't efficient. Can we do better?

We can enhance this by introducing another HashMap, called spotToVehicleMap, to track the reverse mapping from ParkingSpot to Vehicle.

With this approach, we use two HashMaps:

- vehicleToSpotMap: Tracks the parking spot for each vehicle.

- spotToVehicleMap: Tracks the vehicle parked in each spot.

Below is the updated ParkingManager class.

```java
public class ParkingManager {
  private final Map<VehicleSize, List<ParkingSpot>> availableSpots;
  private final Map<Vehicle, ParkingSpot> vehicleToSpotMap;
  private final Map<ParkingSpot, Vehicle> spotToVehicleMap;

  // Create Parking Manager based on a given map of available spots
  public ParkingManager(Map<VehicleSize, List<ParkingSpot>>
    availableSpots) {
    this.availableSpots = availableSpots;
    this.vehicleToSpotMap = new HashMap<>();
    this.spotToVehicleMap = new HashMap<>();
  }

  public ParkingSpot findSpotForVehicle(Vehicle vehicle) {
    // No change in the method
  }

  public ParkingSpot parkVehicle(Vehicle vehicle) {
    ParkingSpot spot = findSpotForVehicle(vehicle);
    if (spot != null) {
      spot.occupy(vehicle);
      // Record bidirectional mapping
      vehicleToSpotMap.put(vehicle, spot);
      spotToVehicleMap.put(spot, vehicle);
      // Remove the spot from the available list
      availableSpots.get(spot.getSize()).remove(spot);
      return spot;   // Parking successful
    }
    return null;   // No spot found for this vehicle
  }

  public void unparkVehicle(Vehicle vehicle) {
    ParkingSpot spot = vehicleToSpotMap.remove(vehicle);
    if (spot != null) {
      spotToVehicleMap.remove(spot);
      spot.vacate();
      availableSpots.get(spot.getSize()).add(spot);
    }
  }

  // Find vehicle's parking spot
  public ParkingSpot findVehicleBySpot(Vehicle vehicle) {
    return vehicleToSpotMap.get(vehicle);
  }

  // Find which vehicle is parked in a spot
```

```
  public Vehicle findSpotByVehicle(ParkingSpot spot) {
    return spotToVehicleMap.get(spot);
  }
}
```

Implementation benefits: The bidirectional mapping in `ParkingManager` enhances performance by adding a `spotToVehicleMap` alongside the `vehicleToSpotMap`, enabling $O(1)$ lookups from a vehicle to a parking spot and vice versa. This eliminates the need to iterate through all parked vehicles to identify the one in a given parking spot. It's especially efficient in large parking lots, where such iterations can be expensive.

With this enhancement explored, let's summarize the key takeaways.

Wrap Up

In this chapter, we gathered requirements for the Parking Lot system through detailed questions and answers. We identified the core objects involved, designed the class structure, and implemented the system's key components.

A key takeaway from this design is the value of modularity and clear separation of concerns. Each component, such as Vehicle, `ParkingSpot`, `ParkingManager`, and `FareCalculator`, handles a distinct responsibility, keeping the system maintainable and open to future enhancements.

Our design choices, like using `ParkingLot` as a facade to coordinate operations or employing the `FareStrategy` interface for flexible pricing, emphasize simplicity and adaptability. An alternative approach, such as embedding spot allocation and fare logic directly in `ParkingLot`, might reduce the number of classes but could complicate scalability by overloading a single class with multiple responsibilities. In an interview, reflecting on these decisions and articulating their benefits showcases your ability to balance trade-offs in object-oriented design.

Congratulations on getting this far! Now give yourself a pat on the back. Good job!

Further Reading: Strategy and Facade Design Patterns

This section gives a quick overview of the design patterns used in this chapter. It's helpful if you're new to these patterns or need a refresher to understand the design choices better.

Strategy design pattern

The Strategy pattern is a behavioral design pattern that defines a family of algorithms, encapsulates each one in a separate class, and allows their objects to be interchangeable.

In the parking lot design, we have used the Strategy pattern to encapsulate pricing rules in the `FareStrategy` interface (e.g., `BaseFareStrategy`, `PeakHoursFareStrategy`), allowing `FareCalculator` to switch between rules dynamically without altering its core logic.

To illustrate the Strategy pattern in another domain, the following example uses an e-commerce payment system.

Problem

Imagine you're developing an e-commerce application that offers various payment methods, such as credit cards, PayPal, and bank transfers. Initially, you might implement each payment method directly within the checkout process. However, as the application grows, this approach can lead to a monolithic design where the payment processing logic becomes tightly coupled with the checkout system. This tight coupling makes it challenging to add new payment methods or modify existing ones without changing the core checkout code, which increases the risk of introducing bugs and makes the system harder to maintain.

Solution

To address this issue, the Strategy design pattern can be employed. This pattern suggests encapsulating each payment algorithm in a separate class, known as a strategy, and making them interchangeable. The main application, referred to as the context, maintains a reference to a strategy object and delegates the payment processing to this object. This design allows the application to switch between different payment methods, without modifying the core checkout logic.

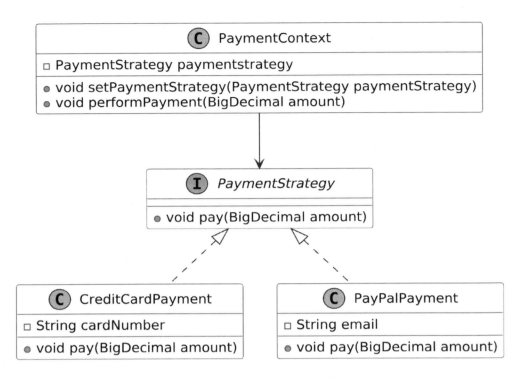

Strategy design pattern class diagram

When to use

The Strategy design pattern is particularly useful in scenarios:

- When an application needs to select different algorithms or behaviors at runtime based on specific conditions, the Strategy pattern is a great fit.
- When a class is cluttered with conditional statements to choose between different algorithm variations, the Strategy pattern simplifies things. It moves each algorithm into its own class, with all classes implementing the same interface. This lets the original object delegate the task to the right class without complex conditionals.
- Use the Strategy pattern to keep your class's business logic separate from the implementation details of the tasks.

Facade design pattern

The Facade pattern is a structural design pattern that provides a simple interface to a complex subsystem, such as a library, framework, or set of classes. It simplifies how clients interact with the system by hiding its underlying complexity.

In the parking lot design, the Facade pattern is used in the ParkingLot class, which streamlines client interactions by managing tasks like vehicle entry, spot assignment, and fee calculation, delegating to subsystems such as ParkingManager and FareCalculator.

To illustrate the Facade pattern in another domain, the following example uses a home theater system.

Problem

Imagine you're setting up a home theater system with multiple components, such as a DVD player, projector, sound system, and lights. To watch a movie, you must turn on each component, adjust settings, and synchronize them. This process is complex, requiring users to understand each component's working. As the system grows, adding new devices (e.g., a streaming device) increases complexity, making it harder to use the system efficiently.

Solution

The Facade pattern addresses this by introducing a single interface, the facade, that encapsulates the subsystem's complexity. For the home theater, a HomeTheaterFacade class could provide methods like watchMovie(), which internally manages all components (e.g., turning on the projector, setting the sound system). Clients interact only with the facade, which delegates tasks to the subsystem, simplifying usage.

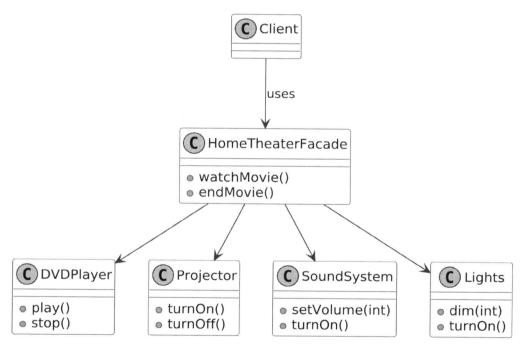

Facade design pattern class diagram

When to use

The Facade design pattern is particularly useful in scenarios:

- When a subsystem is complex, with multiple components or interactions, and you want to provide a simpler interface for clients.

- When you want to layer a system into subsystems, but still offer a unified entry point for common operations.

5

Movie Ticket Booking System

In this chapter, we'll walk through the design of a Movie Ticket Booking System. It's used to assess your ability to model real-world systems and apply object-oriented principles to create a well-structured solution. The goal is to carefully define the classes that represent key entities in a movie booking system, such as rooms, screenings, and movies. We'll aim to build a clear and functional structure that captures the essential interactions between these components, making the system intuitive and scalable.

Let's move on to gathering the specific requirements through a simulated interview scenario.

Movie Theater

Requirements Gathering

Here is an example of a typical prompt an interviewer might give:

"Imagine you're trying to book tickets for a blockbuster movie on a busy weekend. You log into the booking system, browse through the available showtimes, select your preferred seats, and proceed to book them. Within moments, your tickets are confirmed, and you receive a digital ticket. Behind the scenes, the system is efficiently managing seat availability, tracking screenings, and calculating ticket costs. Now, let's design a movie ticket booking system that handles all of this seamlessly."

To refine the system's scope, the candidate might ask the following questions:

Requirements clarification

Here is an example of how a conversation between a candidate and an interviewer might unfold:

Candidate: Does the system support finding and booking tickets across different cinemas and rooms?
Interviewer: Yes, users can search for available tickets across multiple cinemas, each containing multiple rooms.

Candidate: Does the system allow scheduling multiple screenings of the same movie across different rooms and times?
Interviewer: Yes, each movie can have different screenings scheduled across various rooms and times in the same cinema or different cinemas.

Candidate: Does the system support different pricing tiers for seats within the same screening?
Interviewer: Yes, each seat can have its pricing strategy, such as normal, premium, or VIP, affecting the ticket price.

Candidate: Can a user book multiple tickets in a single order, and how does the system calculate the total cost?
Interviewer: Yes, users can combine multiple tickets into one order for a specific screening. The system calculates the total cost by summing the prices of all selected seats based on their rate classes.

Candidate: Does the system need to handle payment processing as part of the booking process?
Interviewer: For this design, we can ignore payment processing and focus on browsing, scheduling, seat selection, and booking tickets.

Candidate: What happens when a user books a ticket for a specific seat?
Interviewer: The system should create a ticket with the screening, seat, and price based on the seat's pricing strategy, then add it to the screening's ticket list, marking the seat as

booked.

Requirements

Based on the questions and answers, the following functional requirements can be identified:

Movie and screening management

- Each cinema is located at a specific location and contains multiple rooms.
- Movies can have multiple screenings scheduled across different rooms, cinemas, and time slots.

Seat management and pricing

- Each room has a grid of seats available for booking.
- Seats within a room can have varying pricing strategies (e.g., normal, premium, VIP) that affect ticket prices.

User search and book flow

- Users can find and book available tickets.
- A ticket represents a specific seat to watch a movie in a room at a particular time.
- A user can book multiple tickets within the same order.
- The total cost for an order is computed by summing the prices of all selected seats, based on their pricing tiers.

Below are the non-functional requirements:

- Fast searches for screenings for a smooth user experience.
- Basic error handling should prevent booking conflicts, such as double-booking the same seat.

With these requirements in hand, the next step is to identify the core objects that will form the backbone of our system.

Identify Core Objects

To build a modular and maintainable system, we'll define objects that represent distinct entities with clear responsibilities. Here are the core objects:

- **Movie:** Represents a specific movie shown in cinemas, capturing its essential details like title and duration.

> ✖ **Design choice:** We separate `Movie` from `Screening` to distinguish fixed movie data from dynamic screening schedules, improving reusability and clarity.

- **Cinema:** Models a physical location where movies are screened, containing multiple rooms.
- **Room:** Defines a screening space within a cinema, tied to a unique layout of seats.

> ✂ **Design choice:** Separating Room from Layout allows rooms to share or customize seating arrangements, enhancing flexibility.

- **Layout:** Organizes the seating arrangement in a room as a grid, managing seat positions.
- **Seat:** Represents an individual seat in a room linked to a pricing strategy.
- **Screening:** Combines a movie, a room, and a time slot to define when and where a movie is shown.
- **Ticket:** Captures a customer's choice of a specific seat for a screening, including its price.
- **Order:** Groups multiple tickets purchased together into a single transaction, tracking the total cost.

Alternative approach: We could merge `Room` and `Layout` into one class, but this limits flexibility if rooms need varied layouts. Another option is adding a `Customer` class, but since the focus is on booking mechanics, we prioritize ticket-related entities.

Interview tip: When presenting objects in an interview, explain why you chose them and how they meet the requirements. Mention alternatives (e.g., combining classes) to show you've considered different options and their trade-offs.

Design Class Diagram

Now that we know the core objects and their roles, the next step is to create classes and methods to build the movie ticket booking system.

Movie

The `Movie` class captures essential details about a specific movie in the system. It focuses on static information, title, genre, and duration, data that remains constant across all screenings of that film. It stands apart from a `Screening`, which ties a movie to a room and time slot for a particular showing.

Below is the UML diagram for the `Movie` class.

Design choice: We designed the `Movie` class to be a standalone entity, independent of cinema-specific or scheduling contexts. This isolation allows the same `Movie` to be reused across multiple cinemas and screenings without data duplication.

Seat

The Seat class holds key details about an individual seat, including its unique number. It uses the strategy pattern, implemented through the `PricingStrategy` interface with concrete classes like `NormalRate`, `PremiumRate`, and `VIPRate`, to manage price calculation flexibly.

The strategy pattern benefits the system in two key ways:

- It promotes extensibility, making it easy to add new rate classes.
- It reduces code redundancy by using a single Seat class for all pricing variations.

The UML diagram below illustrates this structure.

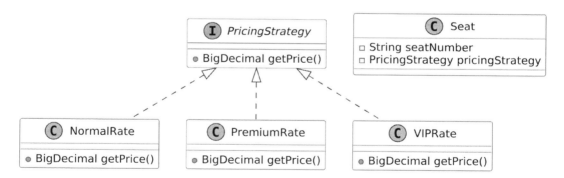

Seat and `PricingStrategy` Design

Alternative approach: We could embed pricing logic directly in Seat, but this reduces flexibility if pricing rules change. The strategy pattern, while more complex, supports future extensions.

The `Seat` class relies on a `Layout` to define its position in a room's seating grid, focusing solely on seat-specific data like its number and pricing strategy.

Note: To learn more about the Strategy pattern and its everyday use cases, refer to the **Parking Lot** chapter of the book.

Layout

The Layout class acts as a bridge between individual seats and cinema rooms. It organizes seats into a grid structure defined by rows and columns. It uses a nested map (Map<Integer, Map<Integer, Seat>>) for efficient seat lookup, where the outer map's key is the row number, the inner map's key is the column number within that row, and the value is the Seat object at that position (row → column → seat).

It also maintains an index (Map<String, Seat>) to locate seats by their seat numbers quickly. This design simplifies managing seats across multiple theater rooms, ensuring easy access to seat data for booking purposes.

The UML diagram below illustrates this structure.

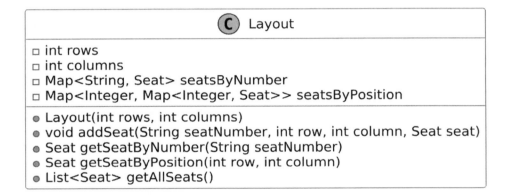

Alternative approach: In Layout, we use a nested map (Map<Integer, Map<Integer, Seat>>) for seat arrangement instead of a 2D array. This allows dynamic row creation with computeIfAbsent and supports variable row sizes. A 2D array for Layout could work for fixed-size rooms but lacks flexibility for irregular layouts or dynamic additions.

Interview tip: When coding, explain why you chose a data structure (e.g., map vs. array) and how it supports your design goals.

Cinema and Room

The Cinema and Room classes structure the cinema system by leveraging the seat and layout framework. A Cinema contains multiple Room instances, exemplifying composition where one class holds another as an attribute. Each Room, in turn, includes a Layout to define its seat arrangement.

Together, these classes form a model of a cinema, with Cinema managing locations and rooms, and Room organizing seat layouts. Their composition ensures a clear hierarchy for managing theater spaces.

Below are the representations of these classes.

Cinema and Room classes

Design choice: We structured the Cinema and Room with a compositional relationship to simulate a real-world cinema with multiple screening rooms. This design allows each Room to operate independently with its layout and schedule, while the Cinema provides a unified context.

Screening

With the cinema structure in place, the Screening class defines a specific showing of a movie in a particular room at a scheduled time. It combines a Movie, a Room, and time details into a single entity.

Design choice: The Screening class centralizes scheduling details, making it easier to manage showtimes across cinemas. It ensures a clear separation of concerns and simplifies schedule management.

Ticket

The Ticket class represents a purchased seat for a specific Screening, combining a Screening and a Seat.

It includes a price attribute, capturing the seat's cost at the time of purchase. This design, despite the Seat class using a strategy pattern for pricing, ensures the ticket price remains fixed, independent of any future changes to the seat's pricing strategy.

Here is the representation of this class.

Order

The Order class groups multiple tickets into a single transaction, capturing all tickets purchased together at a specific time. It tracks the order's timestamp and provides the total cost of the tickets.

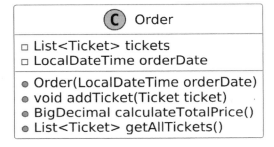

ScreeningManager

Modeling classes like Movie, Seat, and Ticket alone does not create a complete system. To address this, we design a ScreeningManager class that manages key operations, such as searching for screenings of specific movies, identifying available seats, and storing purchased tickets.

The following UML diagram shows the ScreeningManager structure.

C ScreeningManager
☐ Map<Movie, List<Screening>> screeningsByMovie ☐ Map<Screening, List<Ticket>> ticketsByScreening
● void addScreening(Movie movie, Screening screening) ● void addTicket(Screening screening, Ticket ticket) ● List<Screening> getScreeningsForMovie(Movie movie) ● List<Ticket> getTicketsForScreening(Screening screening) ● List<Seat> getAvailableSeats(Screening screening)

✂ **Design choice:** The ScreeningManager class serves as a central coordinator for screening and ticket-related operations. An alternative could be to embed these operations in the Cinema class, with each cinema managing its screenings and tickets. However, this would couple the static cinema attributes (e.g., location and rooms) with the logic for scheduling and booking, reducing the system's modularity and maintainability.

MovieBookingSystem

The MovieBookingSystem class is the final piece that brings all components together. It integrates the list of movies, cinema locations, and an instance of ScreeningManager into a cohesive system. It acts as a facade, streamlining user interactions by delegating tasks to underlying classes like ScreeningManager, Movie, and Cinema.

Through MovieBookingSystem, key operations, such as adding movies or cinemas, finding screenings for a movie, checking available seats, and booking tickets, are centralized. This design enhances usability by offering a single entry point for these functions while preserving modularity, as each task remains handled by its respective class.

Here is the representation of this class.

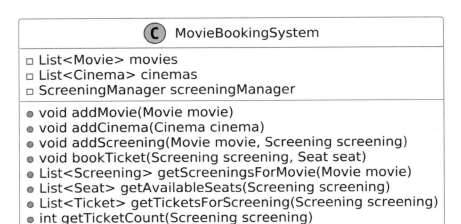

MovieBookingSystem

- ▢ List<Movie> movies
- ▢ List<Cinema> cinemas
- ▢ ScreeningManager screeningManager

- ● void addMovie(Movie movie)
- ● void addCinema(Cinema cinema)
- ● void addScreening(Movie movie, Screening screening)
- ● void bookTicket(Screening screening, Seat seat)
- ● List<Screening> getScreeningsForMovie(Movie movie)
- ● List<Seat> getAvailableSeats(Screening screening)
- ● List<Ticket> getTicketsForScreening(Screening screening)
- ● int getTicketCount(Screening screening)

Alternative approach: We designed the `MovieBookingSystem` class as a facade to provide a simplified interface for client code. An alternative could be to allow client code to directly interact with classes like `ScreeningManager` or Cinema. However, this would increase coupling between clients and internal components, potentially leading to fragile and error-prone interactions. The facade pattern enhances maintainability and simplifies system interactions.

Complete Class Diagram

Below is the class diagram of our movie ticket booking system.

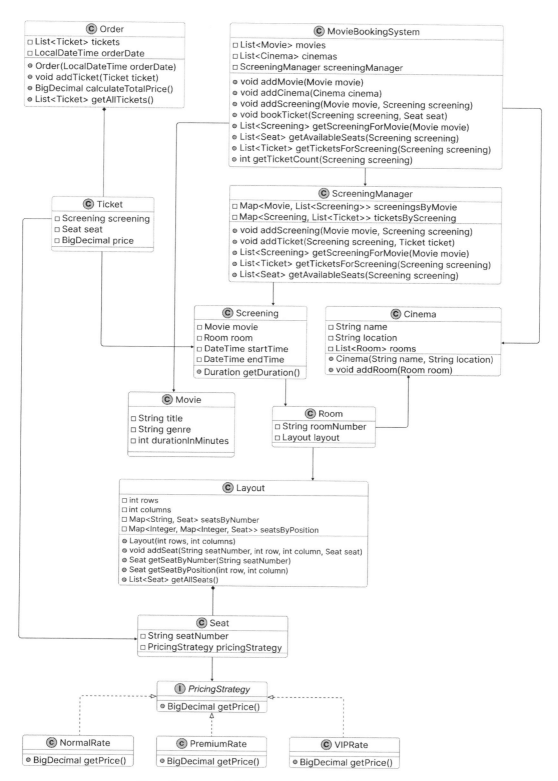

Class Diagram of Movie Ticket Booking System

Code - Movie Ticket Booking System

In this section, we'll implement the core functionalities of the movie ticket booking system, focusing on key areas such as handling cinema and movie listings, scheduling screenings, managing seat selection and availability, and processing ticket bookings through an order system.

Movie

The Movie class represents the static details of a film, such as its title, genre, and duration, which remain consistent across all screenings. The class is designed to be immutable, as it does not include setter methods, ensuring that movie details cannot be altered once the object is created. This immutability guarantees data integrity and reflects the static nature of a movie's attributes.

Below is the code implementation of this class:

```java
public Movie(String title, String genre, int durationInMinutes) {
  this.title = title;
  this.genre = genre;
  this.durationInMinutes = durationInMinutes;
}

public Duration getDuration() {
  return Duration.ofMinutes(durationInMinutes);
}

// getter methods are omitted for brevity
}
```

The getDuration method converts the stored durationInMinutes value into a Duration object, offering a standardized and convenient way to represent and utilize the movie's length for tasks such as scheduling screenings or calculating screening durations.

Cinema

The Cinema class represents a cinema with attributes such as its name, location, and collection of Room objects. The rooms attribute is implemented as a dynamic List, allowing the addition of rooms at runtime using the addRoom method. This design provides flexibility, as cinemas can have varying numbers of rooms.

```java
public class Cinema {
  private final String name;
  private final String location;
  private final List<Room> rooms;

  public Cinema(String name, String location) {
    this.name = name;
    this.location = location;
```

```
    this.rooms = new ArrayList<>();
  }

  public void addRoom(Room room) {
    rooms.add(room);
  }

  // getter and setter methods are omitted for brevity
}
```

Room

The Room class represents a theater room within a cinema, with attributes such as its unique room number and a Layout object that defines its seating arrangement.

```
public class Room {
  private final String roomNumber;
  private final Layout layout;

  public Room(String roomNumber, Layout layout) {
    this.roomNumber = roomNumber;
    this.layout = layout;
  }

  // getter and setter methods are omitted for brevity
}
```

Layout

The Layout class defines the seating arrangement of a cinema room, tracking its rows and columns to form a grid. It uses a nested map (Map<Integer, Map<Integer, Seat>>) for locating seats by row and column positions, and a separate map (Map<String, Seat>) for quick lookup by unique seat numbers.

Below is the implementation of this class.

```
// Represents the seating layout of a cinema room.
public class Layout {
  private final int rows;
  private final int columns;

  // Maps seat numbers (e.g., "0-0") to Seat objects for direct access
  private final Map<String, Seat> seatsByNumber;

  // Nested map for position-based access (row → column → seat)
  private final Map<Integer, Map<Integer, Seat>> seatsByPosition;

  public Layout(int rows, int columns) {
    this.rows = rows;
```

```java
    this.columns = columns;
    this.seatsByNumber = new HashMap<>();
    this.seatsByPosition = new HashMap<>();
    initializeLayout();
  }

  // Creates seats for all positions with default null pricing
  private void initializeLayout() {
    for (int i = 0; i < rows; i++) {
      for (int j = 0; j < columns; j++) {
        String seatNumber = i + "-" + j;
        addSeat(seatNumber, i, j, new Seat(seatNumber, null));
      }
    }
  }

  public void addSeat(String seatNumber, int row, int column, Seat seat)
    {
    // Store seat in number-based lookup map
    seatsByNumber.put(seatNumber, seat);
    // Store seat in position-based lookup map
    seatsByPosition
      .computeIfAbsent(row, k -> new HashMap<>())
      .put(column, seat);
  }

  public Seat getSeatByNumber(String seatNumber) {
    return seatsByNumber.get(seatNumber);
  }

  // Gets a seat by its row and column position
  public Seat getSeatByPosition(int row, int column) {
    Map<Integer, Seat> rowSeats = seatsByPosition.get(row);
    return (rowSeats != null) ? rowSeats.get(column) : null;
  }

  public List<Seat> getAllSeats() {
    return List.copyOf(seatsByNumber.values());
  }
}
```

- The addSeat method employs the computeIfAbsent technique to dynamically create rows in the nested map as needed, streamlining the addition of seats without requiring pre-initialization of the entire grid.

- The getSeatByNumber method retrieves a seat based on its unique string identifier, enhancing lookup efficiency.

- The getSeatByPosition method accesses a seat using its row and column coordinates, supporting precise seat selection.

- The `getAllSeats` method returns an unmodifiable list of all seats, ensuring safe access to the seating data.

`Layout` integrates with the `Room` class to provide the seating structure, working alongside `Seat` objects to support the ticket booking process, such as availability and pricing.

Implementation choice: We used a nested Map<Integer, Map<Integer, Seat>> for the seat grid and a Map<String, Seat> for seat number lookup in the `Layout` class, as these structures provide efficient $O(1)$ access by row-column or seat number. The nested map supports dynamic row creation via `computeIfAbsent`. An alternative could be a 2D array (`Seat[][]`) for the grid, which is simpler for fixed-size layouts and offers direct index-based access. However, arrays lack flexibility for irregular layouts (e.g., missing seats) and require pre-allocation.

Seat

The `Seat` class represents an individual seat in a cinema room with attributes such as its unique `seatNumber` and associated `PricingStrategy`. The `PricingStrategy` provides dynamic pricing for each seat, enabling the system to assign different pricing logic (e.g., normal, premium, VIP) without modifying the `Seat` class itself.

```
public class Seat {
  private final String seatNumber;
  private PricingStrategy pricingStrategy;

  public Seat(String seatNumber, PricingStrategy pricingStrategy) {
    this.seatNumber = seatNumber;
    this.pricingStrategy = pricingStrategy;
  }

  // getter and setter methods are omitted for brevity
}
```

Alternative approach: We implemented the `Seat` class with a `PricingStrategy` interface reference, delegating pricing logic to the strategy pattern. An alternative could be to store the price info directly in `Seat`, with an enum for seat type (e.g., NORMAL, PREMIUM). However, this would embed pricing logic in Seat, making it harder to modify and extend pricing rules without changing the class.

PricingStrategy

The `PricingStrategy` interface establishes a contract requiring the implementation of a `getPrice()` method to provide a seat's price. Concrete classes, like `NormalRate`, `PremiumRate`, and `VIPRate`, encapsulate fixed price values for different seat types, reflecting their respective pricing tiers.

By associating a `PricingStrategy` with each seat, the system achieves flexibility and extensibility in pricing, adhering to the **Open-Closed Principle:** new pricing strategies can be added without modifying existing code.

Here is the implementation of this interface and its concrete classes.

```java
public interface PricingStrategy {
  BigDecimal getPrice();
}

public class NormalRate implements PricingStrategy {
  private final BigDecimal price;

  public NormalRate(BigDecimal price) {
    this.price = price;
  }

  @Override
  public BigDecimal getPrice() {
    return price;
  }
}

public class PremiumRate implements PricingStrategy {
  private final BigDecimal price;

  public PremiumRate(BigDecimal price) {
    this.price = price;
  }

  @Override
  public BigDecimal getPrice() {
    return price;
  }
}

public class VIPRate implements PricingStrategy {
  private final BigDecimal price;

  public VIPRate(BigDecimal price) {
    this.price = price;
  }

  @Override
  public BigDecimal getPrice() {
    return price;
  }
}
```

Screening

The Screening class combines a Movie with a specific room, time, and duration, representing a scheduled instance of that movie being played in a particular cinema room. While the Movie class captures attributes intrinsic to the film itself, the Screening class incorporates contextual details about when and where the movie is being presented, making it specific to a time slot and location.

```java
// Represents a scheduled screening of a movie in a specific cinema room.
public class Screening {
  private final Movie movie;
  private final Room room;
  private final LocalDateTime startTime;
  private final LocalDateTime endTime;

  public Screening(Movie movie, Room room, LocalDateTime startTime,
    LocalDateTime endTime) {
    this.movie = movie;
    this.room = room;
    this.startTime = startTime;
    this.endTime = endTime;
  }

  public Duration getDuration() {
    return Duration.between(startTime, endTime);
  }

  // getter and setter methods are omitted for brevity
}
```

The class provides a getDuration() method to calculate the duration of the screening based on its start and end times.

Ticket

The Ticket class represents a single unit of purchase in the ticket booking system. It connects a Screening (scheduled movie instance) with a specific Seat and assigns a price at the time of booking. This design ensures that the ticket encapsulates all necessary details for a single booking, making it central to the ticketing process.

```java
public class Ticket {
  private final Screening screening;
  private final Seat seat;
  private final BigDecimal price;

  public Ticket(Screening screening, Seat seat, BigDecimal price) {
    this.screening = screening;
    this.seat = seat;
    this.price = price;
```

```
  }

  // getter and setter methods are omitted for brevity
}
```

Order

The `Order` class represents a single transaction in the movie ticket booking system. It encapsulates a collection of `Ticket` objects purchased together and records the date and time of the order (`orderDate`). This design ensures that all tickets associated with a single booking are grouped and tracked cohesively.

```
public class Order {
  private final List<Ticket> tickets;
  private final LocalDateTime orderDate;

  public Order(LocalDateTime orderDate) {
    this.tickets = new ArrayList<>();
    this.orderDate = orderDate;
  }

  public void addTicket(Ticket ticket) {
    tickets.add(ticket);
  }

  // Calculates the total price of all tickets in the order
  public BigDecimal calculateTotalPrice() {
    return tickets.stream()
    .map(Ticket::getPrice)
    .reduce(BigDecimal.ZERO, BigDecimal::add);
  }

  // getter and setter methods are omitted for brevity
}
```

ScreeningManager

The `ScreeningManager` class serves as a centralized manager for showtimes and tickets within the movie ticket booking system. It maintains mappings between `Movie` objects and their corresponding `Screening` instances, as well as between `Screening` objects and their associated `Ticket` objects. This design ensures that the system can dynamically manage showtimes and ticket bookings while maintaining clear relationships between components.

Here is the implementation of this class.

```
// Manages the relationships between movies, screenings, and tickets in
    the booking system
public class ScreeningManager {
  // Maps movies to their scheduled screenings
```

```java
    private final Map<Movie, List<Screening>> screeningsByMovie;
    // Maps screenings to tickets sold for that screening
    private final Map<Screening, List<Ticket>> ticketsByScreening;

    public ScreeningManager() {
      this.screeningsByMovie = new HashMap<>();
      this.ticketsByScreening = new HashMap<>();
    }

    public void addScreening(Movie movie, Screening screening) {
      screeningsByMovie
      .computeIfAbsent(movie, k -> new ArrayList<>())
      .add(screening);
    }

    // Returns all screenings for a specific movie
    public List<Screening> getScreeningsForMovie(Movie movie) {
      return screeningsByMovie.getOrDefault(movie, new ArrayList<>());
    }

    public void addTicket(Screening screening, Ticket ticket) {
      ticketsByScreening
      .computeIfAbsent(screening, k -> new ArrayList<>())
      .add(ticket);
    }

    // Returns all tickets sold for a specific screening
    public List<Ticket> getTicketsForScreening(Screening screening) {
      return ticketsByScreening.getOrDefault(screening, new ArrayList<>());
    }

    // Calculates which seats are still available for a screening
    public List<Seat> getAvailableSeats(Screening screening) {
      List<Seat> allSeats = screening.getRoom().getLayout().getAllSeats();
      List<Ticket> bookedTickets = getTicketsForScreening(screening);

      List<Seat> availableSeats = new ArrayList<>(allSeats);
      for (Ticket ticket : bookedTickets) {
        availableSeats.remove(ticket.getSeat());
      }
      return availableSeats;
    }
  }
}
```

- The addScreening and addTicket methods use computeIfAbsent to dynamically initialize the lists for a movie's screenings or a screening's tickets if they do not already exist.

- The getAvailableSeats method determines which seats are available for a given screening. It retrieves all seats from the room's Layout and removes seats that are already associated with tickets for the screening. This logic ensures accurate seat availability by dynamically reflecting the current booking status.

Implementation choice: We used a `Map<Movie, List<Screening>>` for movie-to-screening mappings and a `Map<Screening, List<Ticket>>` for screening-to-ticket mappings. These maps provide $O(1)$ lookup, optimizing search and booking operations. An alternative could be a `List<Screening>` and `List<Ticket>` with manual filtering to find relevant entries, but this would result in $O(n)$ search times. The map-based approach is more efficient and scalable for managing large numbers of screenings and tickets.

MovieBookingSystem

The `MovieBookingSystem` class serves as a facade for the movie ticket booking system, providing a simplified interface for managing the core data and operations. It abstracts away the complexities of interacting with underlying components, such as `ScreeningManager`, while maintaining seamless integration with `Movie`, `Cinema`, `Screening`, and `Seat`.

Below is the code implementation of this class:

```java
// Manages the complete movie booking system operations
public class MovieBookingSystem {

  private final List<Movie> movies;
  private final List<Cinema> cinemas;
  private final ScreeningManager screeningManager;

  public MovieBookingSystem() {
    this.movies = new ArrayList<>();
    this.cinemas = new ArrayList<>();
    this.screeningManager = new ScreeningManager();
  }

  public void addMovie(Movie movie) {
    movies.add(movie);
  }

  public void addCinema(Cinema cinema) {
    cinemas.add(cinema);
  }

  public void addScreening(Movie movie, Screening screening) {
    screeningManager.addScreening(movie, screening);
  }

  // Books a ticket for a specific seat at a screening
  public void bookTicket(Screening screening, Seat seat) {
    BigDecimal price = seat.getPricingStrategy().getPrice();
    Ticket ticket = new Ticket(screening, seat, price);
    screeningManager.addTicket(screening, ticket);
```

```
  }

  // Returns all screenings for a specific movie
  public List<Screening> getScreeningsForMovie(Movie movie) {
    return screeningManager.getScreeningsForMovie(movie);
  }

  // Returns all available seats for a screening
  public List<Seat> getAvailableSeats(Screening screening) {
    return screeningManager.getAvailableSeats(screening);
  }

  // Returns the number of tickets sold for a screening
  public int getTicketCount(Screening screening) {
    return screeningManager.getTicketsForScreening(screening).size();
  }

  // Returns the list of tickets for a screening
  public List<Ticket> getTicketsForScreening(Screening screening) {
    return screeningManager.getTicketsForScreening(screening);
  }

  // getter and setter methods are omitted for brevity
}
```

Key functionalities include adding movies and cinemas, retrieving available seats for a specific screening, finding screenings for a given movie, and booking tickets.

The bookTicket method dynamically calculates the price of a ticket using the associated seat's PricingStrategy. It then creates a new Ticket instance, associating it with the specified screening and seat, and stores it in the ScreeningManager.

Deep Dive Topics

Now that the basic design is complete, the interviewer might ask you to enhance the movie ticket system's functionality or accommodate more complex use cases.

Handling concurrent bookings

In OOD interviews, concurrency is often discussed for systems like movie ticket booking, where multiple users interact simultaneously. Concurrency adds complexity and requires understanding basic threading concepts. During an interview, ask the interviewer if concurrency needs to be handled in the system.

Problem: Race condition

A race condition occurs when two users attempt to book the same seat at the same time, potentially leading to both receiving confirmation, causing a double-booking. This undermines the system's reliability and user experience.

Solution: Pessimistic and Optimistic locking

To prevent race conditions, we can use locking mechanisms to ensure only one user books a seat at a time, turning parallel actions into sequential ones. There are two common approaches: pessimistic locking and optimistic locking, each with distinct trade-offs.

Pessimistic Locking: This strategy acquires an exclusive lock on a seat at the start of a user's booking process, preventing concurrent access by other users until the lock is released. The lock is held throughout the transaction, spanning seat selection, booking confirmation, or cancellation, ensuring sole access to the seat. For instance, when a user selects a seat, the system locks it until the booking is finalized or abandoned. To mitigate the risk of indefinite locks due to system failures, a timeout mechanism (e.g., 30 seconds) automatically releases the lock if the transaction remains incomplete. Pessimistic locking is well-suited for scenarios with high contention, where multiple users frequently attempt to book the same seat, as it guarantees exclusive access. Its drawback is increased latency due to lock acquisition and release overhead, which can impact system performance under heavy load.

Optimistic Locking: This strategy avoids locking seats during the booking process, instead verifying seat availability at the transaction's final stage. If another user has booked the seat in the interim, the transaction fails, requiring the user to retry. Optimistic locking is lightweight and efficient in low-contention scenarios, where simultaneous booking attempts for the same seat are rare, minimizing the need for retries. However, in high-contention environments, frequent conflicts can lead to multiple retries, degrading user experience, and increasing system load. This approach relies on atomic checks (e.g., using synchronized blocks or database transactions) to ensure consistency during the final validation.

We provide implementation for both locking strategies below.

Implementation: Pessimistic locking

To implement pessimistic locking, we introduce a `SeatLockManager` class that uses Java's concurrency features to manage temporary seat locks. It uses a `ConcurrentHashMap` for thread-safe access and synchronizes critical methods to prevent race conditions during lock creation and cleanup. Each lock has a timeout to prevent permanent holds if a process fails.

```
public class SeatLockManager {
  private final Map<String, SeatLock> lockedSeats = new ConcurrentHashMap
    <>();
  private final Duration lockDuration;

  public SeatLockManager(Duration lockDuration) {
    this.lockDuration = lockDuration;
  }

  public synchronized boolean lockSeat(Screening screening, Seat seat,
    String userId) {
    String lockKey = generateLockKey(screening, seat);
```

```java
    // Clean up lock if expired (on-demand cleanup when another process
    attempts to lock)
    cleanupLockIfExpired(lockKey);
    // Check if a seat is already locked
    if (isLocked(screening, seat)) {
      return false;
    }

    // Create a new lock with expiration time
    SeatLock lock = new SeatLock(userId, LocalDateTime.now().plus(
    lockDuration));
    lockedSeats.put(lockKey, lock);
    return true;
}

public synchronized boolean isLocked(Screening screening, Seat seat) {
  String lockKey = generateLockKey(screening, seat);

  // Clean up lock if expired (on-demand cleanup)
  cleanupLockIfExpired(lockKey);

  // If we reach here, either no lock exists or it's valid
  return lockedSeats.containsKey(lockKey);
}

private void cleanupLockIfExpired(String lockKey) {
  SeatLock lock = lockedSeats.get(lockKey);
  if (lock != null && lock.isExpired()) {
    lockedSeats.remove(lockKey);
  }
}

private String generateLockKey(Screening screening, Seat seat) {
  return screening.getId() + "-" + seat.getSeatNumber();
}

// SeatLock inner class
private static class SeatLock {
  private final String userId;
  private final LocalDateTime expirationTime;

  public SeatLock(String userId, LocalDateTime expirationTime) {
    this.userId = userId;
    this.expirationTime = expirationTime;
  }

  public boolean isExpired() {
    return LocalDateTime.now().isAfter(expirationTime);
  }
```

```
    public String getUserId() {
      return userId;
    }
  }
}
```

- **lockSeat(Screening, Seat, String):** Synchronously attempts to lock a seat for a user by generating a unique lock key, cleaning up any expired locks, and checking if the seat is currently locked. If the seat is available, it creates and stores a new lock with an expiration timestamp to ensure the lock is temporary.

- **isLocked(Screening, Seat):** Checks if a valid lock exists after cleaning up expired locks.

- **cleanupLockIfExpired(String):** Removes expired locks from lockedSeats to free the seat.

Implementation: Optimistic locking

In the optimistic locking approach, the ScreeningManager class is updated to verify seat availability just before finalizing a booking, without acquiring a persistent lock beforehand. The synchronized keyword is used to ensure that the availability check and the booking operation execute atomically, preventing race conditions that could lead to double-booking.

```
// Simplified optimistic locking in ScreeningManager
public synchronized Ticket bookSeatOptimistically(Screening screening,
    Seat seat) {
  // First check if a seat is available (optimistic)
  if (isSeatBooked(screening, seat)) {
    throw new IllegalStateException("Seat is already booked");
  }

  // Create ticket - at this point, we're optimistically assuming
  // the seat is still available
  BigDecimal price = seat.getPricingStrategy().getPrice();
  Ticket ticket = new Ticket(screening, seat, price);

  // Add to booking system - this effectively "reserves" the seat
  ticketsByScreening
  .computeIfAbsent(screening, k -> new ArrayList<>())
  .add(ticket);

  return ticket;
}

// Helper method to check if a seat is already booked
private boolean isSeatBooked(Screening screening, Seat seat) {
  List<Ticket> tickets = getTicketsForScreening(screening);
  return tickets.stream().anyMatch(ticket -> ticket.getSeat().equals(seat
    ));
}
```

bookSeatOptimistically(Screening, Seat): Checks if the seat is booked, creates a `Ticket`, and atomically adds it to the screening's ticket list.

This implementation is lightweight and suitable when race conditions are infrequent, but it may require users to retry if a booking fails due to a conflict.

> 💡 **Interview tip:** In an OOD interview, discussing concurrency shows your ability to handle advanced scenarios. For the movie ticket booking system, pessimistic locking is often preferred for popular screenings with high contention, while optimistic locking suits simpler cases with fewer conflicts. Ask the interviewer which approach aligns with their expectations, and implement a basic solution like those above.

Wrap Up

In this chapter, we gathered requirements for the Movie Ticket Booking System through a series of thoughtful questions and answers. We then identified the core objects involved, designed the class structure, and implemented the key components of the system.

A key takeaway from this design is the significance of modularity and adherence to the single responsibility principle. Each component, such as the `Movie`, `ScreeningManager`, `Seat`, and `Order` classes, handles a distinct responsibility, ensuring the system remains maintainable and adaptable for future enhancements.

Our design choices, such as separating `Movie` and `Screening` or using a strategy pattern for pricing, prioritize flexibility and scalability. An alternative, like merging `Screening` and `Ticket`, might simplify the model but could complicate individual seat management. In an interview, revisiting these decisions and explaining their rationale showcases your critical thinking ability.

Congratulations on getting this far! Now give yourself a pat on the back. Good job!

6

Unix File Search System

In this chapter, we will explore the design of a Unix File Search system. The goal is to design classes that represent abstractions of the key entities in a file search system, such as directories, files, and filter criteria. We'll aim to create a clear and functional structure that captures the essential interactions between these components, ensuring the search system is intuitive and scalable.

```
$ find . -name "* . java"
./Movie_Ticket_Code/movie_ticket/rate/VIPRate.java
./Movie_Ticket_Code/movie_ticket/rate/NormalRate.java
./Movie_Ticket_Code/movie_ticket/rate/PremiumRate.java
./Movie_Ticket_Code/movie_ticket/rate/PricingStrategy.java
```

Unix file search

Let's gather the specific requirements through a simulated interview scenario.

Requirements Gathering

Here is an example of a typical prompt an interviewer might give:

"Imagine you're a developer trying to find specific files on a Unix system, like files owned by a user, or text files matching a pattern, buried deep in a directory structure. You run a search command, specify your criteria, and the system returns matching files quickly. Behind the scenes, it's recursively traversing directories, evaluating file attributes, and applying your filters efficiently. Let's design a Unix File Search system that handles this process."

Requirements clarification

Here is an example of how a conversation between a candidate and an interviewer might unfold:

Candidate: What attributes does the find command use to search for files?

Interviewer: It could be based on criteria like size, file type, filename, and owner.

Candidate: Does it need to handle directories?
Interviewer: Yes, directories are considered as files too, with a distinct file type.

Candidate: What types of comparisons does the command support?
Interviewer: That depends on the type of attribute. For strings, we support 'equals' and 'regex match'. For numbers, we support 'greater than', 'equals', and 'less than'.

Candidate: Can we combine multiple criteria, even on the same attribute?
Interviewer: Yes, with multiple criteria, using 'and', 'or', and 'not' conditions.

Candidate: I assume we're designing a system to search a directory and its sub-directories, returning files that match the given conditions.
Interviewer: Yes, that's a fair assumption.

Constructing concrete examples

With the requirements for our Unix File Search system in hand, let's see them in action through some real-world command-line searches. These examples will show what the system needs to handle and set the stage for designing our classes:

- **Start with a Simple Search:** Find files recursively within / where `size > 10`.
- **Scale Up to a Complex Search:** Find files recursively within / where `((size > 10 and size < 1000 and owner = "alice") or (size > 1000 and !(filename matches /prefix.*/)))`.

Requirements

Based on the questions and answers, the following functional requirements can be identified:

- The search system can search for files based on attributes such as size, type, filename, and owner.
- The search system supports comparison types depending on the attribute: 'equals' and 'regex match' for strings, and 'greater than', 'equals', and 'less than' for numbers.
- The system can combine multiple search criteria using logical operators (and, or, not).
- The file search system can perform recursive searches within directories.
- The search system can apply search criteria to directories as well as files.

Below are the non-functional requirements:

- **Scalability:** Efficiently handle large directory trees with thousands or millions of files using resource-efficient traversal strategies.
- **Extensibility:** Support adding new attributes (e.g., modification time) and comparison

operators without altering core traversal or filtering logic.

- **Separation of concerns:** Keep traversal logic separate from filtering logic for a modular and maintainable design.

With these requirements established, let's move on to identifying the core objects that will bring this system to life.

Identify Core Objects

Now that we've seen how Unix file searches work, it's time to design a system that can handle them. Let's break it down into core objects, each with a clear role, to create a file search system that's both modular and easy to maintain. Here's what we'll need:

- **FileSearch:** The central entity managing the search process, serving as the entry point into our application logic. It recursively traverses the filesystem from a starting `File` (directory) and returns matches based on a `FileSearchCriteria` object.
- **File:** Models a file or directory in the filesystem, storing attributes like size, type, filename, and owner. It supports a hierarchical structure with entries for subdirectories or files.

> ✂ **Design choice:** The `File` object represents files and directories as a single entity. This enables `FileSearch` to perform consistent traversal and evaluation. This design aligns with the Unix principle that treats everything as a file for uniform handling.

- **FileSearchCriteria:** Encapsulates a search condition and determines whether a given `File` matches it by delegating to a `Predicate`. This wrapper class decouples the search execution logic (`FileSearch`) from the condition evaluation logic (`Predicate`), promoting separation of concerns and greater flexibility.
- **Predicate:** An interface defining the contract for evaluating whether a `File` matches a condition, enabling both simple checks (e.g., "size > 10") and composite conditions (e.g., AND, OR, NOT). We separate `Predicate` from `FileSearchCriteria` to isolate comparisons and logical combinations from how `FileSearch` uses the criteria. This keeps `FileSearchCriteria` a lightweight wrapper, while `Predicate` manages the complex logic.
- **SimplePredicate:** Implements `Predicate` to compare one file attribute (e.g., "size > 10") against a value with an operator (e.g., equals, greater than).
- **CompositePredicate:** Extends `Predicate` for combining conditions (e.g., AND, OR, NOT) with implementations like `AndPredicate`, `OrPredicate`, and `NotPredicate`. It supports complex queries, such as "size > 10 AND owner = 'bob'".
- **ComparisonOperator:** An interface defining how attribute values are compared, with implementations like `EqualsOperator`, `RegexMatchOperator`, `GreaterThanOperator`

, and `LessThanOperator`.

Alternative approach: We could merge `FileSearchCriteria` and `Predicate` into a single class, embedding the matching logic directly in `FileSearch`. This simplifies the design by removing one layer but reduces modularity, as the search logic would be tightly coupled to condition evaluation, making it harder to swap criteria. For instance, switching the condition from "`size > 10`" to "`owner = 'bob'`" would require updating `FileSearch`.

Design Class Diagram

We've mapped out the core objects, such as `File` and `FileSearch`, for our Unix File Search system. Now, let's define their classes, pinning down their roles and methods to keep everything clear and modular.

File

To model a filesystem for searching, we need a way to represent files and directories. Rather than relying on a standard library like Java's `java.io.File`, we define a custom `File` class as the core entity, capturing key attributes and supporting hierarchical traversal. It's paired with a `FileAttribute` enum for attributes used in search conditions.

Below is the representation of this class and the enum.

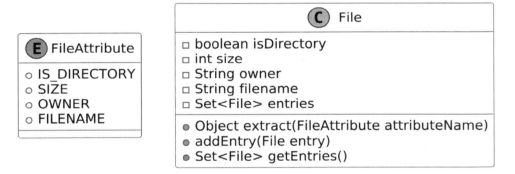

File class

> ✂ **Design choice:** We define `FileAttribute` as an enum to provide a fixed, type-safe set of attributes (e.g., size, owner) for search conditions. This ensures that only valid, predefined attributes are used when evaluating files, preventing runtime errors from invalid attribute names. It also supports scalability: adding a new attribute, such as modification time, requires simply extending the enum, keeping the system extensible without altering existing logic.

FileSearch

The `FileSearch` class is responsible for traversing the file system from a given `File`, using a `FileSearchCriteria` object to select matching files and return them. By separating traversal from filtering logic, the design remains modular, maintainable, and easy to extend. The UML diagram below illustrates this structure.

FileSearchCriteria

The `FileSearchCriteria` class decides which files match our search by connecting `FileSearch` to Predicate. It tells `FileSearch` what qualifies as a match, using `Predicate` to check each `File` against the conditions.

Here is the representation of this class.

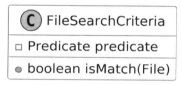

> ✂ **Design choice:** We designed `FileSearchCriteria` to work alongside `Predicate`, allowing it to evaluate whether a file meets the search conditions without handling all the logic itself. This keeps responsibilities clean and modular.
>
> For example, `FileSearchCriteria` delegates to a `Predicate` to check if a file's size is greater than 10 or if the owner is "bob." This delegation enables flexibility. We can change or combine filtering logic (like checking different attributes or using complex conditions) without modifying either `FileSearch` or `FileSearchCriteria`.
>
> By decoupling the search traversal from condition evaluation, we preserve the separation of concerns and make the system easier to extend and maintain.

Predicate and SimplePredicate

A key part of our design is the ability to define conditions that determine whether a file should be included in the search results. These conditions can range from simple to complex. For example, we might want files whose names follow a regular expression like `report.*`, or files with sizes exceeding 10 bytes. To manage this, we introduce the `Predicate` interface as the foundation for evaluating files. It defines a single method that takes a `File` object and returns a boolean: true if the file satisfies the condition, false otherwise.

For straightforward conditions, we implement the `SimplePredicate` class. This concrete class evaluates a single file attribute, such as size or owner, against a specified value using a comparison operator (like greater than or equal). For instance, it can check "is the size bigger than 10?" or "is the owner 'bob'?" by leveraging the `FileAttribute` enum and a `ComparisonOperator` instance. The UML diagram below illustrates how these pieces fit together.

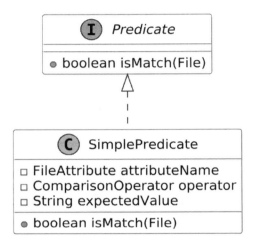

Predicate interface and concrete class

ComparisonOperator

The `ComparisonOperator` interface defines a contract for comparing a file's attribute value (like size or name) to an expected value, answering questions like "is the size greater than 10?" or "does the filename match the pattern `log.*`?" It declares a method that takes two values (the attribute's actual value and the target value), and returns a boolean indicating whether the comparison holds. We implement this interface with concrete classes, such as:

- `EqualsOperator` confirms if two attribute values are the same, like "is the owner 'bob'?"
- `GreaterThanOperator` verifies if one attribute value is larger, like "is the size over 10?"
- `LessThanOperator` ensures one attribute value is smaller, like "is the size under 5?"
- `RegexMatchOperator` evaluates whether a string attribute value satisfies a regular expression pattern, such as checking if the filename matches `log.*` (e.g., `log.txt` or `logger` would return true).

This interface-based design allows `SimplePredicate` to delegate comparisons to specialized classes like `EqualsOperator` or `RegexMatchOperator`, each optimized for its operation, enabling precise and efficient file filtering in `FileSearchCriteria`.

The UML diagram below shows how this structure comes together.

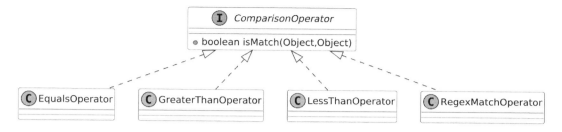

ComparisonOperator interface and concrete classes

Alternative approaches: We could represent operations with strings such as **"equals"** or **">"**. This simplifies initial implementation but shifts validation to runtime. Each string must be parsed and mapped to a comparison function, which increases execution time and risks runtime exceptions if an invalid operator (e.g., **"equals"**) is left unchecked.

Another option is to use enums like `EQUALS` or `GREATER_THAN` to represent comparison operations. This makes the code safer and faster because the operations are checked at compile time, not at runtime. However, if you want to add a new operation, like case-insensitive equality for owner names, you would need to change the enum itself. In contrast, with the interface-based approach, you can just create a new class for the new operation without touching existing code.

Composite Predicate

With `SimplePredicate` and its `ComparisonOperator` implementations in place, we can already test files against single conditions like `size > 10` or `owner = 'alice'`. But real-world searches often demand more, combining multiple conditions with logical operators. To tackle this, we use the Composite design pattern, enabling us to build complex predicates from simpler ones.

Note: To learn more about the Composite Pattern and its common use cases, refer to the **Further Reading** section at the end of this chapter.

Consider a search like this:

Find files where ((`size > 10 and size < 1000 and owner =` "alice") or (`size > 1000 and !(filename matches /prefix.*/)`)).

If we label each simple condition:

- A for "`size > 10`"
- B for "`size < 1000`"
- C for "`owner = 'alice'`"

- D for "`size > 1000`"
- "`filename matches 'prefix.*'`"
- It becomes: `((A and B and C) or (D and !(E)))`

This structure uses "and," "or," and "not" operators, with brackets indicating the order of nested evaluations. This tree-like hierarchy needs a systematic way to evaluate files.

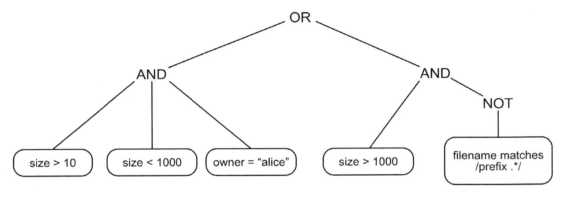

Tree evaluation

To handle this, we define the `CompositePredicate` interface, extending Predicate, with concrete implementations: `AndPredicate`, `OrPredicate`, and `NotPredicate`. These classes compose multiple predicates into a single unit, evaluated recursively:

- `AndPredicate` takes a list of predicates (e.g., A, B, C) and returns true only if all succeed for a given file.
- `OrPredicate` takes a list (e.g., the AndPredicate result and another group) and returns true if at least one succeeds.
- `NotPredicate` wraps a single predicate (e.g., E) and inverts its result.

In our example:

- `AndPredicate` combines "`size > 10`", "`size < 1000`", and "`owner = 'alice'`" into one check.
- Another `AndPredicate` pairs "`size > 1000`" with a `NotPredicate` that negates "`filename matches 'prefix.*'`".
- `OrPredicate` links these two groups, returning true if either holds.

This structure, rooted in CompositePredicate, delivers a boolean result to FileSearchCriteria efficiently by distributing evaluation across the tree, avoiding redundant checks.

The UML diagram below illustrates this recursive composition.

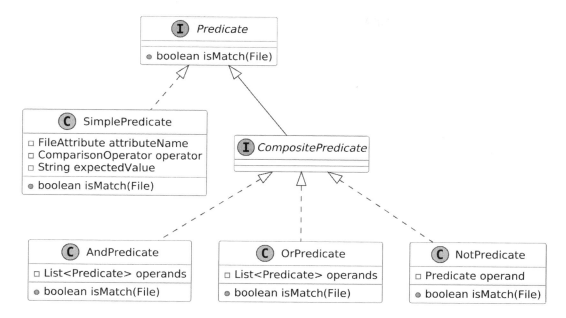

CompositePredicate interface and concrete classes

With all classes defined, let's review how they fit together in the complete class diagram.

Complete Class Diagram

Having built our classes, from the hierarchical `File` structure to the intricate predicate logic, we're ready to see the complete system in a UML class diagram below. The detailed methods and attributes are skipped to make the diagram more readable.

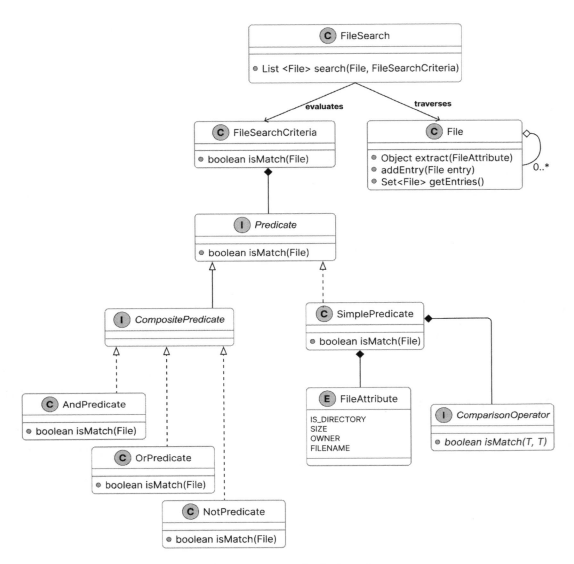

Class Diagram of File Search

Code - Unix File Search

Now that the design is in place, we can move on to implementing the core components: defining files and their attributes, applying conditions to evaluate matches, and performing the actual file search across the directory structure.

File

The File class models both files and directories in our search system, encapsulating attributes such as size, name, owner, and a boolean flag indicating directory status. It maintains a hierarchical structure through a set of child File objects, which represent the contents of subdirectories. Built for immutability, it offers no setters. Attributes are set at construction and remain unchanged, ensuring data consistency throughout the search process.

Tied to this, the `FileAttribute` enum defines the searchable properties, such as `SIZE` or `OWNER`, enabling `SimplePredicate` to extract the correct value (e.g., size for a "`size > 10`" condition) during evaluation.

Below is the code implementation:

```java
// Represents a file or directory in the file system
// Contains basic file attributes and supports hierarchical structure
public class File {
  private final boolean isDirectory;
  private final int size;
  private final String owner;
  private final String filename;
  // Set of directory entries (files and subdirectories)
  private final Set<File> entries = new HashSet<>();

  // Creates a new file with the specified attributes
  public File(final boolean isDirectory, final int size, final String
    owner, final String filename) {
    this.isDirectory = isDirectory;
    this.size = size;
    this.owner = owner;
    this.filename = filename;
  }

  // Extracts the value of a specified file attribute
  public Object extract(final FileAttribute attributeName) {
    switch (attributeName) {
      case SIZE -> {
        return size;
      }
      case OWNER -> {
        return owner;
      }
      case IS_DIRECTORY -> {
        return isDirectory;
      }
      case FILENAME -> {
        return filename;
      }
    }
    throw new IllegalArgumentException("invalid filter criteria type");
  }

  // Adds a file or directory entry to this directory
  public void addEntry(final File entry) {
    entries.add(entry);
```

```
  }

  // getter methods omitted for brevity
}

// Represents the different attributes that can be checked for a file
public enum FileAttribute {
  IS_DIRECTORY,
  SIZE,
  OWNER,
  FILENAME
}
```

- The extract method retrieves a specific attribute's value by mapping a `FileAttribute` enum constant (like `SIZE` or `OWNER`) to its corresponding field. This provides `SimplePredicate` with the value needed to evaluate a condition, such as size for "size > 10".

- Complementing this, the `addEntry` method builds the directory hierarchy by adding a `File` instance to the entries set, enabling the recursive structure essential for file system traversal.

Predicate

The `Predicate` interface defines the contract for evaluating whether a `File` satisfies a search condition, serving as the cornerstone of our system's filtering logic. It declares a single method, `isMatch`, which accepts a `File` instance and returns a boolean: true if the file meets the condition, false otherwise. Here's its implementation:

```
// Base interface for all file search predicates
public interface Predicate {
  // Checks if the given file matches the search condition
  boolean isMatch(final File inputFile);
}
```

This method powers `FileSearchCriteria` by providing the yes-or-no decision needed to filter files during traversal. Its abstract nature ensures flexibility, supporting everything from simple checks like **"size > 10"** to complex combinations, laying the groundwork for both `SimplePredicate` and `CompositePredicate` implementations.

ComparisonOperator

The `ComparisonOperator` interface specifies a contract for comparing a file's attribute value to an expected value, enabling precise condition checks, such as "is the size greater than 10?" or "does the filename match `log.*?`". It defines an `isMatch` method that takes two parameters (the attribute's actual value and the target value) and returns a boolean indicating if the comparison holds.

We use generics (`<T>`) to enforce type safety, ensuring that numeric attributes (e.g., Double for size) are compared only with numbers, and string attributes (e.g., String for names) are compared only with strings.

Below is the implementation of this interface:

```
// Base interface for all comparison operations in the file search system
public interface ComparisonOperator<T> {
  boolean isMatch(final T attributeValue, final T expectedValue);
}
```

Concrete implementations, such as EqualsOperator, GreaterThanOperator, LessThanOperator, and RegexMatchOperator, encapsulate the logic for equality, ordering, and pattern matching, each tailored to its respective type. These are shown below.

```
// Implements exact equality comparison between values
public class EqualsOperator<T> implements ComparisonOperator<T> {
  @Override
  public boolean isMatch(final T attributeValue, final T expectedValue) {
    return Objects.equals(attributeValue, expectedValue);
  }
}

// Implements greater than comparison for numeric values
class GreaterThanOperator<T extends Number> implements ComparisonOperator
    <T> {
  @Override
  public boolean isMatch(final T attributeValue, final T expectedValue) {
    return Double.compare(attributeValue.doubleValue(), expectedValue.
    doubleValue()) > 0;
  }
}

// Implements less than comparison for numeric values
class LessThanOperator<T extends Number> implements ComparisonOperator<T>
    {
  @Override
  public boolean isMatch(final T attributeValue, final T expectedValue) {
    return Double.compare(attributeValue.doubleValue(), expectedValue.
    doubleValue()) < 0;
  }
}

// Implements regular expression pattern matching for string values
public class RegexMatchOperator<T extends String> implements
    ComparisonOperator<T> {
  @Override
  public boolean isMatch(final T attributeValue, final T expectedValue) {
    final Pattern p = Pattern.compile(expectedValue);
    return p.matcher(attributeValue).matches();
```

```
    }
}
```

The `isMatch` method takes an actual value (from a `File` attribute) and an expected value (set in `SimplePredicate`), and returns true if they satisfy the operator's rule.

Implementation choice: We leverage generics (`<T>`) in this design to enforce type safety at compile time, ensuring that attribute values and expected values align in type, such as Double for size or String for filename, making the code robust and readable.

SimplePredicate

The `SimplePredicate` class implements the `Predicate` interface to test a `File` against a single condition, such as whether its size exceeds 10 or its owner is "bob". Designed with generics (`<T>`), it pairs a `FileAttribute` enum value (e.g., `SIZE`, `OWNER`) with a `ComparisonOperator<T>` and an expected value of type `T` to define the check.

Here's how it's structured:

```
// A basic predicate that compares a file attribute with an expected
    value
public class SimplePredicate<T> implements Predicate {
  // The name of the file attribute to check
  private final FileAttribute attributeName;
  // The operator to use for comparison (equals, contains, greater than,
    etc.)
  private final ComparisonOperator<T> operator;
  // The expected value to compare against
  T expectedValue;

  // Creates a new simple predicate with the specified attribute,
    operator, and
  // expected value
  public SimplePredicate(
  final FileAttribute attributeName,
  final ComparisonOperator<T> operator,
  final T expectedValue) {
    this.attributeName = attributeName;
    this.operator = operator;
    this.expectedValue = expectedValue;
  }

  @Override
  public boolean isMatch(final File inputFile) {
    // Extract the actual value of the attribute from the file
    Object actualValue = inputFile.extract(attributeName);
    // Check if the actual value is of the correct type
    if (expectedValue.getClass().isInstance(actualValue)) {
      // Perform the comparison using the specified operator
```

```
      return operator.isMatch((T) actualValue, expectedValue);
    } else {
      return false;
    }
  }
}
```

This implementation of `SimplePredicate` ensures type safety and modularity, allowing `FileSearchCriteria` to apply precise, single-attribute filters across the filesystem traversal.

CompositePredicate

The `CompositePredicate` interface extends `Predicate` to combine multiple predicates into complex conditions, such as "`size > 10 and owner = 'bob'`". We follow the Composite design pattern, which organizes predicates into a tree where simple ones (like `SimplePredicate`) act as leaves and combinations (like `AndPredicate`) act as nodes, all sharing the `Predicate` interface. This lets us evaluate them recursively, treating single and combined conditions the same way.

Here's the code:

```
public interface CompositePredicate extends Predicate {
  // This interface is intentionally empty as it serves as a marker
  // to identify predicates that combine multiple other predicates (AND,
    OR, NOT)
}

// Implements logical AND operation between multiple predicates
public class AndPredicate implements CompositePredicate {
  // List of predicates that must all match for this predicate to match
  private final List<Predicate> operands;

  // Creates a new AND predicate with the specified predicates
  public AndPredicate(final List<Predicate> operands) {
    this.operands = operands;
  }

  // Checks if the given file matches ALL predicates
  @Override
  public boolean isMatch(final File inputFile) {
    return operands.stream().allMatch(predicate -> predicate.isMatch(
    inputFile));
  }
}

// Implements logical OR operation between multiple predicates
public class OrPredicate implements CompositePredicate {
  // List of predicates, at least one of which must match
```

```java
  private final List<Predicate> operands;

  // Creates a new OR predicate with the specified predicates
  public OrPredicate(final List<Predicate> operands) {
    this.operands = operands;
  }

  @Override
  public boolean isMatch(final File inputFile) {
    return operands.stream().anyMatch(predicate -> predicate.isMatch(
    inputFile));
  }
}

// Implements logical NOT operation on a predicate
public class NotPredicate implements CompositePredicate {
  // The predicate to negate
  private final Predicate operand;

  // Creates a new NOT predicate with the specified predicate to negate
  public NotPredicate(final Predicate operand) {
    this.operand = operand;
  }

  @Override
  public boolean isMatch(final File inputFile) {
    return !operand.isMatch(inputFile);
  }
}
```

- AndPredicate checks if all conditions pass (e.g., "size > 10 and owner = 'bob'").
- OrPredicate checks if any condition passes (e.g., "size > 10 or owner = 'bob'").
- NotPredicate takes a single predicate and flips its isMatch result (e.g., "filename not ending with '.txt'").
- AndPredicate and OrPredicate use List<Predicate> to support any number of conditions.
- NotPredicate takes just one condition.
- Combined Impact: Enables FileSearchCriteria to process nested logical conditions efficiently.

FileSearchCriteria

The FileSearchCriteria class acts as a bridge between FileSearch and the predicate-based conditions that determine which files match, delegating the evaluation to a Predicate, whether a SimplePredicate or CompositePredicate. Here's its implementation:

```java
// Wrapper class that encapsulates a search condition for file matching
```

```java
public class FileSearchCriteria {
  // The predicate that defines what makes a file match
  private final Predicate predicate;

  // Constructor that takes a predicate defining the criteria
  public FileSearchCriteria(final Predicate predicate) {
    this.predicate = predicate;
  }

  // Checks if the given file matches the search criteria
  public boolean isMatch(final File inputFile) {
    return predicate.isMatch(inputFile);
  }
}
```

This design centers on the isMatch method, which invokes the Predicate's logic to assess a File and returns true for matches, such as "size > 10" with SimplePredicate or "size > 10 and owner = 'bob'" with CompositePredicate.

Implementation choice: We chose to wrap the Predicate in FileSearchCriteria to keep FileSearch focused solely on filesystem traversal and isolate condition evaluation to a separate, reusable layer.

Alternative implementation: Instead of using FileSearchCriteria, FileSearch could directly invoke the Predicate's logic to evaluate files. However, this would tightly couple traversal and filtering logic, making it harder to modify or extend conditions independently.

FileSearch

The FileSearch class orchestrates the search across the filesystem, starting from a root File and leveraging FileSearchCriteria to identify matching files through recursive traversal. It employs a stack-based approach to explore directories efficiently. Here's the implementation:

```java
// Main class responsible for performing file system searches
public class FileSearch {
  // Performs a recursive search through the file system starting from
  // root
  // Returns a list of files that match the given criteria
  public List<File> search(final File root, final FileSearchCriteria
    criteria) {
    // List to store matching files
    final List<File> result = new ArrayList<>();
    // Stack to handle recursive traversal without actual recursion
    final ArrayDeque<File> recursionStack = new ArrayDeque<>();
    // Start with the root directory
    recursionStack.add(root);
    // Continue until we've processed all files
    while (!recursionStack.isEmpty()) {
```

```
    // Get the next file to process
    File next = recursionStack.pop();
    // Check if the file matches our criteria
    if (criteria.isMatch(next)) {
      result.add(next);
    }
    // Add all directory entries to the stack for processing
    for (File entry : next.getEntries()) {
      recursionStack.push(entry);
    }
  }
  return result;
  }
}
```

This search method begins by initializing a result list and an `ArrayDeque` stack with the root `File`. It then processes each file by popping it from the stack, evaluating it with the `criteria.isMatch`, and adding matches to the result. For directories, it pushes all entries onto the stack, ensuring every file is visited in a depth-first manner. The returned `List<File>` contains all matches, mutable for flexibility in downstream use, by the client code.

Implementation choice: We opted for a stack over recursive calls to prevent stack overflow in deep filesystems, balancing efficiency with robustness. Alternatively, a recursive method could work for smaller structures, but it risks failure on large or deeply nested directories.

Deep Dive Topic

Now that the basic design is complete, the interviewer might ask you some deep dive questions. Let's check out some of these.

File search test

After implementing our classes, it's a good idea to verify the end-to-end logic. The UNIX file search problem is abstract, so we create a test case to demonstrate how it works.

Here's a test case for the condition "non-directories owned by 'ge.*'":

```
public class FileSearchTest {
  @Test
  public void testFileSearch() {
    // Create a root directory and two files with different owners
    final File root = new File(true, 0, "adam", "root");
    final File a = new File(false, 2000, "adam", "a");
    final File b = new File(false, 3000, "george", "b");

    // Add files to the root directory
```

```
    root.addEntry(a);
    root.addEntry(b);

    // Search criteria: Find non-directory files owned by users matching
    "ge.*"
    final FileSearchCriteria criteria = new FileSearchCriteria(
    new AndPredicate(List.of(
    new SimplePredicate<>(FileAttribute.IS_DIRECTORY,
    new EqualsOperator<>(), false),
    new SimplePredicate<>(FileAttribute.OWNER,
    new RegexMatchOperator<>(), "ge.*"))));

    // Execute the search and get results
    final FileSearch fileSearch = new FileSearch();
    final List<File> result = fileSearch.search(root, criteria);

    // Verify that only one file matches the criteria
    assertEquals(1, result.size());
    // Verify that the matching file is "b"
    assertEquals("b", result.get(0).getFilename());

  }
}
```

Wrap Up

With the UNIX file search system fully implemented and tested, it's time to step back and consider what we've achieved. This chapter began by gathering requirements through a structured dialogue, then progressed to defining core objects, crafting their class structure, and coding the essential components.

The system's maintainability and extensibility are ensured by the clear division of responsibilities among the classes: `File`, `FileSearch`, `FileSearchCriteria`, and `Predicate`, which respectively represent files, traverse directories, evaluate conditions, and define match logic. Our choices, such as separating `FileSearch` from `FileSearchCriteria` and using generics in `ComparisonOperator`, improve scalability and maintain type safety throughout processes. We could have merged `FileSearchCriteria` with `Predicate` into one class for a tighter initial design, but this would blur their distinct roles, making it harder to update or swap condition logic without affecting traversal.

Congratulations on getting this far! Now give yourself a pat on the back. Good job!

Further Reading: Composite Design Pattern

This section gives a quick overview of the design patterns used in this chapter. It's helpful if you're new to these patterns or need a refresher to better understand the design choices.

Composite design pattern

Composite is a structural pattern that lets you organize objects into tree structures and then handle these structures as if they were individual objects.

Problem

Imagine you have two types of objects: File and Folder. A Folder can contain several Files as well as many smaller Folders and so on. Say you decide to create a search system that uses these classes. Searches could involve simple Files on their own, as well as Folders packed with Files, and other Folders. How would you find all items matching a specific condition, like "`size > 10`," across this structure?

Solution

The Composite pattern suggests that we work with Files and Folders through a common interface that declares a method for checking conditions.

Here's how this method works:

- **For a File:** It checks if the `File` matches the condition, like "`size > 10`," and gives a yes or no answer.
- **For a Folder:**
    - It examines each item within, testing whether it meets the condition.
    - It recursively applies this process to any nested folders, traversing the entire tree until all items are evaluated.
    - It can also enforce its constraint, such as "not a directory," to refine the result.

Here's a simple diagram showing the Composite pattern for Files and Folders:

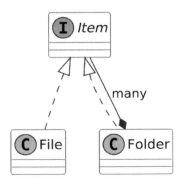

Item interface and concrete classes

`Item` is the common interface that both `File` and `Folder` use. The advantage is that we can treat all objects, `File` or nested `Folder`, the same through the common interface, letting them pass the check down the tree without knowing their types.

When to use

The Composite design pattern is useful in scenarios where:

- You need to build a tree-like object structure.
- When you want the client code to handle both simple and complex elements uniformly.

7

Vending Machine System

In this chapter, we will explore the design of a vending machine system that allows users to select and purchase products, dispense items, manage inventory, and process payments. Although real-world vending machines involve hardware components, like coin dispensers, card readers, and touchscreens, we'll focus on modeling the system's states, data, and core functionality.

Vending Machine

Requirements Gathering

Here is an example of a typical prompt an interviewer might give:

"Imagine you're at a vending machine, craving a snack. You insert some cash, select your favorite item, and within seconds, it drops into the tray. The machine also gives you the right change if needed. Behind the scenes, the system is working smoothly to track inventory, handle payments, and make sure everything runs efficiently. Now, let's design a vending machine that does all this."

Requirements clarification

Here is an example of how a conversation between a candidate and an interviewer might unfold:

Candidate: Does the vending machine support different types of products?
Interviewer: Yes, the vending machine supports a variety of products, such as snacks, beverages, and other items.

Candidate: How are products organized within the vending machine? Are they placed in specific racks or arranged differently? Also, I assume each product needs a unique identifier, like a product code, along with attributes such as its price.
Interviewer: Yes, products are placed in specific racks, with each rack holding only one type of product at a time. Each product also has a unique product code and a price tag.

Candidate: How will payments be processed in the vending machine?
Interviewer: The vending machine should only accept cash payments and calculate change if needed.

Candidate: How does the vending machine handle cases where a user selects a product that is out of stock or unavailable?
Interviewer: In such cases, the system should be able to check if a product is available. If not, it should display an error message to the user.

Candidate: If a user inserts money less than the product's full price, can they add more incrementally?
Interviewer: For this design, let's assume users insert the full amount in one step. If the inserted amount is insufficient, the vending machine should return the money and display an error.

Candidate: Are there any restrictions on who can access the vending machine?
Interviewer: Access to the vending machine is available to users and admins, with different privileges. Users should be able to select and purchase products by specifying the product code. Admins, however, are responsible for adding or removing products from the machine.

Candidate: Are there any security or inventory tracking requirements for the vending machine?
Interviewer: Yes. The vending machine should track inventory, and only the admin can add or remove products.

Requirements

Here are the functional requirements based on the conversation:

- **Product selection:** Users should be able to select from a set of products. Each product has a unique product code, description, and price tag. While description is not talked about, it is a common-sense attribute to make the product model more realistic.

- **Inventory management:** Products are stored in specific racks within the vending machine. The system keeps track of the inventory level for each product in its respective rack.

- **Payment processing:** The system only accepts cash payments and can calculate change when needed.

Below are the non-functional requirements:

- The user interface must be intuitive, allowing users to complete a purchase (insert money, select product, receive product, and change) with minimal instructions, and error messages should be clear and concise to guide users effectively.

- The system must protect against unauthorized access to the vending machine, ensuring only admins can add, remove, or update products, and securely handle cash transactions to prevent tampering or fraud.

Use Case Diagram

A use case diagram illustrates how actors (users or the system) interact with the vending machine system to achieve specific goals. This diagram helps clarify key actions, such as inserting money, selecting a product, dispensing items, and managing inventory.

Below is the use case diagram of the vending machine system.

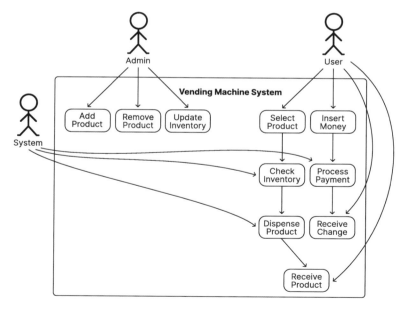

Use Case Diagram of a Vending Machine

The use cases for the **User** actor are as follows:

- Insert Money: The user inserts cash to initiate a purchase.
- Select Product: The user chooses a product by entering its unique product code.
- Receive Product: The user collects the dispensed product from the vending machine.
- Receive Change: The user receives any change if the inserted amount exceeds the product's price.

The use cases for the **Admin** actor are as follows:

- Add Product: The admin adds new products to the vending machine's inventory.
- Remove Product: The admin removes products from the vending machine's inventory.
- Update Inventory: The admin updates the stock levels of existing products in the racks.

The use cases for the **System** actor are as follows.

- Process Payment: The system validates the inserted cash and calculates change if necessary.
- Dispense Product: The system releases the selected product from the appropriate rack.
- Check Inventory: The system verifies the availability of a product before dispensing.

Identify Core Objects

Before diving into the design, it's important to enumerate the core objects and give them appropriate names. These objects will form the foundation of the vending machine's structure and functionality.

- **VendingMachine:** This is the central entity that coordinates the vending machine's operations and serves as the main entry point for user interactions. We will ensure this entity does not become a god object (antipattern) by appropriately delegating responsibilities to other components. The Facade design pattern is very helpful in this case, as it allows a single class to orchestrate end-to-end functionality.
- **Product:** Represents the items stored in the vending machine. Each product has attributes like an identifier, a price, and a description. Products are also linked to the racks where they are stored.
- **Rack:** Represents a designated slot in the vending machine that holds a single product type and stores multiple units of that product. It also includes the dispenser hardware to release one unit of a product at a time upon selection.

- **InventoryManager:** Keeps track of the inventory level within the vending machine.
- **PaymentProcessor:** Interacts with coin dispensers to process payment. It also keeps track of the vending machine balance and calculates change when needed.

Design Class Diagram

Now that we know the core objects and their roles, the next step is to create classes and methods to build the vending machine system.

Product

The first component in our class diagram is the Product class, which represents a basic product within the vending machine. It includes attributes such as product code, description, and the price of the product.

While additional attributes could be added for completeness, we skip them for this exercise. During the interview, it's a good idea to acknowledge these other attributes but focus on the essential attributes to save time and stay aligned with requirements.

Below is the representation of this class.

Rack

Next, we will look at the Rack class, which models a single rack space within the vending machine. Each rack is associated with a single product and can hold multiple units of that product.

We will put multiple racks together via the *composition* technique to represent the inventory spaces within the vending machine.

Here is the representation of this class.

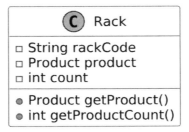

> ✂ **Design choice:** We chose not to have the Rack class include methods like `dispenseProductFromRack`. Instead, we kept the Rack class focused on managing inventory count and product information, delegating actions like dispensing to a higher-level class, such as `InventoryManager`, which aligns with the single responsibility principle.

InventoryManager

Building on the Rack class, the `InventoryManager` class handles the tracking and storage of products in the vending machine. It supports operations such as adding, removing, and dispensing products during user interactions. It will interface with hardware mechanisms that dispense items from the rack.

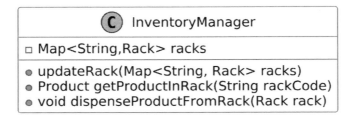

Key method: The `dispenseProductFromRack` method executes the action of dispensing product from the rack and decrements the inventory level. Pay attention to the naming of `dispenseProductFromRack` and `getProductInRack`. To avoid ambiguity, we should follow conventions and reserve the "get" prefix for getters that return attributes.

The `updateRack` method allows for editing product offerings or inventory levels. This allows an admin to edit the state of the rack.

> ✂ **Design choice:** When managing collections like racks in `InventoryManager`, we must decide whether to expose the collection directly, a copy, or specific methods. The choice should balance flexibility and control. Here, we use `updateRack(Map racks)` to allow administrative components to replace the entire rack structure in one operation, suitable for bulk updates. For most cases, we prefer granular methods like `addRack(Rack rack)` and `removeRack(Rack rack)` to limit modifications to individual racks, reducing the risk of unintended changes. These methods are used for read access, aligning with the vending machine's needs. To enhance safety, consider immutable collections or defensive copying to prevent unintended modifications and ensure thread safety in multi-threaded environments.

PaymentProcessor

With inventory management addressed, we now turn to the `PaymentProcessor` class. This class manages payment acceptance, including tracking the current balance and returning change. This will interface with a coin receptacle or a credit card processing unit if supported.

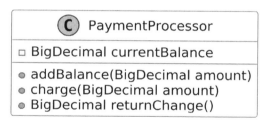

Transaction

In a vending machine system, purchases involve multiple steps, including product selection, payment processing, and confirmation. While components like `PaymentProcessor` handle payments and `InventoryManager` manage stock, the Transaction class acts as a data structure that tracks the current state of a purchase.

This design provides several benefits.

- It encapsulates key details such as the selected product, the rack it belongs to, and the total cost required for the purchase.
- By maintaining a structured record, the vending machine can track an in-progress

transaction before finalizing or canceling it.

- The Transaction class improves coordination between different components. While PaymentProcessor is responsible for deducting the required amount, and InventoryManager ensures the selected product is available and dispenses it, the Transaction object ensures that the vending machine keeps all necessary purchase details in one place so that the system can reference them throughout the transaction process.

Below is the representation of this class.

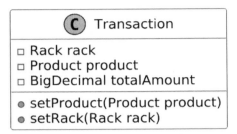

VendingMachine

This class serves as the core component of the system. Here is the representation of the class:

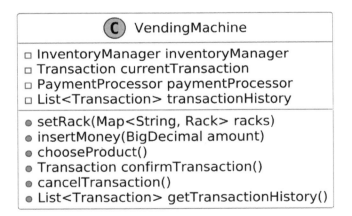

The VendingMachine class models a vending machine's behavior, processes payments, and manages inventory.

Design pattern: The Vending Machine uses the *Facade* pattern to provide a single interface to the clients of the Vending Machine. The term client refers to the software or hardware interfaces of the vending machine rather than any individual users.

Note: To learn more about the Facade pattern and its common use cases, refer to the Parking Lot chapter of this book.

Complete Class Diagram

Below is the complete class diagram of our vending machine system:

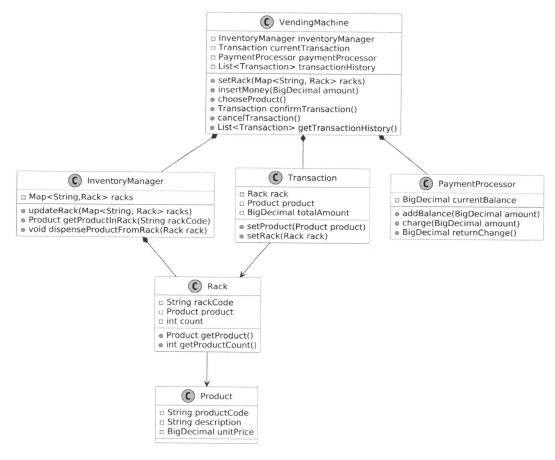

Class Diagram of Vending Machine

Code - Vending Machine

In this section, we'll implement the core functionalities of the vending machine system, focusing on key areas such as managing product inventory, processing cash payments, and handling product selection and dispensing.

Product

We will start by implementing the Product class, which represents a basic unit of a product in the context of a vending machine. The definition of the Product class is given below:

```
class Product {
  final String productCode;
  final String description;
  final BigDecimal unitPrice;

  public Product(String productCode, String description, BigDecimal
    unitPrice) {
    this.productCode = productCode;
    this.description = description;
    this.unitPrice = unitPrice;
  }
}
```

Implementation choice: For monetary values like the unitPrice attribute, we recommend using BigDecimal for its precision and rounding control. For an interview, it is also acceptable to use an integer to represent the smallest unit of currency (e.g., cents for US dollars) to save time. Avoid using float or double for currency, as they introduce precision/rounding errors. For identifiers like productCode, we recommend using a string rather than a numeric type in your code, even if the values are digits, you will most likely not be performing calculations, but string operations.

InventoryManager and Rack

Next, we implement the InventoryManager and Rack classes, which work together to manage the vending machine's inventory. By using the Composite design pattern, we create a hierarchical structure for handling inventory at multiple levels. The InventoryManager class manages the overall inventory, while the Rack class handles individual storage units.

We use a HashMap<String, Rack> to store racks because it allows for efficient lookups by rack code. Since each rack has a unique identifier, a hash map provides constant-time ($O(1)$) access when retrieving or updating a rack. This makes it well-suited for managing inventory in a vending machine, where quick access to product storage is important.

Below is the representation of the two classes:

```
public class InventoryManager {
  // Maps rack codes to their corresponding rack objects
  private Map<String, Rack> racks;

  public InventoryManager() {
    racks = new HashMap<>();
  }

  // Retrieves the product from a specific rack using its code
```

```java
  public Product getProductInRack(String rackCode) {
    return racks.get(rackCode).getProduct();
  }

  // Dispenses a product from the specified rack and decrements its count
  public void dispenseProductFromRack(Rack rack) {
    if (rack.getProductCount() > 0) {
      rack.setCount(rack.getProductCount() - 1);
    } else {
      throw new IllegalStateException("Cannot dispense product. Rack is
    empty.");
    }
  }


  public void updateRack(Map<String, Rack> racks) {
    this.racks = racks;
  }

  public Rack getRack(String name) {
    return racks.get(name);
  }
}
```

Rack class

The Rack class represents individual storage units in the vending machine, each associated with a single product type.

```java
public class Rack {
  private final String rackCode;
  private final Product product;
  private int count;

  public Rack(final String rackCode,
  final Product product,
  final int count) {
    this.rackCode = rackCode;
    this.product = product;
    this.count = count;
  }

  public Product getProduct() {
    return product;
  }

  public int getProductCount() {
    return count;
  }
}
```

PaymentProcessor

The `PaymentProcessor` class handles payment-related operations, such as adding funds, charging for purchases, and returning change. This ensures the vending machine's financial logic is encapsulated and easily maintainable.

```
public class PaymentProcessor {
  // Tracks the current balance in the payment processor
  private BigDecimal currentBalance = BigDecimal.ZERO;

  // Adds the specified amount to the current balance
  public void addBalance(BigDecimal amount){
    currentBalance = currentBalance.add(amount);
  }

  // Deducts the specified amount from the current balance
  public void charge(BigDecimal amount){
    currentBalance = currentBalance.subtract(amount);
  }

  // Returns the current balance as change and resets the balance to zero
  public BigDecimal returnChange() {
    BigDecimal change = currentBalance;
    System.out.println("Trigger giving change: " + change);
    currentBalance = BigDecimal.ZERO;
    return change;
  }

  // Returns the current balance
  public BigDecimal getCurrentBalance() {
    return currentBalance;
  }
}
```

VendingMachine

Finally, we implement the `VendingMachine` class, a central component in the vending machine that is responsible for modeling the vending machine's behavior and handling user interactions.

Below is the implementation of this class.

```
class VendingMachine {
  // Stores the history of all completed transactions
  final private List<Transaction> transactionHistory;
  // Manages the inventory of products in the vending machine
  final private InventoryManager inventoryManager;
  // Handles all payment-related operations
```

```java
final private PaymentProcessor paymentProcessor;

// Tracks the current ongoing transaction
private Transaction currentTransaction;
// Represents the current state of the vending machine
private VendingMachineState currentState;
// Tracks the current balance in the machine
private double balance;
// Stores the currently selected product code
private String selectedProduct;

public VendingMachine() {
  transactionHistory = new ArrayList<>();
  currentTransaction = new Transaction();
  inventoryManager = new InventoryManager();
  paymentProcessor = new PaymentProcessor();
  this.currentState = new NoMoneyInsertedState();
  this.balance = 0.0;
  this.selectedProduct = null;
}

// Updates the rack configuration with new product racks
void setRack(Map<String, Rack> rack) {
  inventoryManager.updateRack(rack);
}

// Adds money to the payment processor
void insertMoney(final BigDecimal amount) {
  paymentProcessor.addBalance(amount);
}

// Selects a product from a specific rack
void chooseProduct(String rackId) {
  final Product product = inventoryManager.getProductInRack(rackId);
  currentTransaction.setRack(inventoryManager.getRack(rackId));
  currentTransaction.setProduct(product);
}

// Processes and completes the current transaction
Transaction confirmTransaction() throws InvalidTransactionException {
  // Step 1: Validate the transaction before processing
  validateTransaction();

  // Step 2: Charge the customer for the product
  paymentProcessor.charge(currentTransaction.getProduct().getUnitPrice
());

  // Step 3: Dispense the product from the rack
  inventoryManager.dispenseProductFromRack(currentTransaction.getRack()
);
```

```java
    // Step 4: Return the change to the customer
    currentTransaction.setTotalAmount(paymentProcessor.returnChange());

    // Step 5: Add the completed transaction to the history
    transactionHistory.add(currentTransaction);
    Transaction completedTransaction = currentTransaction;

    // Reset the current transaction for the next purchase.
    currentTransaction = new Transaction();
    return completedTransaction;
  }

  // Validates the current transaction for product availability and
    sufficient funds
  private void validateTransaction() throws InvalidTransactionException {
    if (currentTransaction.getProduct() == null) {
      throw new InvalidTransactionException("Invalid product selection");
    } else if (currentTransaction.getRack().getProductCount() == 0) {
      System.out.println(currentTransaction);
      throw new InvalidTransactionException("Insufficient inventory for
    product.");
    } else if (paymentProcessor.getCurrentBalance().compareTo(
    currentTransaction.getProduct().getUnitPrice()) < 0) {
      throw new InvalidTransactionException("Insufficient fund");
    }
  }

  // Returns an unmodifiable list of all completed transactions
  public List<Transaction> getTransactionHistory() {
    return Collections.unmodifiableList(transactionHistory);
  }

  // Cancels the current transaction and returns any inserted money
  public void cancelTransaction() {
    paymentProcessor.returnChange();
    currentTransaction = new Transaction(); // Reset the current
    transaction for the next purchase.
  }

  // Returns the inventory manager instance
  public InventoryManager getInventoryManager() {
    return inventoryManager;
  }

}
```

Let's walk through the purchase process and highlight the methods' roles.

- insertMoney(BigDecimal amount): Adds the specified amount to the machine's balance via the `PaymentProcessor` class.

- `chooseProduct()`: Retrieves the product and its corresponding rack from the `InventoryManager` and associates them with the current transaction.

- `confirmTransaction()`: Validates the transaction (e.g., checks for sufficient funds and product availability), processes payment, dispenses the product, and updates the machine's inventory and transaction history.

Deep Dive Topics

Now that the basic design is complete, the interviewer might ask you to enhance the vending machine's functionality or accommodate more complex use cases.

Enforcing task sequences

What if the interviewer asks: "How would you ensure that users insert money before selecting a product?" This is a common requirement in vending machines to prevent invalid actions, such as selecting a product without committing to payment.

To address this, we need to enforce a strict sequence of actions:

1. Users must insert money first.
2. The system checks if the inserted amount is enough for a purchase.
3. If the amount is sufficient, the user can select a product.
4. Finally, the machine dispenses the product.

Additionally, the vending machine should provide feedback at each stage to guide the user. For instance, it might display messages like "Insert money to proceed," "Select a product," or "Please collect your change." How would you go about implementing this?

To handle these requirements, we can introduce the State Pattern. This pattern allows us to model the vending machine's behavior as a set of well-defined states. Let's break it down.

Note: To learn more about the State Pattern and its common use cases, refer to the Further Reading section at the end of this chapter.

Design changes

To enforce task sequences and display state-dependent messages, we will define three distinct states:

NoMoneyInsertedState:

- Represents the initial state where no money has been inserted.
- Displays prompts like *"Insert money to proceed."*
- Users are only allowed to insert money. If a user attempts to select a product without inserting money, it raises an exception.

- Transitions to `MoneyInsertedState` upon successful money insertion.

MoneyInsertedState:

- Represents the state where money has been inserted.
- Displays prompts like *"Select a product."*
- Enables product selection while preventing additional money insertion to avoid overpayment.
- Validates if the selected product is available and the inserted amount covers the product's cost.
- Transitions to `DispenseState` upon successful product selection.

DispenseState:

- Represents the state where the vending machine is prepared to dispense the selected product.
- Displays prompts like *"Dispensing product..."* or *"Please collect your change."*
- Handles product dispensing and resets the machine to the initial state after completion.
- Prevents further actions (e.g., inserting money or selecting another product) until the process is complete.

Why does this work?

The State Pattern explicitly defines the transitions between states, ensuring that actions follow the required order. Here's how it works:

- In `NoMoneyInsertedState`, users can only insert money. If they try to select a product, the system raises an error.
- In `MoneyInsertedState`, users must select a product before the system dispenses anything.
- In `DispenseState`, the vending machine completes the transaction and prevents further actions until it resets.

This approach guarantees the sequence: **Insert Money → Select Product → Dispense Product**.

Each state provides user feedback based on its context:

- `NoMoneyInsertedState`: "Insert money to proceed."
- `MoneyInsertedState`: "Select a product."
- `DispenseState`: "Dispensing product..." or "Please collect your change."

We now define a `VendingMachineState` interface that serves as a blueprint for the three states (`NoMoneyInsertedState`, `MoneyInsertedState`, and `DispenseState`).

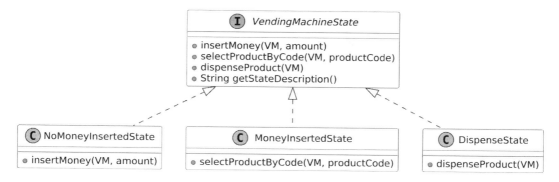

VendingMachineState interface

Code changes

The `VendingMachineState` interface sets the rules for all states of the vending machine. It includes the behaviors that different states of the vending machine should implement, such as inserting money, selecting products, dispensing products, and describing the current state.

```java
public interface VendingMachineState {
  // Handles money insertion in the current state
  void insertMoney(VendingMachine VM, double amount);

  // Handles product selection in the current state
  void selectProductByCode(VendingMachine VM, String productCode) throws
    InvalidStateException;

  // Handles product dispensing in the current state
  void dispenseProduct(VendingMachine VM) throws InvalidStateException;

  // Returns a description of the current state
  String getStateDescription();
}
```

Here is the code for the `NoMoneyInsertedState` class:

```java
public class NoMoneyInsertedState implements VendingMachineState {
  // Adds money to the machine and transitions to MoneyInsertedState
  @Override
  public void insertMoney(VendingMachine VM, double amount) {
    VM.addBalance(amount);
    VM.setState(new MoneyInsertedState());
  }

  // Throws exception as product selection is not allowed without money
  @Override
```

```java
public void selectProductByCode(VendingMachine VM, String productCode)
  throws InvalidStateException {
  throw new InvalidStateException("Cannot select a product without
  inserting money.");
}

// Throws exception as product dispensing is not allowed without money
@Override
public void dispenseProduct(VendingMachine VM) throws
  InvalidStateException {
  throw new InvalidStateException("Cannot dispense product without
  inserting money.");
}

// Returns a description of the current state
@Override
public String getStateDescription() {
  return "No Money Inserted State - Please insert money to proceed";
}
}
```

For brevity, the implementation of the `MoneyInsertedState` and `DispenseState` classes is omitted, but they follow the same structure.

Wrap Up

In this chapter, we have designed and implemented a Vending Machine system. The most important takeaway from this chapter is how we divided responsibilities across classes, such as Product, Rack, `InventoryManager`, and `PaymentProcessor`, while unifying them under a facade for a clear and simple-to-access API. This approach not only simplified the system's external interface but also adhered to the Single Responsibility Principle, ensuring each component focused on a specific responsibility. For instance, the `InventoryManager` managed stock levels, while the `PaymentProcessor` handled cash payments and calculated change.

In the deep dive section, we explored state-based control using the State Pattern to enforce a strict sequence of actions and prevent invalid behaviors like dispensing without payment.

In interviews, remember to emphasize validation and error handling after implementing core functionality, especially for systems where improper behavior could cause damage or financial loss.

Congratulations on getting this far! Now give yourself a pat on the back. Good job!

Further Reading: State Design Pattern

This section gives a quick overview of the design patterns used in this chapter. It's helpful if you're new to these patterns or need a refresher to better understand the design choices.

State design pattern

The State pattern is a behavioral pattern that allows an object to alter its behavior when its internal state changes, making it appear as though the object is behaving like a different class.

In the vending machine design, we use the State pattern to manage states like `NoMoneyInsertedState`, `MoneyInsertedState`, and `DispenseState`, enabling the `VendingMachine` to switch behaviors dynamically without modifying its core logic.

To illustrate the State pattern in another domain, the following example uses the traffic light system.

Problem

Imagine we have a `TrafficLight` class. The traffic light can be in one of three states: Red, Yellow, or Green. The behavior of the traffic light changes depending on its current state:

- In the Red state, the light stays red for a set duration.
- In the Yellow state, the light blinks yellow, signaling cars to slow down and prepare to stop.
- In the Green state, the light stays green to allow traffic to pass.

If we were to implement this logic using conditionals, we would need to check the current state of the traffic light every time an action occurs.

While the solution works initially, several issues arise as the system becomes more complex:

Scalability: As the number of states increases, the conditionals grow larger. For example, adding a new state (like a flashing state for emergency vehicles) would require adding more checks to the existing logic, making the code increasingly hard to manage and prone to errors.

Maintainability: The duplication of code and the need to update the same conditional logic in multiple places make the system difficult to maintain over time. This is a crucial problem because it impacts long-term code quality and increases the chance of introducing bugs when modifying the logic.

Solution

Instead of relying on conditionals to manage state transitions, we can use the State pattern, which encapsulates the behavior associated with each state into separate classes.

Rather than handling all behaviors on its own, the original object, known as the context, holds a reference to one of the state objects that represents its current state, delegating the state-related tasks to that object.

For example, a `TrafficLight` context can delegate its behavior to a state object, like `RedLightState`, `GreenLightState`, or `YellowLightState`. Each of these states knows how to handle the actions specific to that state, such as changing the light or transitioning to the next state.

To transition to a new state, the context simply replaces the current state object with another one that represents the new state. For instance, when the light is Green, the system transitions to Yellow, and then to Red, without needing complex conditionals.

Here is the representation of the state pattern.

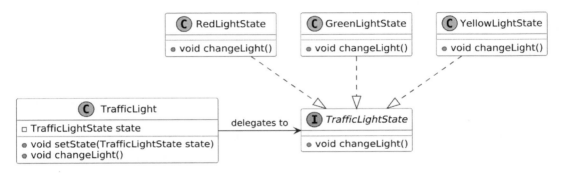

State design pattern

8

Elevator System

In this chapter, we will explore the object-oriented design of an Elevator System. Compared to some of the other popular interview problems, this one places a stronger emphasis on modeling behavior, rather than on modeling data. Our approach will focus on designing key components such as how to represent real-world elevators, the elevator's state, incoming hallway call requests, and the algorithm that determines the elevator's movement.

Elevator System

Requirements Gathering

Here is an example of a typical prompt an interviewer might give:

"Imagine you are in an office building with a bunch of identical elevator cars, and they all go to the same set of floors. You press the "up" or "down" button on your floor, and an elevator arrives promptly. Inside, you select your desired floor from a panel of buttons, and the elevator takes you there. Behind the scenes, the system efficiently manages elevator assignments and ignores requests in the wrong direction. Now, let's design an elevator system that handles all of this."

Requirements clarification

Here is an example of how a conversation between a candidate and an interviewer might unfold:

Candidate: Are we designing an elevator system for an office building, or do we need to consider other types of elevators as well, such as industrial elevators for factories or freight elevators for heavy goods?
Interviewer: Only for office buildings.

Candidate: Do all elevator cars serve the same set of floors?
Interviewer: Yes, all elevator cars can serve every floor.

Candidate: When a user presses the "up" or "down" button on a particular floor, what strategy should the system use to determine which elevator to dispatch?
Interviewer: The specific strategy is up to you. Ideally, it could be configurable. We should be able to easily swap strategies to see which one fits best for the building's traffic. It could be a first-come, first-served strategy for fairness or other strategies.

> 💡 **Tip:** The top floor should only have a "down" button, and the bottom floor should only have an "up" button. While it's great to recognize this detail during design, it's not critical if it isn't the primary focus.

Requirements

Based on the conversation and how elevator systems work in the real world, here are the key functional requirements we've identified.

- The system manages multiple elevator cars, all of which serve the same set of floors.
- On each floor, there are "up" and "down" buttons that users press to call an elevator car before getting in.
- Each elevator car should display its current floor and state (e.g., moving up, down, or idle).
- Each elevator car has an internal control panel that includes buttons for every floor. Users inside the car press the button corresponding to the floor they want to go to.
- If a user inside the elevator car presses a floor button in a direction opposite to the

elevator's current movement, the request should be ignored.

Below are the non-functional requirements:

- The dispatching algorithm should be configurable, allowing the system to easily switch between different optimization strategies.

Some of the requirements above are based on common sense in elevator systems. It's a good idea to list them briefly during an interview to ensure everyone is on the same page. This way, the interviewer can step in if they want to adjust or clarify any assumptions. It helps save time and keeps the conversation aligned with the interviewer's expectations.

Understanding elevator control panels

Elevator systems typically include two types of buttons, each serving a distinct purpose for controlling elevator operations:

- **Hallway buttons (Outside the Elevator):**
  Hallway buttons are located on each floor outside the elevator. Typically, there are two buttons: an "up" button to call the elevator to go up and a "down" button to call the elevator to go down.
- **Floor buttons (Inside the Elevator):**
  Floor buttons are located on the control panel inside the elevator car. Each button corresponds to a specific floor.

Note: From this point onward, we will use the terms "hallway buttons" and "floor buttons" in our discussions.

Use Case Diagram

A use case diagram shows how actors (users or systems) interact with a system to achieve specific goals. In the elevator system, this will help us clarify key actions, such as requesting an elevator, selecting a floor, and dispatching an elevator.

Below is the use case diagram of the elevator system.

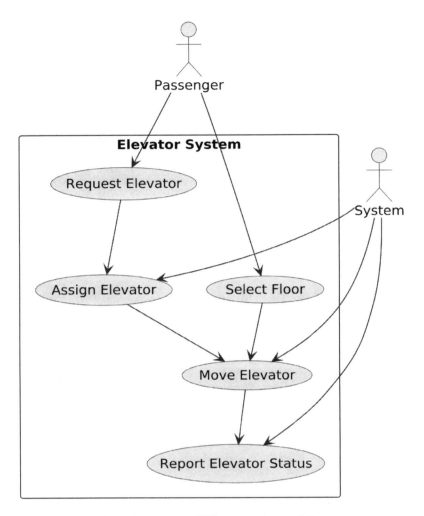

Use Case Diagram of Elevator Control System

The use cases for the **Passenger** actor are as follows:

- **Request Elevator:** This represents the action of a passenger on a specific floor pressing the hallway button to request an elevator.
- **Select Floor:** After entering the elevator, the passenger selects the destination floor using the floor button.

The use cases for the **System** actor are as follows. Note that actors are not necessarily humans:

- **Assign Elevator:** This represents the system selecting the most appropriate elevator car based on factors like availability and suitability.
- **Move Elevator:** This represents the elevator moving between floors to pick up and drop off users as needed.

- **Report Elevator Status:** This represents the system updating and reporting the elevator's current status (floor and direction).

Identify Core Objects

Before diving into the design, it's important to enumerate the core objects.

- **Elevator System:** This is the facade class that provides the main interface to the elevator system. It coordinates the overall operation by tracking the status of all elevator cars and delegating hallway call requests to the Elevator Dispatch for assignment and movement.
- **Elevator Dispatch:** This class handles hallway calls by assigning the most appropriate elevator. When a user presses a hallway button, the system evaluates the available elevators using the dispatching strategy and selects the most suitable elevator to fulfill the request.
- **Elevator Car:** An elevator car is a single unit that transports passengers between floors in a building. Each car operates independently and contains its internal control panel with buttons for selecting destination floors.

Design Class Diagram

To choose the right strategy for modeling our system, let's first consider whether the elevator problem is more centered around logic or data. The use cases for the elevator are pretty straightforward. We can easily picture a user calling an elevator, getting inside, and selecting a floor. However, when it comes to the data model, it's less clear which entities require detailed modeling. For example, do we need to model the doors, individual buttons, or passengers?

Since the use cases are clearer than the underlying data model, we'll start with the system's behaviors and user interactions (captured through use cases) and then use them to guide the definition of classes and methods. With the core use cases already defined, we can now directly translate their responsibilities into the key classes that implement the system's functionality.

Elevator System

The `ElevatorSystem` class serves as the central controller, providing an API for controlling all the elevator cars, tracking their status, and handling dispatching requests efficiently.

By looking at the use case diagram, we can identify three core responsibilities of the system, each tied to specific APIs.

- **Get status:** Check the current state of each elevator (e.g., which floor it's on, and its direction of movement). This is used in displays both in and out of the elevator.
- **Request elevator:** When a user presses the hallway button on a floor, the system

triggers a request to assign an elevator to that floor.

- **Select destination:** Once inside the elevator, users press the floor button on the control panel for their destination floor.

To prevent the `ElevatorSystem` class from becoming overly complex and difficult to maintain, we delegate the task of assigning elevators to a separate `ElevatorDispatch` controller using composition.

Below is the UML diagram for the `ElevatorSystem` class.

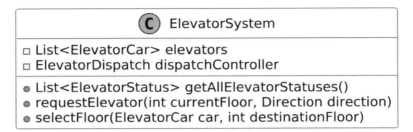

Elevator Car

The `ElevatorCar` class models the behaviors of an elevator car within the system. It maintains a queue of target floors to track requested stops and delegates state management to the `ElevatorStatus` class for modularity.

This delegation allows the `ElevatorStatus` class to encapsulate dynamic attributes, such as the elevator's current floor and movement direction. The `Direction` enum further simplifies this by defining movement as `UP`, `DOWN`, or `IDLE`.

The UML diagram below illustrates this structure.

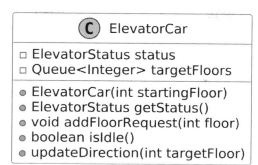

Elevator Status

The `ElevatorStatus` class provides a snapshot of the current state of an elevator car, encapsulating its `currentFloor` and `currentDirection` in a single object. It is a simple class but crucial for tracking the elevator's real-time state.

The status is updated dynamically as the elevator moves between floors, providing real-time information to the system.

Alternative approach: We could have used a generic data structure, such as a key-value collection, to store elevator state attributes like floor and direction. However, a dedicated `ElevatorStatus` class was chosen for its type safety and its extensibility, allowing new attributes (e.g., maintenance status) to be added without affecting other system components.

Direction

The Direction enum provides a type-safe way to represent an elevator's movement direction. It includes three possible values.

- **UP:** The elevator is moving upwards.
- **DOWN:** The elevator is moving downwards.

- **IDLE:** The elevator is stationary.

By using an enum instead of arbitrary values, the system minimizes ambiguity and ensures consistent, predictable behavior across all elevator cars. It plays a key role in optimizing elevator operation, helping prevent unnecessary direction changes, and minimizing wait times for users. For example:

- The system can prevent assigning requests in the opposite direction of an elevator's current movement, avoiding unnecessary reversals that cause delays.
- The system can prioritize elevators already moving toward the requested floor, reducing passenger wait times.

The UML diagram for the `Direction` enum is shown below:

Elevator Dispatch and Dispatching Strategy

The `ElevatorDispatch` class plays a critical role in managing user requests from hallway buttons and floor buttons, determining and selecting the appropriate elevator car to handle each request efficiently. To clarify what "dispatch" means in this context, it refers to assigning an elevator to handle a hallway call request and directing it to make a stop. From the perspective of an elevator car, both picking up and dropping off users are treated as stops along its path.

The dispatch logic relies on the **Strategy Pattern**, which enables the system to dynamically select and swap between different algorithms for optimizing elevator allocation.

Note: To learn more about the Strategy Pattern and its common use cases, refer to the **Parking Lot** chapter of the book.

The general dispatching process follows three main steps:

1. **Review the request and elevator status:** The system evaluates the incoming request, which includes details like the floor from which the request has been made, the direction of travel, and the status of all elevator cars (e.g., idle, moving, at a specific floor).

2. **Select the best elevator car:** Based on the selected `DispatchingStrategy`, the system determines which elevator car is most suited to fulfill the request. Strategies may prioritize factors such as:
   - **Proximity:** Assign an elevator based on its closeness to the requested floor. If

multiple elevators are available, the closer one may be prioritized.

- **Direction of travel:** If the elevator is already moving in the requested direction, it may be prioritized.
- **Minimizing wait time:** Selecting the car that reduces the overall waiting time for passengers.

3. **Update next stops:** Once the correct elevator car is selected, the requested floor is added to that car's list of upcoming stops. The elevator car adjusts its path to accommodate the request, ensuring it serves the user efficiently.

Below is the representation of this class.

- `dispatchElevatorCar(int floor, Direction direction, List<ElevatorCar> elevators)`: Processes the request from a hallway button by evaluating the current state of all elevators and assigning the most suitable one to respond.

DispatchingStrategy interface:

The `DispatchingStrategy` defines the specific rules for selecting an elevator car when a hallway button is pressed.

By abstracting the selection logic, the system is adaptable to various strategies, allowing flexibility in optimizing the dispatch process.

Common dispatching strategies

First Come, First Serve (FCFS): The system assigns the request to the next available elevator in the system's dispatch queue, regardless of its direction or proximity to the request. This strategy is simple but might not always be the most efficient in a busy system.

Shortest Seek Time First (SSTF): The system assigns the request to the elevator that can reach the requested floor the fastest by evaluating two key factors. It first checks whether the elevator is either idle or moving in the direction of the request. Among these elevators, it then selects the elevator closest to the requested floor, minimizing the user's wait time.

Dynamic strategies: The dispatch strategy of the system can be dynamically configurable based on traffic patterns. For example, a "high throughput" strategy may optimize for speed during busy periods, while a "first-come, first-served" strategy can be used during quieter hours.

Complete Class Diagram

Below is the complete class diagram of the elevator system:

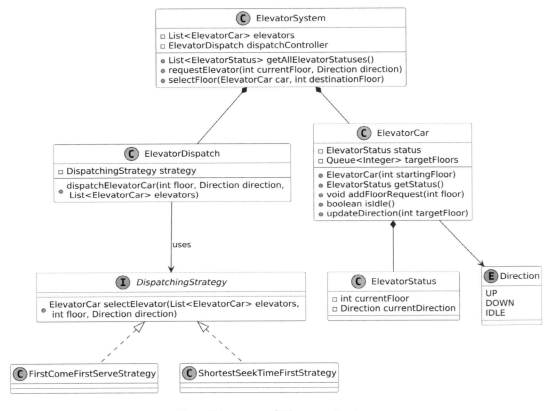

Class Diagram of Elevator System

Code - Elevator System

In this section, we'll implement the core functionalities of the elevator system, focusing on key areas such as tracking elevator status, dispatching elevators efficiently, and simulating elevator movement.

- **ElevatorSystem:** Manages multiple elevator cars, tracks their statuses, and handles requests from hallway buttons (to call an elevator) and floor buttons (to select a destination floor).

- **ElevatorCar:** Represents an individual elevator car.

- **ElevatorDispatch:** Manages requests from hallway buttons and ensures the right elevator is assigned. It uses the dispatching strategy to evaluate all available elevators and select the best one to respond to the request.

- **DispatchingStrategy interface and implementations:** Defines the contract for elevator selection and provides implementations such as First-Come-First-Serve and Shortest-Seek-Time-First strategies.

Now, let's define these classes and their key functionalities in detail.

Elevator System

The `ElevatorSystem` class is responsible for managing multiple `ElevatorCar` objects, using composition to simplify the management of these cars. It delegates the core task of dispatching requests to an instance of `ElevatorDispatch`.

The constructor of `ElevatorSystem` accepts two parameters:

- A list of `ElevatorCar` objects, which represents all the elevator cars in the system.

- A `DispatchingStrategy` object that defines how requests are dispatched.

By allowing the `DispatchingStrategy` to be passed into the constructor, the system can easily adapt to different dispatching strategies at runtime. This flexibility makes it easy to test different strategies and optimize the system's performance based on traffic patterns.

Here is the implementation of this class.

```
public class ElevatorSystem {

  private final List<ElevatorCar> elevators;
  private final ElevatorDispatch dispatchController;

  public ElevatorSystem(List<ElevatorCar> elevators, DispatchingStrategy
    strategy) {
    this.elevators = elevators;
    this.dispatchController = new ElevatorDispatch(strategy);
  }

  // Returns the current status of all elevators in the system
  public List<ElevatorStatus> getAllElevatorStatuses() {
    List<ElevatorStatus> statuses = new ArrayList<>();
    for (ElevatorCar elevator : elevators) {
      statuses.add(elevator.getStatus());
    }
    return statuses;
  }
}
```

```
  // Handles a request for an elevator from a specific floor and
  //   direction
  public void requestElevator(int currentFloor, Direction direction) {
    dispatchController.dispatchElevatorCar(currentFloor, direction,
    elevators);
  }

  // Handles a floor selection request from inside an elevator
  public void selectFloor(ElevatorCar car, int destinationFloor) {
    car.addFloorRequest(destinationFloor);
  }

}
```

The `getAllElevatorStatuses` method is designed to provide a consolidated view of the status of all elevators in the system. These statuses reflect real-time information about the elevator car, including its current floor and movement direction.

The `ElevatorSystem` class offers two primary methods for handling requests from users:

- **requestElevator:** A user on a specific floor presses a hallway button (up or down) to request an elevator. The method passes the request to the ElevatorDispatch instance, which decides which elevator is best suited to fulfill the request.

- **selectFloor:** A user selects a destination floor by pressing the floor button on the control panel inside an elevator car. This is handled directly by the elevator car.

Elevator Car

The `ElevatorCar` class models an individual elevator in the system. It keeps track of the elevator's current floor, its movement direction, and the list of floors it needs to visit. The elevator uses a queue (`targetFloors`) to manage requests from hallway and floor buttons and ensures that no duplicate requests are added to the queue.

Below is the implementation of this class.

```
public class ElevatorCar {
  private ElevatorStatus status;
  private final Queue<Integer> targetFloors;

  public ElevatorCar(int startingFloor) {
    this.status = new ElevatorStatus(startingFloor, Direction.IDLE);
    this.targetFloors = new LinkedList<>();
  }

  // Returns the current state of the elevator
  public ElevatorStatus getStatus() {
    return status;
```

```
    }

    // Adds a new floor request if it's not already in the queue
    public void addFloorRequest(int floor) {
      if (!targetFloors.contains(floor)) {
        targetFloors.offer(floor);
        updateDirection(floor);
      }
    }

    // Checks if elevator has no pending floor requests
    public boolean isIdle() {
      return targetFloors.isEmpty();
    }

    // Updates elevator direction based on target floor position
    private void updateDirection(int targetFloor) {
      if (status.getCurrentFloor() < targetFloor) {
        status = new ElevatorStatus(status.getCurrentFloor(), Direction.UP)
    ;
      } else if (status.getCurrentFloor() > targetFloor) {
        status = new ElevatorStatus(status.getCurrentFloor(), Direction.
    DOWN);
      }
    }

    // getters are omitted for brevity
}
```

- Once the elevator reaches the target floor, it removes that floor from the queue and checks if there are any more requests in the queue. If the queue is empty, the elevator becomes idle.

- The elevator enters the IDLE state when there are no more floors in the targetFloors queue to visit. This state indicates that the elevator is stationary, waiting for new requests.

Implementation choice: We implemented the targetFloors collection as a Queue to manage the sequence of floors the elevator must visit. The Queue was chosen for its first-in-first-out (FIFO) behavior, which ensures that floor requests are processed in the order they are received, maintaining fairness for passengers. This structure supports constant-time operations for adding new floor requests and removing the next floor upon arrival.

Alternative approach: A PriorityQueue could have been used to sort floors by closeness or direction, saving travel time. However, reordering floors might confuse passengers expecting stops in request order and requires extra logic to prevent stops in the opposite direction of travel. A Queue may take slightly longer but is simpler, fairer, and matches how elevators typically work.

Elevator Dispatch

The `ElevatorDispatch` class is responsible for assigning and directing elevator cars to handle hallway requests using a specified dispatching strategy.

Below is the implementation of this class.

```
public class ElevatorDispatch {

  private final DispatchingStrategy strategy;

  public ElevatorDispatch(DispatchingStrategy strategy) {
    this.strategy = strategy;
  }

  // Handles requests from the hallway button and assigns an elevator
    based on the dispatching strategy.
  public void dispatchElevatorCar(int floor, Direction direction, List<
    ElevatorCar> elevators) {
    ElevatorCar selectedElevator = strategy.selectElevator(elevators,
    floor, direction);
    if (selectedElevator != null) {
      selectedElevator.addFloorRequest(floor);
    }
  }
}
```

dispatchElevatorCar: This method is used when a user on a floor presses the hallway button. It uses the `DispatchingStrategy` to select the most appropriate elevator. Once an elevator is selected, the floor where the request was made is added to the elevator's list of stops.

Alternative approach: An alternative could have been to maintain a priority queue of elevators, ordered by suitability (e.g., distance to the requested floor), to reduce selection time. However, maintaining a priority queue requires continuous updates as elevators move, adding overhead that outweighs the benefits for small elevator counts. The trade-off is that iterating over a list has linear time complexity, but this is acceptable given the typically small number of elevators and the need for strategy flexibility.

Dispatching Strategy

The `DispatchingStrategy` interface defines a contract for selecting an elevator from a list of available elevators based on a requested floor and desired direction. This interface abstracts the logic for handling requests and enables the system to switch between different dispatching algorithms.

First-Come-First-Serve Strategy

The `FirstComeFirstServeStrategy` selects the first elevator that is either idle (not moving) or moving in the direction of the request. If no idle or direction-compatible elevators are found, the strategy randomly selects an elevator from the list. This ensures that every request is fulfilled, even if no perfect match is available.

```java
public class FirstComeFirstServeStrategy implements DispatchingStrategy {
  // Selects the first available elevator that is either idle or moving
    in the same direction
  @Override
  public ElevatorCar selectElevator(List<ElevatorCar> elevators, int
    floor, Direction direction) {
    for (ElevatorCar elevator : elevators) {
      // Return first elevator that is idle or moving in the same
      direction
      if (elevator.isIdle() || elevator.getCurrentDirection() ==
      direction) {
        return elevator;
      }
    }
    // If no suitable elevator is found, randomly select one
    return elevators.get((int) (Math.random() * elevators.size()));
  }
}
```

Shortest-Seek-Time-First Strategy

The ShortestSeekTimeFirstStrategy prioritizes the elevator that is closest to the requested floor. It calculates the absolute distance between the current floor of each elevator and the requested floor and selects the elevator that can reach the requested floor the quickest. This strategy also takes into account whether the elevator is idle or moving in the correct direction.

- Elevators that are idle or moving in the correct direction are prioritized.

- If multiple elevators are equidistant to the requested floor, the first one encountered is selected.

```java
public class ShortestSeekTimeFirstStrategy implements DispatchingStrategy
    {
  // Selects the elevator that is closest to the requested floor and
    moving in the same direction
  @Override
  public ElevatorCar selectElevator(List<ElevatorCar> elevators, int
    floor, Direction direction) {
    ElevatorCar bestElevator = null;
    int shortestDistance = Integer.MAX_VALUE;

    for (ElevatorCar elevator : elevators) {
      // Calculate distance between elevator and requested floor
      int distance = Math.abs(elevator.getCurrentFloor() - floor);
```

```
    // Select elevator if it's idle or moving in the same direction and
   closer than the current best
    if ((elevator.isIdle() || elevator.getCurrentDirection() ==
   direction)
      && distance < shortestDistance) {
        bestElevator = elevator;
        shortestDistance = distance;
      }
    }

    return bestElevator;
  }
}
```

Deep Dive Topics

In the current design, both hallway button requests and floor button requests are added to the same queue of pending stops within the elevator car. When a user presses a hallway button, the dispatch controller assigns the most suitable elevator and adds the request to that elevator's queue. Similarly, when a user selects a destination floor using the floor buttons inside the elevator, the request is directly added to the same queue.

While this design works, it has some limitations:

- **Tightly coupled components:** Button presses, whether from the hallway or inside the elevator, add requests directly to a queue processed by the dispatch controller. Since the button logic and controller processing are interconnected through this queue, modifying one component requires changes to the other, making the system harder to maintain or extend.

- **Potential delays under heavy load:** In periods of high traffic, processing requests sequentially can introduce slight delays before an elevator is assigned.

Event-driven elevator request handling

To address these limitations, we introduce an event-driven approach using the **Observer Pattern**. This approach decouples the hallway buttons from the dispatch controller, allowing them to interact through event-driven notifications instead of relying on the sequential processing of a queue.

How it works?

- **Observable subject:** The hallway buttons act as subjects. When an "up" or a "down" button is pressed, it triggers an observer event that automatically notifies the dispatch controller.

- **Observer:** The dispatch controller listens to these button-press events and responds by allocating an appropriate elevator car.

Note: To learn more about the Observer Pattern and its common use cases, refer to the **Further Reading** section at the end of this chapter.

Code changes

Below is the implementation of the observer pattern for handling hallway call requests:

```java
// Observable Subject: HallwayButtonPanel
public class HallwayButtonPanel {
  private final int floor;
  private final List<ElevatorObserver> observers;

  public HallwayButtonPanel(int floor) {
    this.floor = floor;
    this.observers = new ArrayList<>();
  }

  // Handles button press event and notifies all registered observers
  public void pressButton(Direction direction) {
    System.out.println("Button pressed on floor " + floor + " for
    direction " + direction);
    notifyObservers(direction);
  }

  // Registers a new observer to receive button press notifications
  public void addObserver(ElevatorObserver observer) {
    observers.add(observer);
  }

  // Notifies all registered observers about the button press
  private void notifyObservers(Direction direction) {
    for (ElevatorObserver observer : observers) {
      observer.update(floor, direction);
    }
  }
}


// Observer Interface
public interface ElevatorObserver {
  void update(int floor, Direction direction);
}


// Observer Implementation: ElevatorDispatchController
public class ElevatorDispatchController implements ElevatorObserver {
  @Override
  public void update(int floor, Direction direction) {
    System.out.println("Received request: Floor " + floor + ", Direction
    " + direction);
    // Logic to handle the floor request
  }
}
```

Why it's better?

- **Decoupled architecture:** The Observer Pattern separates the hallway buttons and dispatch logic, making it easier to maintain, test, and extend the system.
- **Faster response time during rush hours:** By treating hallway button presses as discrete events, the system bypasses any queue buildup during rush hours, ensuring that requests are handled without noticeable delays.

Handling elevators serving different floor sets

In the existing design, all elevators can stop at every floor. What if the building has certain elevators that only stop at specific floors?

In order to fulfill such a requirement, the design should allow each elevator car to be assigned a defined set of accessible floors and ensure the system assigns hallway button requests only to elevators that can stop at the requested floor.

How it works?

- **Defining accessible floors:** Each elevator car will have a list of floors it can serve. This can be set during the system initialization.
- **Validating hallway call requests:** Before an elevator is assigned or a hallway call request is added to its queue, the system checks whether the requested floor is accessible by the elevator.
- **Updating dispatching logic:** The dispatching strategy must ensure that only elevators that can reach the requested floor are considered for assignment.

Example scenario: Suppose the building has 20 floors. **Elevator 1** serves only floors 1, 5, 10, 15, and 20. **Elevator 2** serves all the floors. When a user on the 3rd floor presses the "up" button, the system avoids assigning **Elevator 1** since it cannot stop at floor 3. **Elevator 2** will be chosen instead.

Design and code changes:

Update the `ElevatorCar` class:

We introduce the `accessibleFloors` attribute to store the list of floors each elevator can serve.

```
// Set of floors this elevator can service
private final Set<Integer> accessibleFloors;
```

Modify the `addFloorRequest` method:

Before adding a floor to the elevator's list of stops, check whether the floor is part of the elevator's accessible set.

```
public void addFloorRequest(int floor) {
  // Only add the request if the floor is accessible by this elevator and
    not already in the queue
  if (accessibleFloors.contains(floor) && !targetFloors.contains(floor))
  {
    targetFloors.offer(floor);
    updateDirection(floor);
  }
}
```

Update dispatching strategies:

The `DispatchingStrategy` implementations will ensure that only elevators capable of reaching the requested floor are considered for assignment. For example, in the **Shortest Seek Time First** strategy, add an additional check:

```
public class ShortestSeekTimeFirstStrategy implements DispatchingStrategy
    {
  @Override
  public ElevatorCar selectElevator(List<ElevatorCar> elevators, int
    floor, Direction direction) {
    ElevatorCar bestElevator = null;
    int shortestDistance = Integer.MAX_VALUE;

    for (ElevatorCar elevator : elevators) {
      // Calculate distance between elevator and requested floor
      int distance = Math.abs(elevator.getCurrentFloor() - floor);
      // Select elevator if it's idle or moving in the same direction and
      closer than the current best
      if ((elevator.isIdle() || elevator.getCurrentDirection() ==
      direction)
        // Only consider elevators that can actually reach the requested
      floor
        && elevator.getAccessibleFloors().contains(floor)
        && distance < shortestDistance) {
        bestElevator = elevator;
        shortestDistance = distance;
      }
    }

    return bestElevator;
  }
}
```

Wrap Up

In this chapter, we designed an Elevator System by following a structured approach, similar to how a candidate would solve this problem during an OOD interview. We began by gathering and clarifying requirements through a series of questions and answers with the interviewer. This was followed by identifying the core objects involved, designing the class diagram, and implementing key components of the system.

A key takeaway from this design is the importance of modularity and clear separation of concerns. Each component, such as `ElevatorSystem`, `ElevatorCar`, `ElevatorDispatch`, and `DispatchingStrategy`, focuses on a specific responsibility, ensuring that the system is maintainable, scalable, and flexible. This modular design allows the system to easily adapt to different dispatching strategies and optimize performance for various building traffic conditions.

In the deep dive section, we explored advanced topics, including using the Observer Pattern for event-driven hallway call requests, where pressing the hallway buttons instantly notifies the dispatch controller, enabling faster elevator assignments. We also discussed handling elevators that serve different sets of floors.

Congratulations on getting this far! Now give yourself a pat on the back. Good job!

Further Reading: Observer Design Pattern

This section gives a quick overview of the design patterns used in this chapter. It's helpful if you're new to these patterns or need a refresher to better understand the design choices.

Observer design pattern

The Observer is a behavioral pattern that lets you define a subscription mechanism, allowing multiple objects to receive notifications and updates automatically whenever the object they are observing changes state.

In the elevator system design, we use the Observer pattern to decouple hallway button presses from the dispatch controller, enabling efficient event-driven request handling. To illustrate the Observer pattern in another domain, the following example uses a news application.

Problem

Imagine you're developing a news application that delivers real-time updates to its users. Whenever a breaking news story is published, all users who have subscribed to that category should receive immediate notifications. Implementing this functionality can be challenging as directly linking the news publisher to each user would result in a tightly coupled design, making the system rigid and difficult to maintain. Additionally, as the user base grows, the system must efficiently manage the distribution of updates without becoming a bottleneck.

Solution

The Observer design pattern offers an elegant solution to this problem by establishing a one-to-many relationship between the publisher (news provider) and subscribers (users).

In this pattern:

- The "subject" (or "publisher") is the news application, which holds the core business logic and the breaking news content.
- The "observers" (or "subscribers") are the users who have subscribed to specific news categories and need to be notified when new content is published in those categories.
- The news application (subject) maintains a list of subscribed users (observers), and when a new breaking news story is published (state change), it notifies all subscribed users (observers) by calling an update method on each.

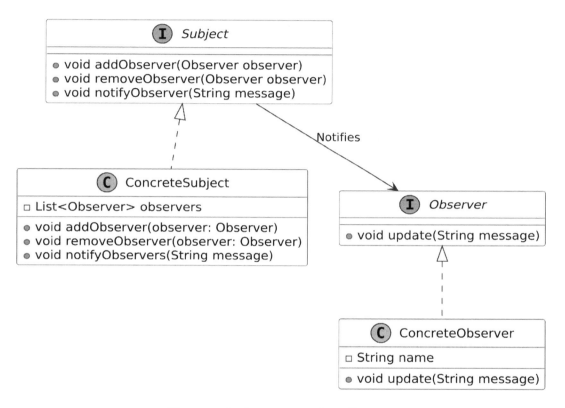

Observer design pattern class diagram

When to use

The Observer design pattern is particularly useful in scenarios where:

- Changes in one object require notifying other objects, especially when the set of objects that need to be notified isn't known in advance or can change dynamically.
- When objects in your application need to observe other objects (subjects), but only under specific conditions or for a limited time.

Grocery Store System

Grocery Store System

9

Grocery Store System

In this chapter, we will explore the design of a grocery store system. This system is tailored for grocery store workers to streamline operations like managing the item catalog, configuring pricing, and applying discounts.

Grocery Store System

Requirements Gathering

Here is an example of a typical prompt an interviewer might give:

"Imagine you're at a grocery store, filling your cart with fresh produce, snacks, and household essentials. At the checkout, the cashier scans each item, and the system instantly tracks the order, applies any discounts, and displays the final total. Behind the scenes, the system is seamlessly managing the item catalog, updating inventory as stock arrives or sells, and ensuring every transaction is smooth and accurate. Now, let's design a grocery store system that does all this."

Requirements clarification

Here is an example of how a conversation between a candidate and an interviewer might unfold:

Candidate: What are the primary operations the grocery store system needs to support?
Interviewer: The system should support store workers, including shipment handlers and cashiers, in managing the item catalog, tracking inventory, and processing customer checkouts with applicable discounts.

Candidate: I'd like to confirm my understanding of the checkout process. The cashier scans or enters a code for each item, and the system keeps track of the order. It calculates the subtotal, applies any discounts, and updates the total. Once all items are entered, the cashier sees the final amount, accepts payment, and provides change if needed. A receipt is then generated. Does this sound correct?
Interviewer: Yes, that's an accurate understanding of the system.

Candidate: How should the system handle inventory management?
Interviewer: The system should track inventory for all items, increasing inventory when new stock arrives and automatically decreasing inventory during checkout for items sold.

Candidate: Should the system categorize items into different categories, such as food, beverages, etc.?
Interviewer: Yes, that's a good idea.

Candidate: For discounts, can I assume it works this way? The system should track discount campaigns, which can apply to specific items or categories. If multiple discounts apply to the same item, the system should automatically apply the highest discount.
Interviewer: That sounds great.

Requirements

This question has multiple requirements, so grouping similar ones makes it easier to manage and track. The requirements can be broken down into four groups.

Catalog management

- Admins can add, update, and remove items from the catalog.
- The catalog tracks item details, including name, category, price, and barcode.

Inventory management

- Shipment handlers can update inventory when shipments arrive.
- The system should automatically decrease inventory when items are sold.

Checkout process

- Cashiers can scan barcodes or manually enter item codes to build an order.
- Cashiers can view details of the active order, including items, discounts, and the subtotal.
- The system calculates and applies relevant discounts automatically.
- Cashiers can finalize an order, calculate the total, handle payments, and calculate change.
- A detailed receipt is generated.

Discount campaigns

- Admins can define discount campaigns for specific items or categories.
- If multiple discounts apply to an item, the system selects the highest discount.

Below are the non-functional requirements:

- The system should provide clear, user-friendly error messages (e.g., for invalid barcodes or insufficient inventory) to the cashier.
- The system's components (catalog, inventory, checkout, discounts) must be modular to allow updates or replacements of individual modules without affecting the entire system.

Identify Core Objects

Before diving into the design, it's important to enumerate the core objects.

- **Item:** Represents an individual product in the grocery store, encapsulating details such as name, barcode, category, and price.
- **Catalog:** Acts as the central repository for all items, managing the collection of products and supporting operations like adding, updating, and removing items.
- **Inventory:** Tracks the stock levels for each item. It updates the count of available items when new stock arrives (via shipments) or when items are sold during the checkout process.
- **Order:** This object tracks the ongoing checkout process. It manages details such as the items in the order, active discounts, and the calculation of subtotals and total prices. This data is used to generate a receipt once the order is finalized.
- **DiscountCampaign:** The `DiscountCampaign` object defines promotional rules for applying discounts.

Design Class Diagram

Now that we know the core objects and their roles, the next step is to create classes and methods that turn the requirements into an easy-to-maintain system. Let's take a closer look.

Item

The first component in our class diagram is the `Item` class, which represents individual products in the store. It encapsulates attributes like name, barcode, category, and price.

Below is the representation of this class.

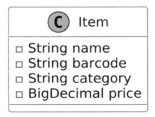

Catalog

The `Catalog` class is responsible for maintaining a structured list of all available products, each uniquely identified by a barcode. It provides methods to add, update, remove, and retrieve items.

The UML diagram below illustrates this structure.

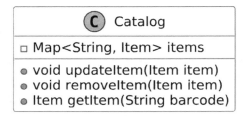

Inventory

Building on the `Catalog` class, the Inventory class is a critical component of the grocery store system, responsible for managing stock levels of items. It maintains a mapping between each item's barcode and its corresponding stock quantity.

Here is the representation of this class.

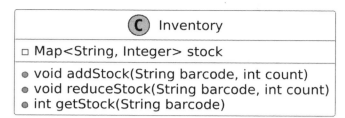

- **Static Data (Catalog):** Product metadata, such as name, category, and price, is managed by the Catalog class. This allows consistent, centralized handling of product information that does not change frequently.

- **Dynamic Data (Inventory):** Stock levels, which change frequently due to operations like sales and shipments, are managed independently in the Inventory class.

This separation simplifies both classes and adheres to the Single Responsibility Principle, ensuring each class focuses on a distinct aspect of the system.

DiscountCriteria

The `DiscountCriteria` interface encapsulates the logic to determine whether a discount applies to an item. It provides a flexible, extensible framework for defining applicability checks, such as item-based and category-based criteria, allowing the system to support diverse discount rules without modifying existing code.

The UML diagram below illustrates this structure.

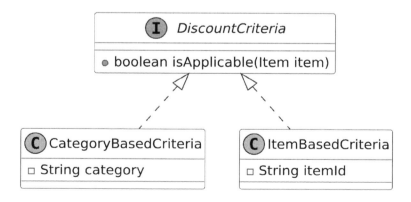

DiscountCriteria interface and concrete classes

CategoryBasedCriteria: The `CategoryBasedCriteria` determines whether a discount is applicable by verifying if an item belongs to a specific category. For example, if the discount targets the "Beverages" category and the item's category is "Beverages," the discount is applicable. This approach is ideal for campaigns that focus on broad groups of products, such as category-wide promotions.

ItemBasedCriteria: The ItemBasedCriteria checks whether a discount applies to a specific item by matching its unique identifier. For instance, if the discount applies to an item with ID 12345 and the item's ID is 12345, the discount is considered applicable. This criterion is particularly useful for campaigns targeting specific products, such as special promotions or clearance discounts for individual items.

DiscountCalculationStrategy

The DiscountCalculationStrategy interface encapsulates the logic for calculating discounts. It uses the Strategy Pattern to provide flexibility in applying a variety of discount types, such as fixed amount-based or percentage-based discounts.

Below is the representation of this interface.

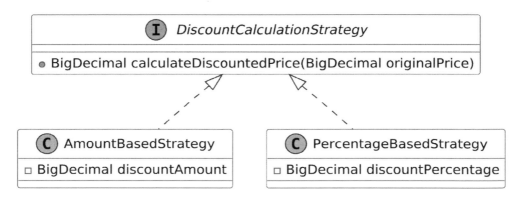

DiscountCalculationStrategy interface and concrete classes

AmountBasedStrategy: This strategy applies a fixed discount amount to the original price. For example, if the original price is $100 and the discount amount is $20, the resulting price after the discount will be $80. This approach is straightforward and is ideal for campaigns offering a constant monetary reduction.

PercentageBasedStrategy: This strategy applies a percentage-based discount to the original price. For instance, if the original price is $100 and the discount percentage is 20%, the price after the discount will be $80. This strategy is particularly useful for campaigns offering proportional reductions, such as seasonal or category-based discounts.

DiscountCampaign

Now, we design the `DiscountCampaign` class, which models active discount campaigns and is a key component for applying discounts. It leverages the Strategy Pattern to encapsulate different calculation strategies (e.g., percentage-based or fixed-amount discounts), ensuring flexibility in how discounts are computed. The class uses a `DiscountCriteria` interface to specify which items qualify for a discount, such as those in a particular category or with a specific barcode, allowing precise targeting of promotions while maintaining extensibility for new applicability rules.

The UML diagram below illustrates this structure.

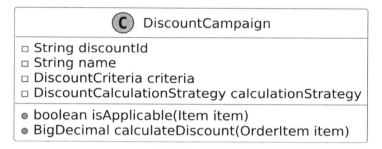

OrderItem

The next component is the `OrderItem` class, which represents a specific item in an order, along with its quantity. It encapsulates methods to calculate the total price for the item, based on its unit price and quantity.

Below is the representation of this class.

C OrderItem
▢ Item item ▢ int quantity
● BigDecimal calculatePrice() ● BigDecimal calculatePriceWithDiscount(DiscountCampaign newDiscount)

> ✂ **Design choice:** The OrderItem class separates item-level details from the higher-level order. This ensures that each item's quantity and price logic are encapsulated, making the design modular and easier to maintain.

Order

The Order class represents an active transaction during the checkout process. It tracks the list of items in order, along with any applied discounts. The class provides methods to calculate the subtotal (before discounts) and the total amount (after discounts).

Below is the representation of this class.

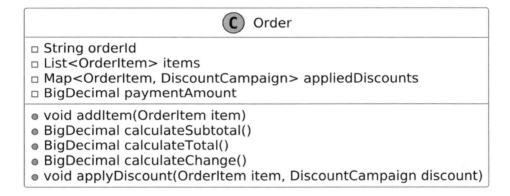

C Order
▢ String orderId ▢ List<OrderItem> items ▢ Map<OrderItem, DiscountCampaign> appliedDiscounts ▢ BigDecimal paymentAmount
● void addItem(OrderItem item) ● BigDecimal calculateSubtotal() ● BigDecimal calculateTotal() ● BigDecimal calculateChange() ● void applyDiscount(OrderItem item, DiscountCampaign discount)

> ✂ **Design choice:** The Order class focuses on managing transactional data for the checkout process. It delegates the handling of individual item quantities to the OrderItem class, ensuring a clean separation of responsibilities.

Receipt

The Receipt class acts as the final record of a completed transaction, consolidating all relevant details into a formatted output for the customer. It includes essential transaction information such as the order summary, payment details, and any changes to be given to the customer.

Below is the representation of this class.

Design choice: The `Receipt` class focuses solely on presenting transaction data in a customer-friendly format. It delegates all business logic, such as order calculations and discount handling, to the `Order` and `OrderItem` classes. This ensures the receipt remains lightweight and dedicated to its role as a transaction summary.

Checkout

Moving on to the `Checkout` class, which encapsulates the logic for handling the checkout process within the grocery store system. It maintains an active `Order` object to track the transaction details. Additionally, it applies active discount campaigns by determining their applicability and performing calculations.

Below is the representation of this class.

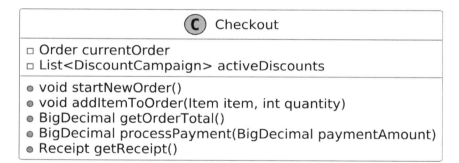

Design choice: Despite its central role, the `Checkout` class remains lightweight because the responsibilities for managing items, discounts, and calculations are delegated to well-separated components such as Order, `DiscountCampaign`, and the underlying strategy classes. This modular design ensures a clean separation of concerns and keeps the checkout logic manageable.

GroceryStoreSystem

Finally, we design the `GroceryStoreSystem` class, which serves as a facade that simplifies interaction with the components of the system, such as the `Catalog`, `Inventory`, and

Checkout. By providing a unified interface, it abstracts away the underlying complexity, making the system easier for clients to use. In an interview, this facade also allows us to validate that we have addressed the requirements by mapping them to the facade methods.

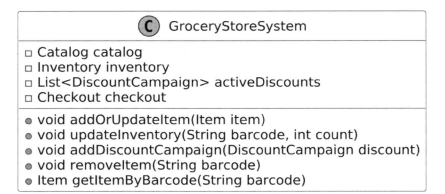

Complete Class Diagram

Below is the complete class diagram of our grocery store system. The detailed methods and attributes are skipped to make the diagram more readable.

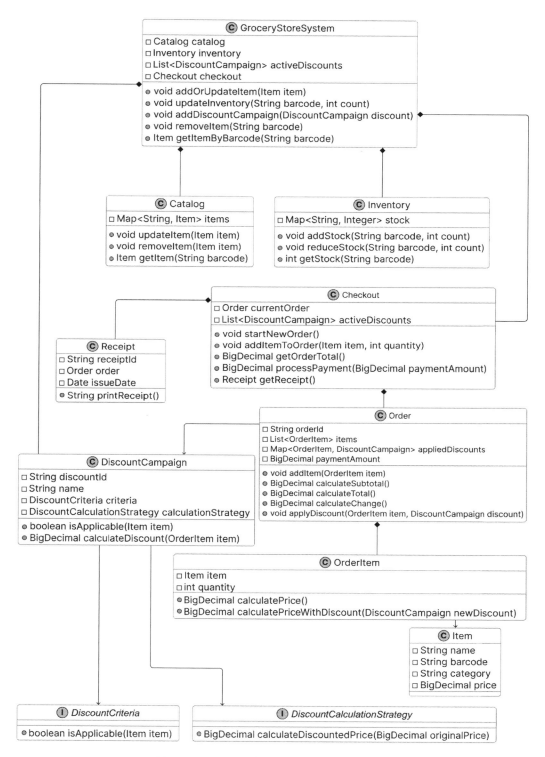

Class Diagram of Grocery Store System

Code - Grocery Store System

In this section, we'll implement the core functionality of the grocery store system, focusing on key areas such as managing products and inventory, and streamlining the checkout process, including discount handling.

Item

We implement the Item class, which encapsulates product attributes, including the name, barcode, category, and price. It is designed as a simple data container with no business logic, making it easy to use and maintain.

Here is the implementation of this class.

```java
public class Item {
  private final String name;
  private final String barcode;
  private final String category;
  private BigDecimal price;

  public Item(String name, String barcode, String category, BigDecimal
    price) {
    this.name = name;
    this.barcode = barcode;
    this.category = category;
    this.price = price;
  }

  // getter and setter methods are omitted for brevity
}
```

Catalog

We define the Catalog class, which acts as the centralized repository for managing the store's item inventory. Below is the implementation of this class.

```java
public class Catalog {
  // Map of barcodes to their corresponding items
  private final Map<String, Item> items = new HashMap<>();

  public void updateItem(Item item) {
    items.put(item.getBarcode(), item);
  }

  public void removeItem(String barcode) {
    items.remove(barcode);
  }

  public Item getItem(String barcode) {
    return items.get(barcode);
  }
}
```

```
}
```

Implementation note: The class uses a `Map<String, Item>` to store items, where the barcode serves as the key. The hash map ensures efficient lookups, updates, and deletions.

Inventory

The `Inventory` class manages the stock levels of items, associating each item's barcode with its available quantity. It provides methods to handle stock operations, such as adding new stock, decreasing stock for sales, and querying the current stock levels for a specific item.

Here is the implementation of this class.

```java
public class Inventory {
  // Map of barcodes to their stock quantities
  private final Map<String, Integer> stock = new HashMap<>();

  public void addStock(String barcode, int count) {
    stock.put(barcode, stock.getOrDefault(barcode, 0) + count);
  }

  public void reduceStock(String barcode, int count) {
    stock.put(barcode, stock.getOrDefault(barcode, 0) - count);
  }

  public int getStock(String barcode) {
    return stock.getOrDefault(barcode, 0);
  }
}
```

- **addStock(String barcode, int count):** Increases the stock for the specified barcode.
- **reduceStock(String barcode, int count):** Decreases the stock for the specified barcode.
- **getStock(String barcode):** Returns the current stock count for the specified barcode.

Implementation choice: The Inventory class uses a `HashMap` to map barcodes to stock quantities, enabling $O(1)$ average-case time complexity for updates and queries. This supports efficient inventory management during sales and shipments, which is crucial for maintaining accurate stock levels in a busy store.

DiscountCampaign

The `DiscountCampaign` class models promotional rules for applying discounts. It separates the logic for determining discount applicability (using `DiscountCriteria`) from the calculation of discount values (using `DiscountCalculationStrategy`). This design ensures flexibility and extensibility for various discount configurations.

Below is the implementation of this class.

```java
public class DiscountCampaign {
  // Unique identifier for the discount campaign
  private final String discountId;
  // Name of the discount campaign
  private final String name;
  // Criteria that determines if the discount applies to an item or
    category
  private final DiscountCriteria criteria;
  // Strategy for calculating the discounted price
  private final DiscountCalculationStrategy calculationStrategy;

  // Creates a new discount campaign with the specified details
  public DiscountCampaign(String discountId,
  String name,
  DiscountCriteria criteria,
  DiscountCalculationStrategy calculationStrategy) {
    this.discountId = discountId;
    this.name = name;
    this.criteria = criteria;
    this.calculationStrategy = calculationStrategy;
  }

  // Checks if this discount applies to the given item
  public boolean isApplicable(Item item) {
    return criteria.isApplicable(item);
  }

  // Calculates the discounted price for the given order item
  public BigDecimal calculateDiscount(OrderItem item) {
    return calculationStrategy.calculateDiscountedPrice(item.
    calculatePrice());
  }

  // getter and setter methods are omitted for brevity
}
```

isApplicable(Item item): Check if the discount applies to a given item based on the defined criteria. Returns true if applicable; otherwise, false.

calculateDiscount(BigDecimal price): Computes the discount amount using the specified calculationStrategy. Supports both percentage-based and fixed-amount calculations.

Implementation choice: The DiscountCampaign class uses composition to hold a single DiscountCriteria and DiscountCalculationStrategy, leveraging polymorphism for flexible discount configurations. This allows each campaign to combine one applicability rule and one calculation method, simplifying the implementation while supporting diverse promotions.

Note: For brevity, the code for `DiscountCriteria` and `DiscountCalculationStrategy` is omitted. These interfaces define applicability checks (e.g., category or item matching) and discount calculations (e.g., percentage-based), respectively.

OrderItem

The `OrderItem` class tracks an individual product within an order, along with its quantity. It calculates the total cost for the item by multiplying its unit price by the quantity, enabling seamless integration with the order's subtotal and total calculations.

Here is the implementation of this class.

```java
public class OrderItem {
  // The item being ordered
  private final Item item;
  // Quantity of the item
  private final int quantity;

  // Creates a new order item with the specified item and quantity
  public OrderItem(Item item, int quantity) {
    this.item = item;
    this.quantity = quantity;
  }

  // Calculates the total price for this order item without any discount
  public BigDecimal calculatePrice() {
    return item.getPrice().multiply(BigDecimal.valueOf(quantity));
  }

  // Calculates the total price for this order item with the given
  //   discount
  public BigDecimal calculatePriceWithDiscount(DiscountCampaign
    newDiscount) {
    return newDiscount.calculateDiscount(this);
  }

  // getter and setter methods are omitted for brevity
}
```

`calculatePriceWithDiscount(DiscountCampaign newDiscount)`: This method computes the item's total price after applying a given discount campaign. Instead of simply returning the base price (unit price × quantity), it factors in the discount to determine the adjusted price.

Order

The Order class handles customer transactions by maintaining a list of purchased items and their associated discounts. It dynamically calculates the subtotal and total amounts based on the items currently included in the order and the discounts applied to them at the time of calculation.

```java
public class Order {
  // Unique identifier for the order
  private final String orderId;
  // List of items in the order
  private final List<OrderItem> items = new ArrayList<>();
  // Map of items to their applied discounts
  private final Map<OrderItem, DiscountCampaign> appliedDiscounts = new
    HashMap<>();
  // Amount paid by the customer
  private BigDecimal paymentAmount = BigDecimal.ZERO;

  // Creates a new order with a random UUID
  public Order() {
    this.orderId = String.valueOf(UUID.randomUUID());
  }

  // Adds an item to the order
  public void addItem(OrderItem item) {
    items.add(item);
  }

  // Calculates the subtotal of all items without discounts
  public BigDecimal calculateSubtotal() {
    return items.stream()
    .map(OrderItem::calculatePrice)
    .reduce(BigDecimal.ZERO, BigDecimal::add);
  }

  // Calculates the total price including all applied discounts
  public BigDecimal calculateTotal() {
    return items.stream()
    .map(item -> {
      DiscountCampaign discount = appliedDiscounts.get(item);
      return discount != null ? item.calculatePriceWithDiscount(discount)
      : item.calculatePrice();
    })
    .reduce(BigDecimal.ZERO, BigDecimal::add);
  }

  // Applies a discount to a specific item in the order
  public void applyDiscount(OrderItem item, DiscountCampaign discount) {
    appliedDiscounts.put(item, discount);
  }
```

```
// Calculates the change to be returned to the customer
public BigDecimal calculateChange() {
  return paymentAmount.subtract(calculateTotal());
}


// getter and setter methods are omitted for brevity
}
```

Implementation choice: The Order class uses an `ArrayList` for fast $O(1)$ item additions via `addItem` and efficient $O(n)$ iteration for `calculateSubtotal` and `calculateTotal`, ideal for small grocery orders. Similarly, a `HashMap<OrderItem, DiscountCampaign>` tracks discounts per item, providing $O(1)$ average-case lookups and updates.

Checkout

The `Checkout` class orchestrates the transaction process by integrating the order and discount campaigns. It allows items to be added to an order, applies relevant discounts, and finalizes the payment.

```
public class Checkout {
  // Current order being processed
  private Order currentOrder;
  // List of active discount campaigns
  private final List<DiscountCampaign> activeDiscounts;

  // Creates a new checkout with the given active discounts
  public Checkout(List<DiscountCampaign> activeDiscounts) {
    this.activeDiscounts = activeDiscounts;
    startNewOrder();
  }

  // Starts a new order
  public void startNewOrder() {
    this.currentOrder = new Order();
  }

  // Processes the payment and returns the change
  public BigDecimal processPayment(BigDecimal paymentAmount) {
    currentOrder.setPayment(paymentAmount);
    return currentOrder.calculateChange();
  }

  // Adds an item to the current order and applies applicable discounts
  public void addItemToOrder(Item item, int quantity) {
    OrderItem orderItem = new OrderItem(item, quantity);
    currentOrder.addItem(orderItem);

    for (DiscountCampaign newDiscount : activeDiscounts) {
      if (newDiscount.isApplicable(item)) {
```

```
        // if there are multiple newDiscount that apply to item, apply
    the higher one
        if (currentOrder.getAppliedDiscounts().containsKey(orderItem)) {
            DiscountCampaign existingDiscount = currentOrder.
    getAppliedDiscounts().get(orderItem);
            if (orderItem.calculatePriceWithDiscount(newDiscount)
            .compareTo(orderItem.calculatePriceWithDiscount(
    existingDiscount)) > 0) {
                currentOrder.applyDiscount(orderItem, newDiscount);
            }
        } else {
            currentOrder.applyDiscount(orderItem, newDiscount);
        }
      }
    }
  }

  // Generates a receipt for the current order
  public Receipt getReceipt() {
    return new Receipt(currentOrder);
  }

  // Calculates the total amount for the current order
  public BigDecimal getOrderTotal() {
    return currentOrder.calculateTotal();
  }
}
```

Implementation choice: The Checkout class uses an `ArrayList` to store active discounts, enabling linear iteration ($O(n)$) to evaluate applicability and select the highest discount. This is efficient given the small number of active campaigns.

GroceryStoreSystem

Finally, we implement the `GroceryStoreSystem` class that provides a unified interface to interact with the system's other components, including the catalog, inventory, discount campaigns, and checkout. It simplifies client interactions and ensures consistency across operations such as managing products, applying discounts, and processing customer transactions.

Here is the implementation of this class.

```
public class GroceryStoreSystem {
  // Product catalog containing all available items
  private final Catalog catalog;
  // Inventory tracking system
  private final Inventory inventory;
  // List of active discount campaigns
  private List<DiscountCampaign> activeDiscounts = new ArrayList<>();
  // Checkout system for processing orders
```

```
    private final Checkout checkout;

    public GroceryStoreSystem(){
      this.catalog = new Catalog();
      this.inventory = new Inventory();
      this.checkout = new Checkout(activeDiscounts);
    }

    // Adds or updates an item in the catalog
    public void addOrUpdateItem(Item item) {
      catalog.updateItem(item);
    }

    // Updates the inventory count for an item
    public void updateInventory(String barcode, int count) {
      inventory.addStock(barcode, count);
    }

    // Adds a new discount campaign to the system
    public void addDiscountCampaign(DiscountCampaign discount) {
      activeDiscounts.add(discount);
    }

    // Retrieves an item from the catalog by its barcode
    public Item getItemByBarcode(String barcode) {
      return catalog.getItem(barcode);
    }

    // Removes an item from the catalog
    public void removeItem(String barcode) {
      catalog.removeItem(barcode);
    }
}
```

Deep Dive Topics

In this section, we'll explore some common follow-up topics interviewers may ask about the grocery store system.

Flexible Discount Criteria

The current design encapsulates discount logic into two components:

- **Criteria:** Determines whether an item qualifies for a discount.
- **Price calculation strategy:** Computes the discounted price for eligible items.

This design provides reusability by allowing different combinations of discount policies to be expressed without duplicating code. However, what if the interviewer asks you to implement more complex composite discounts, such as:

- "If total electronics purchases exceed \$100, apply a 10% discount; if they exceed \$200, apply a 20% discount."
- "Buy at least 3 units of the same item in the food category for a special price."

These scenarios require combining multiple criteria and calculations. We can handle such complexity by enhancing the design using the Composite Pattern for criteria and the Decorator Pattern for sequential calculations.

Note: To learn more about the Composite Pattern and its common use cases, refer to the **Unix File Search** chapter of the book.

Combining Multiple Criteria

To address nested or combined criteria, we will use the Composite Pattern, which is particularly well-suited for scenarios where hierarchical structures or combinations of logic are required. Composite criteria allow us to combine multiple rules (e.g., category-based, item-based) using logical operators like **AND** and **OR**, without hardcoding the logic. For example, it can check if an item belongs to a specific category and meets a minimum price threshold.

Design changes

Add a `CompositeCriteria` class to support combining criteria.

Code changes

Below is an example of how to implement `CompositeCriteria`:

```
// Composite criteria that combines multiple discount criteria
public class CompositeCriteria implements DiscountCriteria {
  // List of criteria to be combined
  private final List<DiscountCriteria> criteriaList;

  // Creates a new composite criteria with the given list of criteria
  public CompositeCriteria(List<DiscountCriteria> criteriaList) {
    this.criteriaList = new ArrayList<>(criteriaList);
  }

  // Checks if the item satisfies all the criteria in the list
  @Override
  public boolean isApplicable(Item item) {
    return criteriaList.stream().allMatch(criteria -> criteria.
    isApplicable(item));
  }

  // Adds a new criteria to the composite
  public void addCriteria(DiscountCriteria criteria) {
    criteriaList.add(criteria);
  }

  // Removes a criteria from the composite
```

```
  public void removeCriteria(DiscountCriteria criteria) {
    criteriaList.remove(criteria);
  }
}
```

Layering Discount Calculations

To manage sequential discount calculations, we can use the **Decorator Pattern**. By wrapping multiple calculation strategies, we can apply discounts in a specific order without modifying the underlying strategy logic. For example:

- Apply a fixed discount first.
- Then apply a percentage-based discount to the remaining price.

Note: To learn more about the Decorator Pattern and its common use cases, refer to the **Further Reading** section at the end of this chapter.

Design changes

- Introduce decorators like `FixedDiscountDecorator` and `PercentageDiscountDecorator` to wrap existing strategies.

Code changes

Below are examples of implementing decorators:

FixedDiscountDecorator

```
public class FixedDiscountDecorator implements
    DiscountCalculationStrategy {
  // The strategy being decorated
  private final DiscountCalculationStrategy strategy;
  // The fixed amount to be added to the discount
  private final BigDecimal fixedAmount;

  public FixedDiscountDecorator(DiscountCalculationStrategy strategy,
    BigDecimal fixedAmount) {
    this.strategy = strategy;
    this.fixedAmount = fixedAmount;
  }

  // Calculates the discounted price by applying both the base strategy
    and the fixed amount
  @Override
  public BigDecimal calculateDiscountedPrice(BigDecimal originalPrice) {
    return strategy.calculateDiscountedPrice(originalPrice).subtract(
    fixedAmount);
  }
}
```

PercentageDiscountDecorator

```java
public class PercentageDiscountDecorator implements
    DiscountCalculationStrategy {
  // The strategy being decorated
  private final DiscountCalculationStrategy strategy;
  // The additional percentage to be discounted
  private final BigDecimal additionalPercentage;

  public PercentageDiscountDecorator(DiscountCalculationStrategy strategy
    , BigDecimal additionalPercentage) {
    this.strategy = strategy;
    this.additionalPercentage = additionalPercentage;
  }

  // Calculates the discounted price by applying both the base strategy
    and the additional percentage
  @Override
  public BigDecimal calculateDiscountedPrice(BigDecimal originalPrice) {
    BigDecimal baseDiscountedPrice = strategy.calculateDiscountedPrice(
    originalPrice);
    return baseDiscountedPrice.multiply(BigDecimal.ONE.subtract(
    additionalPercentage.divide(BigDecimal.valueOf(100))));
  }
}
```

By combining nested criteria and sequential calculation strategies, we can design a highly flexible discount system capable of handling even the most complex scenarios. This design approach not only simplifies implementation but also demonstrates a deep understanding of abstraction and extensibility principles, which are crucial in object-oriented design interviews.

Wrap Up

In this chapter, we designed a grocery store system. We tried to solve the grocery store problem in a step-by-step manner, just like a candidate would do in an actual object-oriented design interview. We started off by listing down the requirements through a series of question/answer formats between the candidate and the interviewer. We then identified the core objects, followed by the class diagram of the grocery store, and presented the implementation code.

The most important takeaway is the clear separation of concerns, where each component, such as Catalog, Inventory, Order, and DiscountCampaign, focuses on a specific responsibility. This modularity not only simplifies individual components but also ensures they integrate seamlessly.

In the deep dive section, we explored advanced topics like implementing composite discounts and layering multiple calculation strategies. These enhancements showcase how abstraction and extensibility can handle complex real-world scenarios, such as applying tiered discounts or combining fixed and percentage-based discounts.

Congratulations on getting this far! Now give yourself a pat on the back. Good job!

Further Reading: Decorator Design Pattern

This section gives a quick overview of the design patterns used in this chapter. It's helpful if you're new to these patterns or need a refresher to better understand the design choices.

Decorator design pattern

Decorator is a structural design pattern that allows you to add new behaviors to an object by wrapping it in another object that provides the additional functionality, without modifying the original object's code.

In the grocery store system design, we have used the Decorator pattern to layer multiple discount calculations by wrapping a `DiscountCalculationStrategy` object in decorator classes like `FixedDiscountDecorator` and `PercentageDiscountDecorator`. This allows the system to apply discounts sequentially, such as a fixed amount followed by a percentage reduction, during checkout without altering the core discount strategy.

To illustrate the Decorator pattern in another domain, consider a text formatting system where a document editor applies styles like bold or italic to text content to enhance its appearance.

Problem

Imagine you're developing a text editor where users can format text with styles like bold, italic, or underline. Initially, you might handle these by modifying the Text class with conditional logic or creating subclasses for each style combination (e.g., `BoldText`, `BoldItalicText`). However, this leads to complex code or an explosion of subclasses, making it difficult to add new styles (e.g., strikethrough) or combine multiple styles (e.g., bold and italic).

Solution

The Decorator Pattern addresses this by creating decorator classes that implement the same interface as the Text class and wrap a Text object to add new behaviors. For example, a `BoldDecorator` wraps a Text object to add bold formatting to its display, while an `ItalicDecorator` adds italic formatting. The editor interacts with the decorated text through the same interface, enabling seamless style application. Decorators can be stacked to combine styles (e.g., bold and italic), providing flexibility without altering the Text class.

Here's a simple diagram showing the Decorator pattern for text formatting:

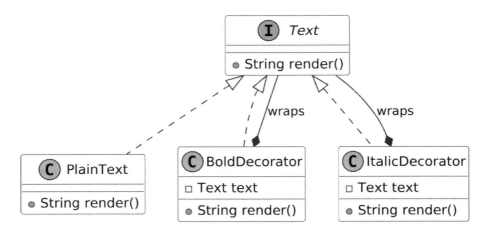

Text interface and concrete classes

Text is the common interface that `PlainText`, `BoldDecorator`, and `ItalicDecorator` implement. The advantage is that we can treat all objects uniformly through the Text interface, allowing decorators to wrap and enhance text formatting, like bold or italic, without knowing the underlying object's type.

When to use

The Decorator design pattern is useful in scenarios:

- When you need to add features or behaviors to objects dynamically at runtime without modifying their code.
- When subclassing results in too many combinations of features (e.g., BoldItalicText), composition is a simpler alternative.

10

Tic-Tac-Toe Game

In this chapter, we will explore the object-oriented design of a Tic-Tac-Toe game. We aim to create an interactive platform where two players alternate turns, placing their symbols on a virtual board. We'll design key components such as the game board, player move tracking, outcome determination, and a score tracker for managing player ratings.

How Tic-Tac-Toe works: Tic-Tac-Toe is a classic two-player game played on a 3×3 grid. Each player selects a symbol ("X" or "O") and takes turns placing it in an empty cell. The goal is to align three identical symbols horizontally, vertically, or diagonally. The game concludes with a win if a player achieves this alignment, or a draw if all nine cells are filled without a winner.

Let's gather the key requirements through a mock interview scenario.

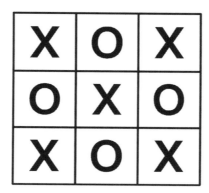

Tic-Tac-Toe

Requirements Gathering

Here's an example of a typical prompt an interviewer might present:

"Imagine you and a friend are sitting down for a quick game of Tic-Tac-Toe. You each choose a symbol (e.g., "X" or "O") and take turns placing your symbol on a board. After each move, the game checks if someone has won or if the board is full, signaling a draw. Behind the scenes, the game tracks your moves, updates a scoreboard to reflect wins, and maintains player rankings for future matches. Let's design a Tic-Tac-Toe game system that handles all this."

Requirements clarification

Here is an example of how a conversation between a candidate and an interviewer might unfold:

Candidate: Does the game support different board sizes?
Interviewer: No, let's stick to the standard 3x3 board for simplicity.

Candidate: How should the game handle outcomes like wins, losses, and draws?
Interviewer: The system must detect winning patterns and notify players of the result: win, draw, or ongoing.

Candidate: Should the game track player ratings?
Interviewer: Yes, the game should maintain a score tracker that updates player ratings based on game outcomes (win, loss, or draw).

Candidate: How does the game handle invalid moves?
Interviewer: If a player attempts a move in an occupied or invalid position, notify them and prompt them for a new move.

Based on this discussion, let's nail down the key functional requirements.

Requirements

Here are the key functional requirements we've identified.

- The game is played on a 3x3 board.
- The system determines the game's status:
  - a win (three identical symbols aligned in a row, column, or diagonal)
  - a draw (a full board with no winner)
  - In progress.
- A score tracker records player performance, updates ratings based on wins, and supports queries like rankings or top players.
- Invalid moves (e.g., placing a symbol in an occupied cell) are rejected with feedback to the player.

Below are the non-functional requirements:

- The user interface should be intuitive, providing clear feedback for invalid moves and game outcomes, with easily accessible gameplay instructions.

- The system should support future enhancements, such as different board sizes or game modes, without major architectural changes.

Identify Core Objects

Before diving into the design, it's important to identify the core objects.

- **Board:** The Board class models the 3x3 game grid where players place their symbols (e.g., "X" or "O"). It handles updates to the grid, checks for a winner by examining rows, columns, and diagonals, and determines if the board is full.
- **Player:** This class represents an individual playing the game.
- **Game:** The central entity of the Tic-Tac-Toe game is the Game class. It coordinates turn-taking between players, validates moves (e.g., ensuring a cell isn't occupied), and tracks the game's status, whether it's in progress or ended with a winner or draw.

> ✂ **Design choice:** The Game class can become overloaded because it handles multiple operations. To keep it manageable, we delegate the Board to manage the grid and ScoreTracker to handle player ratings. This modularity enhances maintainability and scalability.

- **ScoreTracker:** Tracks player ratings across games, updating them based on outcomes.

Now that we've identified the core objects, let's design their relationships in a class diagram.

Design Class Diagram

In this section, we'll define the class structure for a Tic-Tac-Toe game. The goal is to create a cohesive design that adheres to OOD principles, such as the Single Responsibility Principle (SRP), while remaining flexible for future extensions. We'll also explain the reasoning behind design choices and consider alternatives to provide insight into the decision-making process.

Game

The Game class is the central coordinator of the Tic-Tac-Toe game. It manages the flow of gameplay, including initializing components, handling turns, and determining the outcome. To keep the design modular and manageable, certain responsibilities are delegated to other classes.

For instance, the ScoreTracker class is solely responsible for tracking player performance, updating win counts based on game outcomes. The Board class manages the game grid, ensuring moves are valid by checking for empty spaces and staying within bounds. The Player class remains stateless. It does not store win counts directly. This separation allows the centralized ScoreTracker to monitor player performance across multiple games, setting the stage for a scalable ranking system, which we'll explore in more depth later.

Below is the representation of the Game class.

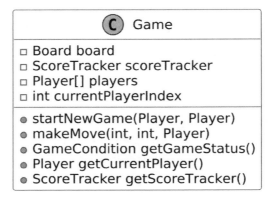

Board

The Board class represents the 3×3 game grid, which is modeled as a two-dimensional array of Player objects. It is responsible for enforcing game rules at the board level, ensuring that moves are made within valid positions. It determines if a player has won by checking for three matching symbols in a row, column, or diagonal. Additionally, it provides functionality to reset the grid for a new game and allows retrieval of player symbols at specific grid positions.

Here is the design of this class.

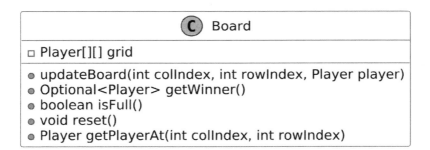

> ✂ **Design choice:** The choice to include win-checking logic within the Board class, rather than the Game class, aligns with Single Responsibility Principle (SRP), as the Board is the owner of grid-related rules.

ScoreTracker

The ScoreTracker class is designed to monitor player performance across multiple games by maintaining a centralized scoreboard for a group of players. While real-world systems often employ complex methods that dynamically adjust scores based on performance distributions and other factors, a more straightforward approach suits an interview setting. Here, we can rate players based solely on their number of wins, keeping the logic straightforward yet effective.

Instead of embedding ratings as an attribute within the Player class, we delegate this responsibility to ScoreTracker. This design choice stems from the nature of ratings: unlike a player's name (an inherent trait), ratings are contextual, reflecting performance relative to others in a group. They shift as games are played, impacting multiple players simultaneously, and in advanced systems, they may even evolve over time. By isolating this logic in ScoreTracker, we also open the door to future enhancements, such as supporting players in multiple leagues with distinct ratings.

To achieve this, ScoreTracker employs a HashMap<Player, Integer> named playerRatings to store win counts for all players. This centralized structure enables efficient management of the population's ratings and supports key operations: updating scores after the game ends, identifying the top-ranked player, and determining any player's rank. This modular approach not only encapsulates rating logic but also enhances maintainability and scalability.

Here is the representation of this class.

When a game ends, the reportGameResult method determines the winner and updates the score tracker. If the game results in a draw, no score changes are made.

Move

The Move class acts as a straightforward data structure designed to capture a player's move in the game. It stores the row and column indices where the player placed their symbol, along with a reference to the player who made the move.

By bundling these details (row, column, and player) into a single Move object, rather than passing them as separate parameters across various methods, the code becomes more readable and easier to maintain.

Player

The `Player` class encapsulates the core attributes of a player in the game: their name and assigned symbol (such as "X" or "O"). These attributes make it simple to identify which player is responsible for a given move.

While it might seem intuitive to include real-world actions like making moves or updating ratings within the `Player` class, this would violate the Single Responsibility Principle (SRP). In a well-designed system, responsibilities are clearly divided:

- The `Board` class is the sole source of truth for validating and placing moves on the grid.
- The `ScoreTracker` class tracks and updates player ratings, as ratings depend on the broader context of a group of players and require uniform updates across all players.

Complete Class Diagram

Below is the complete class diagram of the Tic-Tac-Toe game:

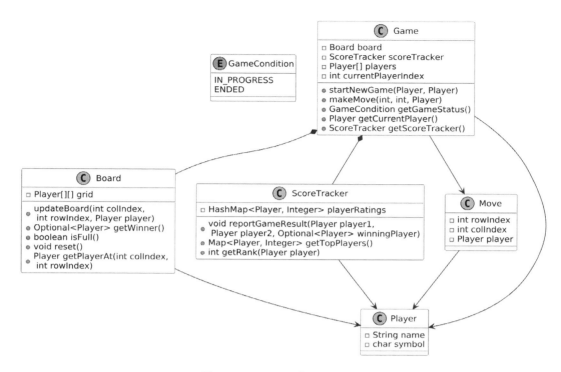

Class Diagram of Tic-Tac-Toe

Let's now bring our design to life with the code implementation!

Code - Tic-Tac-Toe Game

In this section, we'll implement the core functionalities of the Tic-Tac-Toe game, focusing on key areas such as managing the game board, handling player turns, determining the winner, and tracking player ratings through a score tracker.

Game

The Game class manages the flow of a Tic-Tac-Toe game. It manages the game board, player turns, and score tracker updates. After each move, the game checks for win conditions (three matching symbols in a row, column, or diagonal) and for a draw (when the board is full, but no winner exists).

Check out the code implementation of the Game class below.

```java
public class Game {
  // Core game components
  private final Board board;               // Manages the game board state
  private final ScoreTracker scoreTracker; // Keeps track of player scores
  private Player[] players;                // Array of players in the game
  private int currentPlayerIndex;          // Index of the current player'
    s turn
```

```java
// Constructor initializes game components and starts a new game
public Game(Player playerX, Player playerY) {
  board = new Board();
  scoreTracker = new ScoreTracker();
  startNewGame(playerX, playerY);
}

// Resets the game state and initializes players for a new game
public void startNewGame(Player playerX, Player playerY) {
  board.reset();
  players = new Player[]{playerX, playerY};
  currentPlayerIndex = 0;
}

// Processes a player's move, validates it, and updates game state
public void makeMove(int colIndex, int rowIndex, Player player) {
  if (getGameStatus().equals(GameCondition.ENDED)) {
    throw new IllegalStateException("game ended");
  }
  if (players[currentPlayerIndex] != player) {
    throw new IllegalArgumentException("not the current player");
  }
  if(board.getPlayerAt(colIndex, rowIndex) != null) {
    throw new IllegalArgumentException("board position is taken");
  }
  board.updateBoard(colIndex, rowIndex, player);
  final Move newMove = new Move(colIndex, rowIndex, player);
  currentPlayerIndex = (currentPlayerIndex + 1) % players.length;
  if (getGameStatus().equals(GameCondition.ENDED)) {
    scoreTracker.reportGameResult(players[0], players[1], board.
  getWinner());
  }
}

// Determines if the game is in progress or has ended
public GameCondition getGameStatus() {
  Optional<Player> winner = board.getWinner();
  if (winner.isPresent()) {
    return GameCondition.ENDED;
  }
  return board.isFull() ? GameCondition.ENDED : GameCondition.
  IN_PROGRESS;
}

// Returns the player whose turn it is
public Player getCurrentPlayer() {
  return players[currentPlayerIndex];
}
```

```
    // Returns the score tracker for accessing game statistics
    public ScoreTracker getScoreTracker() {
      return scoreTracker;
    }
}
```

- **makeMove(int colIndex, int rowIndex, Player player):** This method handles the player's move by checking if the game is still ongoing, whether the correct player is making a move, and if the selected board position is empty. If all checks pass, the board is updated, and the turn is passed to the next player. If the move results in a win or a draw, the score tracker is updated accordingly.
- **getGameStatus():** Determines the game's status by checking for a winner or a full board. Returns GameCondition.ENDED if either condition is met, otherwise GameCondition.IN_PROGRESS.

Implementation choice: The Game class uses a state machine-like approach to manage game flow, tracking the current player and game status (INPROGRESS or ENDED) with an enum (GameCondition). This was chosen for its simplicity and clarity in handling turn-based logic, as it ensures only one player moves at a time and the game stops when a win or draw occurs.

Board

The Board class represents the game board for a two-player Tic-Tac-Toe game. It uses a 3×3 grid to encapsulate the state of play within a 3x3 grid, where each position holds either a Player object or null if it's empty. The definition of the Board class is given below.

```
public class Board {
  // 3x3 grid to store player moves
  private final Player[][] grid = new Player[3][3];

  // Updates the board with a player's move at the specified position
  public void updateBoard(int colIndex, int rowIndex, Player player) {
    if (grid[colIndex][rowIndex] == null) {
      grid[colIndex][rowIndex] = player;
    }
  }

  // Checks for a winner by examining rows, columns, and diagonals
  public Optional<Player> getWinner() {
    // Check rows for three in a row
    for (int i = 0; i < grid.length; i++) {
      Player first = grid[i][0];
      if (first != null && Arrays.stream(grid[i]).allMatch(p -> p ==
    first))
      {
        return Optional.of(first);
      }
```

```
    }

    // Check columns for three in a column
    for (int j = 0; j < grid[0].length; j++) {
      final Player first = grid[0][j];
      int finalJ = j; //streams require a final object
      if (first != null && Arrays.stream(grid).allMatch(row -> row[finalJ
    ] == first))
      {
        return Optional.of(first);
      }
    }

    // Check main diagonal (top-left to bottom-right)
    Player topLeft = grid[0][0];
    if (topLeft != null && IntStream.range(0, grid.length).allMatch(i ->
    grid[i][i] == topLeft)) {
      return Optional.of(topLeft);
    }

    // Check anti-diagonal (top-right to bottom-left)
    Player topRight = grid[0][grid[0].length - 1];
    if (topRight != null && IntStream.range(0, grid.length).allMatch(i ->
     grid[i][grid[0].length - 1 - i] == topRight)) {
      return Optional.of(topRight);
    }

    // No winner found
    return Optional.empty();
  }

  // Checks if all positions on the board are filled
  public boolean isFull() {
    return Arrays.stream(grid).flatMap(Arrays::stream).noneMatch(Objects
    ::isNull);
  }

  // Resets the board by clearing all positions
  public void reset() {
    for (Player[] players : grid) {
      Arrays.fill(players, null);
    }
  }

  // Returns the player at the specified position, or null if empty
  public Player getPlayerAt(int colIndex, int rowIndex) {
    return grid[colIndex][rowIndex];
  }
}
```

The class provides several methods to manage the game, including:

- `updateBoard(int colIndex, int rowIndex, Player player)`: Updates the board by placing the specified player's symbol at the given `colIndex` and `rowIndex`, provided the position is empty.
- `Optional<Player> getWinner()`: This method checks for a winner by looking at the rows, columns, and diagonals. If any row, column, or diagonal contains the same symbol, the player is declared the winner.
- `Player getPlayerAt(int colIndex, int rowIndex)`: Returns the `Player` object at the specified board position, or null if the position is unoccupied.

Implementation choice: The Board uses a 2D array (`Player[][]`) to represent the 3×3 grid, chosen for its direct mapping to the game's spatial structure and $O(1)$ access time for reading or updating positions.

Player

The `Player` class represents a player in the game, with key attributes like their name and symbol. These attributes help identify the player and their move on the board.

```java
public class Player {
  private final String name;
  private final char symbol;

  public Player(String name, char symbol) {
    this.name = name;
    this.symbol = symbol;
  }
  public String getName() {
    return name;
  }
  public char getSymbol() {
    return symbol;
  }
}
```

ScoreTracker

The `ScoreTracker` class manages player rankings across multiple Tic-Tac-Toe games by tracking and updating scores for a group of players. It uses a `HashMap<Player, Integer>` to store player ratings, where each Player is mapped to an integer score based on a simple victory count system. Here is the implementation of this class.

```java
class ScoreTracker {
  // Stores player ratings in a map where key is player and value is
    their score
  private HashMap<Player, Integer> playerRatings = new HashMap<>();
```

```java
// This logic is customizable and, in reality, will use a complex
  ranking algorithm. For the interview, we use a simple victory count
  system where the winner gets one point, the loser loses a point, and
  no changes occur for a draw.
public void reportGameResult(Player player1, Player player2, Optional<
  Player> winningPlayer) {
  if (winningPlayer.isPresent())
  {
    Player winner = winningPlayer.get();
    Player loser = player1 == winner ? player2 : player1;
    playerRatings.putIfAbsent(winner, 0);
    playerRatings.put(winner, playerRatings.get(winner) + 1);
    playerRatings.putIfAbsent(loser, 0);
    playerRatings.put(loser, playerRatings.get(loser) - 1);
  }
}


// Returns a map of players sorted by their ratings in descending order
public Map<Player, Integer> getTopPlayers() {
  return playerRatings.entrySet()
  .stream()
  .sorted(Map.Entry.comparingByValue(Comparator.reverseOrder()))
  .map(Map.Entry::getKey)
  .collect(Collectors.toMap(player -> player, player -> playerRatings.
  get(player)));
}


// Returns the rank of a player based on their rating
public int getRank(Player player)
{
  List<Player> sortedPlayers = playerRatings.entrySet()
  .stream()
  .sorted(Map.Entry.comparingByValue(Comparator.reverseOrder()))
  .map(Map.Entry::getKey)
  .collect(Collectors.toList());
  return sortedPlayers.indexOf(player) + 1;
}


// getters are omitted for brevity
}
```

Implementation choice: The ScoreTracker uses a HashMap<Player, Integer> to store player ratings, which is chosen for its $O(1)$ average-case lookup and update performance, making it ideal for frequent score updates and queries (e.g., top-ranked player).

Deep Dive Topic

At this point, you have met the basic requirements of the question. In this section, we will explore some potential extensions in more detail.

Implement undo functionality in Tic-Tac-Toe

Imagine you're playing Tic-Tac-Toe, and you accidentally place your 'X' in the wrong spot. Wouldn't it be great to hit an undo button and try again? Let's dive into how we can implement undo functionality in a Tic-Tac-Toe game, step by step.

Step 1: Track move history

- Every time a player makes a move, we store that move so it can be undone later.
- The `Move` class (which we've already designed as part of the main game logic) serves this purpose by capturing details such as `rowIndex`, `colIndex`, and the `player`.

Below is the representation of the `Move` class.

Step 2: Store Moves with a Stack

- Since moves occur in a last-in, first-out (LIFO) order (i.e., the last move is undone first), we can use a stack (`ArrayDeque<Move>`).
- When a move is made, we push it onto the stack.
- When undo is requested, we pop the most recent move from the stack and revert the board to its previous state.

Below is the representation of the `MoveHistory` class, which records the move and implements the undo functionality.

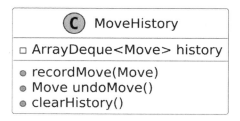

Here's the code for the `MoveHistory` class:

```
class MoveHistory {
  // Stack-like structure to store moves in chronological order
  private final ArrayDeque<Move> history = new ArrayDeque<>();
```

```
  // Adds a new move to the history stack
  public void recordMove(Move move) {
    history.push(move);
  }

  // Removes and returns the most recent move from the history
  public Move undoMove() {
    return history.pop();
  }

  // Clears all moves from the history
  public void clearHistory() {
    history.clear();
  }
}
```

Step 3: Reverse the Board state

The final step is to clear that spot on the board, and switch the current player back to whoever's turn it was before.

Here's the updated code from the Game class:

```
public void makeMove(int colIndex, int rowIndex, Player player) {
  // Validate that game hasn't ended
  if (getGameStatus().equals(GameCondition.ENDED)) {
    throw new IllegalStateException("game ended");
  }
  // Validate that it's the correct player's turn
  if (players[currentPlayerIndex] != player) {
    throw new IllegalArgumentException("not the current player");
  }
  // Validate that the position is not already taken
  if(board.getPlayerAt(colIndex, rowIndex) != null) {
    throw new IllegalArgumentException("board position is taken");
  }
  // Update the board with the player's move
  board.updateBoard(colIndex, rowIndex, player);
  // Record the move in history
  final Move newMove = new Move(colIndex, rowIndex, player);
  moveHistory.recordMove(newMove);
  // Switch to the next player
  currentPlayerIndex = (currentPlayerIndex + 1) % players.length;
  // If game has ended, update the score
  if (getGameStatus().equals(GameCondition.ENDED)) {
    scoreTracker.reportGameResult(players[0], players[1], board.getWinner
    ());
  }
}
```

```java
// Reverts the last move made in the game
public void undoMove() {
  // Check if game has ended to prevent undoing after winner is reported
  if (getGameStatus().equals(GameCondition.ENDED)) {
    throw new IllegalStateException("game ended and winner already
    reported");
  }
  // Get the last move from history
  final Move lastMove = moveHistory.undoMove();

  // Update current player index to previous player
  if (currentPlayerIndex == 0) {
    currentPlayerIndex = players.length - 1;
  }
  else {
    currentPlayerIndex--;
  }

  // Clear the board position of the undone move
  board.updateBoard(lastMove.getColIndex(), lastMove.getRowIndex(), null)
    ;
}
```

What we discussed above is the essence of a well-known software design pattern called the **Memento Pattern**.

> 📖 **Definition:** The Memento Pattern is a behavioral design pattern that allows an object to save and restore its previous state without exposing the details of its implementation. This pattern is useful in scenarios where undo or rollback functionality is needed, as it maintains a complete event history.

In this pattern:

- The Memento is an object that stores the state of another object at a specific point in time, acting as a snapshot. In our design, the Move class served as the Memento, capturing the state of a single move in the Tic-Tac-Toe game.

- The Caretaker is responsible for storing and managing Memento objects, typically keeping them in a collection and providing mechanisms to save or retrieve them. The MoveHistory class played the role of the Caretaker, maintaining a stack of Move objects (Mementos) and offering an undoMove() method to retrieve the last move for reversal.

- The Originator is the object whose state is being captured and restored. It creates Memento objects to save its state and can use them to restore a previous state. The Game class acted as the Originator, creating Move objects during each makeMove() call to capture the move's state and using the undoMove() method to restore the game state by clearing the board position of the last move.

The UML diagram below illustrates this structure.

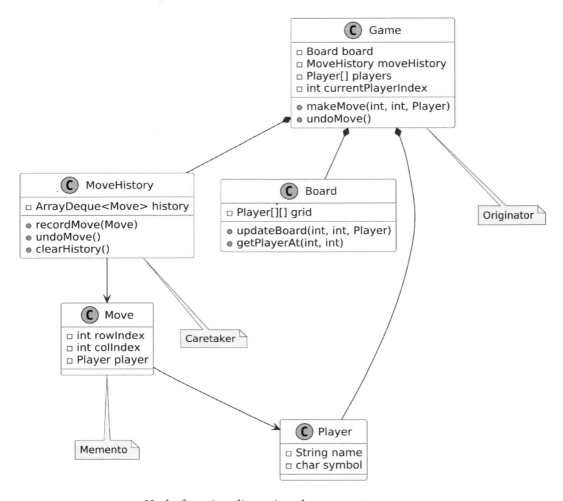

Undo functionality using the memento pattern

However, one potential challenge of using the Memento Pattern is memory overhead. Every time a move is made, we store the entire move in the history. In Tic-Tac-Toe, this isn't much of a problem because the board is small, but in more complex games with larger states, the memory required to store each memento could become a bottleneck.

With our Tic-Tac-Toe game designed and implemented, let's wrap up with key takeaways.

Wrap Up

In this chapter, we designed the Tic-Tac-Toe game. We started by gathering and clarifying the requirements through a series of questions and answers. Next, we identified the core objects involved, designed the class diagram, and implemented the key components of the game.

A key takeaway from this design is the importance of modularity and clear separation of concerns. Each component, such as the `Board`, `Game`, `Player`, and `ScoreTracker` classes, focuses on a specific responsibility, ensuring the system is maintainable and easy to extend.

In the deep dive section, we explored advanced topics, including using the Memento Pattern to handle undo functionality, enabling players to revert their moves while maintaining the integrity of the game state.

Congratulations on getting this far! Now give yourself a pat on the back. Good job!

11

Blackjack Game

In this chapter, we will discuss the object-oriented design of the Blackjack game (also called "21"). Blackjack is a popular card game where the goal is to get a hand of cards that adds up to 21, or as close as possible, without going over. The game is a mix of strategy (deciding when to hit or stand) and luck (the cards you get), making it a captivating and iconic casino game.

Let's gather the game's requirements through a typical interview-style conversation.

Blackjack Game

Requirements Gathering

Here's an example of a typical prompt an interviewer might present:

"Picture yourself at a casino table, ready to play a round of Blackjack, also known as '21.' At the start, you and other players place bets, and the dealer distributes two cards to each player, including themselves. You evaluate your hand, aiming to get as close to 21 as possible without going over, and decide whether to hit or stand. After all players make their moves, the dealer reveals their hand and hits until reaching at least 17, then stands. Behind the scenes, the game manages a deck of cards, tracks player actions, ensures fair dealing, and updates balances. Let's design a Blackjack game system that handles all this."

Note: Blackjack has various rules (e.g., soft 17, double down, splitting). This document focuses on the technical design and object-oriented implementation of a simplified standard Blackjack game.

Requirements clarification

Here is an example of how a conversation between a candidate and an interviewer might unfold:

Candidate: Should I design the game to support multiple players or just one player competing against the dealer?
Interviewer: The game should support multiple players.

Candidate: What happens after a player takes their turn?
Interviewer: After each player takes their turn ("hit" or "stand"), the game should check if all players have either stood or busted (hand value exceeding 21). When this happens, the game should determine the winner by comparing each player's hand value and settle the bets.

Candidate: Should the dealer follow any specific rules for when to hit or stand?
Interviewer: Yes, the dealer should continue to "hit" until their hand totals at least 17. Once they reach 17 or higher, they must "stand."

Candidate: How are bets handled in the game, and how are players paid?
Interviewer: Players place their bets before the initial cards are dealt. Players who win receive a payout equal to their bet (e.g., a $10 bet wins $10, plus their original bet returned), while players who bust lose their bet.

Requirements

Based on the conversation, here are the key functional requirements we've identified.

- The game should support multiple players and a dealer.
- Players should be dealt two cards at the beginning of the game.
- Players should have the option to "hit" (request an additional card) or "stand" (keep their current hand).
- Aces should be valued as 1 or 11, with the value chosen to optimize the player's hand.
- After each player's turn, the game checks if all players have stood or busted. Once all players have completed their turns, the dealer takes their turn, hitting until their hand totals at least 17, then standing. The game then determines the winner and settles the bets.
- Players who win receive a payout equal to their bet (1:1), while players who bust lose

their bet.

Below are the non-functional requirements:

- The user interface must be intuitive, with clear prompts and visual feedback on game state to accommodate users with minimal Blackjack experience.

With these requirements in hand, let's map out the game's flow using an activity diagram to visualize how it all comes together.

Activity Diagram

Understanding the flow of a game like Blackjack is crucial when designing its object-oriented structure, especially given the game's mix of sequential steps and decision points. This is where an activity diagram comes into play. An activity diagram visually maps out the workflow of the game, capturing each action, decision, and transition in a clear, step-by-step manner.

In the context of Blackjack, this means outlining everything from dealing cards to determining winners, ensuring we account for all possible paths, such as a player busting or the dealer hitting until 17. Let's look at the activity diagram for Blackjack, which captures this process in detail.

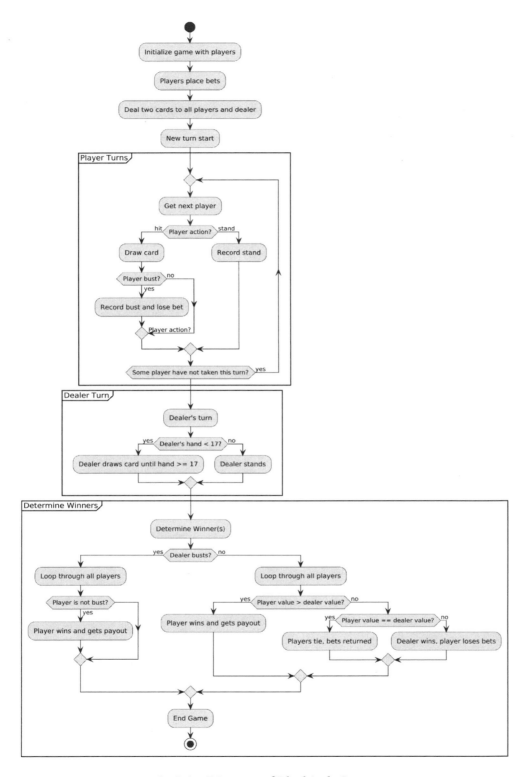

Activity Diagram of Blackjack Game

Now that we've got a clear picture of the game's flow, let's break down the core objects we'll need to bring this design to life.

Identify Core Objects

As we have done in earlier chapters, let's enumerate the core objects.

- **BlackJackGame:** The `BlackJackGame` class acts as the central entity of the game, managing the overall flow from start to finish. It is responsible for dealing cards, tracking player actions ("hit", or "stand"), and determining the winner.

- **Player:** The `Player` interface represents each participant in the game, with concrete implementations as `RealPlayer` for humans tracking bets and balance, and `DealerPlayer` for the dealer, who does not place bets and must hit until reaching a hand value of 17 or higher, as per Blackjack rules.

- **Hand:** Each player is associated with a Hand class, which manages the cards they receive during the game. This class calculates all possible hand values based on the cards held. This is especially important when handling Aces, which can count to 1 or 11, depending on which value keeps the player's hand value closer to 21 without exceeding it.

- **Deck:** The `Deck` class is responsible for managing the collection of cards used in the game. It shuffles the cards when a new round begins and provides a new card when a player requests a hit.

- **Card:** Each individual card is represented by the `Card` class, which is defined by its `Rank` and `Suit` enums. The `Rank` determines the card's value in the game, while the `Suit` provides its identity, such as "Hearts" or "Spades".

Design Class Diagram

Now that we know the core objects and their roles, the next step is to create classes and methods to build the Blackjack game.

Card

The `Card` class is a straightforward, immutable building block that holds a rank and a suit. It acts as a data-only entity with no behavior. This ensures immutability to prevent accidental changes and maintain game consistency.

Note: Immutability means that once a card is created, its rank and suit cannot be changed.

Below is the representation of this class.

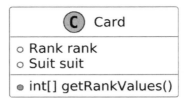

The `Card` class is kept simple, it uses `getRankValues()` to fetch values from Rank. It leaves the heavy lifting of value calculations to the Hand class, sticking to a clean separation of duties. Note that the return value is a list of integers rather than a single value because Ace has two possible values (1 or 11).

> ✂ **Design choice:** The Card class is designed as a standalone entity to represent individual cards, enabling reuse across multiple decks or game variants.

Since `Card` relies on `Rank` and `Suit` to define its value and identity, let's explore those next.

Rank and Suit enumerations

When modeling `Rank` and `Suit`, enums are the ideal choice as they're type-safe, readable, and easy to maintain.

- `Rank` captures card values: numbers 2 through 10 are worth face value, Jack, Queen, and King are each worth 10, and an Ace can be either 1 or 11, depending on what benefits the hand most.
- `Suit` lists the standard four options: Hearts, Diamonds, Clubs, and Spades.

Suit and Rank Enums

> ✂ **Design choice: Why enums over other approaches?** Consider using strings instead. You'd have a lot of flexibility, but that comes at a cost: extra validation to avoid invalid inputs, messy conversions when calculating hand values, and potentially higher memory usage. Integers might seem like a better alternative because they allow simple numeric representation (e.g., 1 for Ace, 10 for Jack), but they're error-prone, developers might accidentally assign invalid values like 0 or 15, and their lack of inherent meaning requires additional checks, reducing the clarity that enums provide with named constants.

For a card game like Blackjack, where precise values and clear representations are key, enums make the design both robust and easy to follow.

With cards defined, let's see how they come together in the Deck class.

Deck

The `Deck` class serves as the backbone of Blackjack's card management, handling a standard 52-card deck. It uses a `List<Card>` to mimic a physical deck's order, providing essential methods like shuffling to randomize the cards, drawing cards for players, counting the remaining cards, checking if the deck is empty, and resetting for a new round. This reset process shuffles the deck to ensure fair dealing.

Below is the representation of this class:

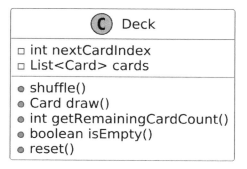

Now that we've got a deck to draw from, let's define the players who'll use it.

Player

The `Player` interface serves as the blueprint for all participants in Blackjack, laying the foundation for both human players and the dealer. For human players, the `RealPlayer` class tracks essential details like a player's name, hand, current bet, and balance, while providing methods for placing bets, receiving payouts, and retrieving key information. `DealerPlayer`, on the other hand, represents the house (no betting or balance here), just hitting until reaching 17 or higher, per Blackjack rules.

Here is the representation of this interface with concrete classes:

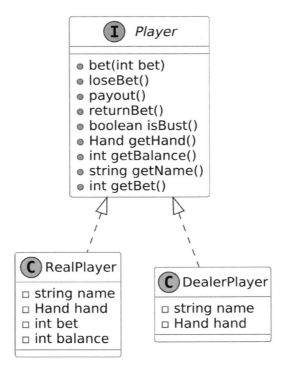

Player interface with concrete classes

> ✂ **Design choice:** An interface-based design for `Player` is chosen to abstract common behaviors across human players and the dealer, promoting extensibility.

Now that our players are set, let's look at how they'll manage their cards with the `Hand` class.

Hand

The `Hand` class manages the cards for a player or dealer in Blackjack, keeping track of a list of cards and calculating all possible hand values. It smartly handles Aces as either 1 or 11 to keep the hand as close to 21 as possible without going over. To support this, the class offers methods to add cards, access the card list, retrieve the possible values (stored as a sorted set to avoid duplicates), clear the hand for a new round, and determine if the hand is bust using `isBust()`.

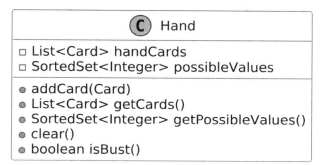

With hands managing cards and totals, let's see how the BlackjackGame class ties it all together.

BlackJackGame

The BlackJackGame class is the central entity in our Blackjack game, orchestrating the action from the initial card dealing to the end of each round. It oversees the game's deck, the players, and the dealer, handling card distribution, tracking turns, and wrapping up rounds by deciding winners and settling bets. To keep things fair, it ensures the dealer keeps hitting until reaching 17, then holds, while players get to choose whether to hit or stand.

Here is the representation of this class.

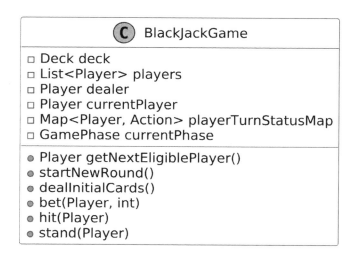

Now that we've detailed our key classes, let's put them together in a complete class diagram to see the full picture.

Complete Class Diagram

Below is the complete class diagram of the Blackjack game:

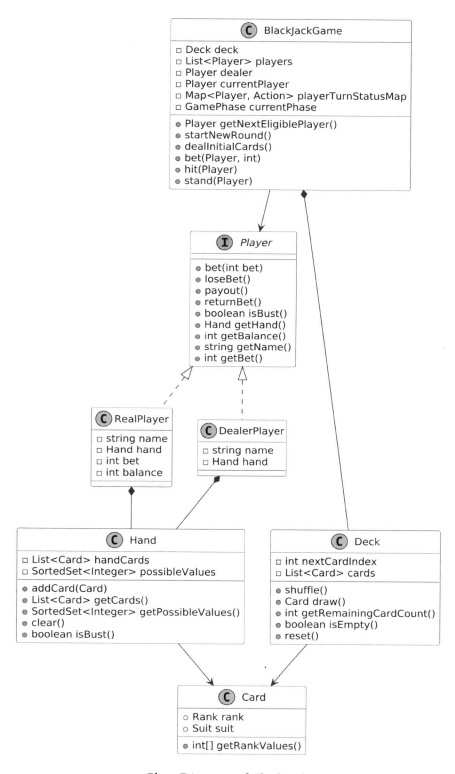

Class Diagram of Blackjack

Let's turn this design into working code.

Code - Blackjack

In this section, we will implement the core functionality of the Blackjack game, emphasizing critical components such as deck management for card distribution, turn coordination for players and the dealer, bet resolution, and winner determination through hand value comparison.

Card

The Card class is a straightforward representation of a playing card, combining a Rank and a Suit. It's designed to be immutable. Its attributes stay fixed once created. The getRankValues() method retrieves the card's possible values from Rank (e.g., 1 or 11 for an Ace).

Below is the code implementation of this class:

```
public class Card {
  public final Rank rank;
  public final Suit suit;

  public Card(Rank rank, Suit suit) {
    this.rank = rank;
    this.suit = suit;
  }

  public int[] getRankValues() {
    return rank.getRankValues();
  }
}
```

Rank is an enum that defines card values: Aces can be 1 or 11, numbered cards retain their face value, and face cards (Jack, Queen, King) are all worth 10. It stores these values in an array and provides them through getRankValues().

```
public enum Rank {
  ACE(new int[]{1, 11}),
  TWO(new int[]{2}),
  THREE(new int[]{3}),
  FOUR(new int[]{4}),
  FIVE(new int[]{5}),
  SIX(new int[]{6}),
  SEVEN(new int[]{7}),
  EIGHT(new int[]{8}),
  NINE(new int[]{9}),
  TEN(new int[]{10}),
  JACK(new int[]{10}),
  QUEEN(new int[]{10}),
```

```
  KING(new int[]{10});

  private final int[] rankValues;

  Rank(int[] rankValues) {
    this.rankValues = rankValues;
  }

  // Returns the possible values for the rank
  public int[] getRankValues() {
    return this.rankValues;
  }
}
```

For Rank, we define Ace with [1, 11] from the start, rather than defaulting to 11 and adjusting later if the hand busts. This allows the Hand class to calculate all possible totals upfront, which is useful for handling multiple Aces.

Suit is a simple enum representing the four standard suits, Hearts, Spades, Clubs, and Diamonds. It acts purely as a label, giving each card its suit without additional logic.

```
public enum Suit {
  HEARTS,
  SPADES,
  CLUBS,
  DIAMONDS
}
```

With cards ready, let's bundle them into a Deck for gameplay.

Deck

The Deck class represents a full deck of playing cards and provides essential operations such as shuffling, drawing, and resetting. It maintains a structured collection of Card objects and ensures that cards are drawn in the correct sequence.

Here is the implementation of this class:

```
public class Deck {
  int nextCardIndex = 0;
  List<Card> cards;

  // Constructor initializes the deck
  public Deck() {
    initializeDeck();
  }

  // Initializes the deck with all cards
  private void initializeDeck() {
```

```java
    cards = new ArrayList<>();
    for (Suit suit : Suit.values()) {
      for (Rank rank : Rank.values()) {
        cards.add(new Card(rank, suit));
      }
    }
    nextCardIndex = 0; // Reset to start drawing from the first card
  }

  // Shuffles the deck using current time as seed
  public void shuffle() {
    Collections.shuffle(cards, new Random(System.currentTimeMillis()));
  }

  // Draws the next card from the deck
  public Card draw() {
    if (isEmpty() || nextCardIndex >= cards.size()) {
      throw new IllegalStateException("No more cards in deck");
    }
    Card drawCard = cards.get(nextCardIndex);
    nextCardIndex++;
    return drawCard;
  }

  // Returns the number of remaining cards in the deck
  public int getRemainingCardCount() {
    return cards.size() - nextCardIndex;
  }

  // Checks if the deck is empty
  public boolean isEmpty() {
    return getRemainingCardCount() == 0;
  }

  // Resets the deck to start drawing from the beginning
  public void reset() {
    nextCardIndex = 0;
  }

  // getter methods are omitted for brevity
}
```

The deck is initialized by pairing each Suit with every Rank, creating a complete set of 52 cards. These cards are stored in a List<Card>, which provides an efficient way to manage them.

Implementation choice: Instead of removing cards when drawn, the deck tracks the next available card using nextCardIndex. This avoids the costly list operation of removing elements from an ArrayList, which requires shifting all remaining elements ($O(n)$ complexity).

By simply incrementing an index, drawing a card becomes an $O(1)$ operation, improving performance.

Now that we've got cards flowing from the deck, let's see how they land in a player's Hand.

Hand

The Hand class is responsible for managing a player's cards and computing possible hand totals, particularly when dealing with Aces, which can be worth 1 or 11. To achieve this, it maintains a List<Card> for tracking the cards in the hand and a SortedSet<Integer> to store all possible hand values dynamically.

When a new card is added via addCard(), it updates both the list of cards and the possible hand values. Handling Aces correctly is crucial:

- If the card is an Ace, both 1 and 11 are introduced as potential hand values.
- If it's a non-Ace, its value is added to every existing total, generating all possible hand values.

This approach precomputes all valid hand scores upfront, avoiding unnecessary recalculations during gameplay and ensuring that multiple Aces are handled efficiently.

```
public class Hand {
  final List<Card> handCards = new ArrayList<>();

  // Sorted set of all possible hand values, accounting for Ace
    flexibility (1 or 11).
  final SortedSet<Integer> possibleValues = new TreeSet<>();

  public Hand() {
  }

  // Adds a card to the hand and updates the set of possible total values
    .
  // For Aces (1 or 11), computes all combinations with existing totals;
    for other cards, adds their value to each total.
  public void addCard(Card card) {
    if (card == null) {
      throw new IllegalArgumentException("Cannot add null card to hand");
    }
    handCards.add(card);

    // card.getRankValues() returns [1, 11] for Aces or a single value (e
    .g., [10]) for others.
    if (possibleValues.isEmpty()) {
      // Initialize with the card's values
      for (int value : card.getRankValues()) {
        possibleValues.add(value);
      }
```

```java
    } else {
      // Add all possible card values to each existing total
      SortedSet<Integer> newPossibleValue = new TreeSet<>();
      for (int value : possibleValues) {
        for (int cardValue : card.getRankValues()) {
          newPossibleValue.add(value + cardValue);
        }
      }
      possibleValues.clear();
      possibleValues.addAll(newPossibleValue);
    }
  }

  // Returns an unmodifiable list of cards in the hand
  public List<Card> getCards() {
    return Collections.unmodifiableList(handCards);
  }

  // Returns an unmodifiable sorted set of possible hand values
  public SortedSet<Integer> getPossibleValues() {
    return Collections.unmodifiableSortedSet(possibleValues);
  }

  // Clears the hand and possible values
  public void clear() {
    handCards.clear();
    possibleValues.clear();
  }

  // Checks if the hand is bust (all possible values > 21)
  public boolean isBust() {
    // check if all possible value of the player's hand is busted
    if (possibleValues.isEmpty()) {
      return false;
    }
    else {
      return possibleValues.first() > 21;
    }
  }
}
```

The isBust() method determines whether a player has exceeded 21. It evaluates the lowest value in possibleValue, and if all options are above 21, the hand is considered bust. This is a critical check that immediately signals when a player is out of the game.

Implementation strategy: Handling Aces efficiently is the biggest challenge in Blackjack hand management. Instead of recalculating Ace values dynamically each time a hand is evaluated, the Hand class precomputes all possible totals upfront. This allows for faster, more efficient scoring and ensures that Blackjack's unique Ace logic is handled seamlessly without requiring mid-game adjustments.

Data structure choice: A `SortedSet` (implemented as `TreeSet`) is used for `possibleValues` to maintain sorted hand values, enabling $O(\log n)$ insertion and $O(1)$ access to the lowest value for `isBust()`. Alternatively, a `HashSet` offers $O(1)$ insertion but lacks sorting, requiring $O(n)$ to find the minimum. Similarly, a `List` could store values but would need $O(n)$ for sorting or searching, which is less efficient for frequent checks in Blackjack's fast-paced gameplay.

With hands tracking cards and totals, let's define the `Players` who'll hold them.

Player

In Blackjack, players fall into two distinct categories: human players, who place bets and manage their funds, and the dealer, who follows fixed rules and does not participate in betting. The Player interface and its concrete implementations, `RealPlayer` and `DealerPlayer`, provide a structured way to model these roles.

Below is the implementation of this interface.

```java
public interface Player {
  void bet(int bet);

  void loseBet();

  void returnBet();

  void payout();

  boolean isBust();

  Hand getHand();

  int getBalance();

  String getName();

  int getBet();
}
```

The `RealPlayer` class models a human player who engages in betting and managing their funds. It implements the `Player` interface, ensuring that bet handling is managed separately from the core game logic. When placing a bet, the `bet()` method ensures that the bet does not exceed the player's available balance before deducting the amount.

To maintain a clear separation of concerns, `RealPlayer` does not handle card evaluation directly. Instead, it delegates all card-related operations to the `Hand` class. This ensures that the player's bet handling and card logic remain separate, making the class more modular and maintainable.

```java
public RealPlayer(String name, int startBalance) {
  this.name = name;
  this.hand = new Hand();
  this.bet = 0;
  this.balance = startBalance;
}

// Places a bet for the player
@Override
public void bet(int bet) {
  if(bet > balance) {
    throw new IllegalArgumentException("Bet is greater than balance");
  }
  this.bet = bet;
  this.balance -= bet;
}

// Handles the player losing a bet
@Override
public void loseBet() {
  System.out.println("Player " + name + " lost " + bet + " with card
    value " + hand.getPossibleValues().last());
  this.bet = 0;
}

// Handles returning the player's bet
@Override
public void returnBet() {
  System.out.println("Player " + name + " return " + bet + " with card
    value " + hand.getPossibleValues().last());
  this.balance += bet;
  this.bet = 0;
}

// Handles the player winning a payout
@Override
public void payout() {
  System.out.println("Player " + name + " won " + bet * 2 + " with card
    value " + hand.getPossibleValues().last());
  this.balance += bet * 2;  // Return bet plus equal amount
  this.bet = 0;
}

// getter methods are omitted for brevity
}
```

The DealerPlayer class represents the house and follows predefined rules that differ from those of human players. Since the dealer does not participate in betting, the bet-handling methods, `bet()`, and `loseBet()` are implemented as empty functions, as they are never invoked in gameplay. Similarly, `getBalance()` and `getBet()` always return 0, reflecting the fact that the dealer does not manage a balance or place bets.

```java
public class DealerPlayer implements Player {
  private final String name = "Dealer";
  private final Hand hand;

  public DealerPlayer() {
    this.hand = new Hand();
  }

  // Bet-handling methods for Dealer (bet, loseBet, returnBet) are
    implemented as empty functions.

  @Override
  public void payout() {
    // Dealer does not get a payout, so this method only prints the
    winning hand
    System.out.println("Player " + name + " won with card value " + hand.
    getPossibleValues().last());
  }

  // getter methods are omitted for brevity
}
```

With players and their hands set, let's orchestrate the whole game in `BlackJackGame`.

BlackjackGame

The `BlackJackGame` class serves as the central orchestrator of the game, handling players, the dealer, the deck, turn management, and enforcing the game rules. It ensures that the game follows a structured flow, with each player's actions and the final outcome being resolved according to the rules of Blackjack.

Below is the implementation of this class.

```java
public class BlackJackGame {
  private final Deck deck = new Deck();
  private final List<Player> players = new ArrayList<>();
  protected final Player dealer = new DealerPlayer();
  private Player currentPlayer = null;

  // Tracks the current status of each player's turn (e.g., HIT or STAND)
  Map<Player, Action> playerTurnStatusMap = new HashMap<>();
  GamePhase currentPhase = GamePhase.STARTED;

  public BlackJackGame(List<Player> players){
    for (Player player : players) {
```

```java
    if (player == null) throw new IllegalArgumentException();
    this.players.add(player);
    this.playerTurnStatusMap.put(player, null);
  }
  this.playerTurnStatusMap.put(dealer, null);
  deck.shuffle();  // Shuffle the deck when game starts
}

// Determines the next player who can take an action (i.e., has not
// stood or bust). If the current player is the dealer, it triggers the
// dealer's turn.
public Player getNextEligiblePlayer() {
  // If current player hasn't stood or bust, they can continue their
  // turn
  if (currentPlayer != null &&
  !Action.STAND.equals(playerTurnStatusMap.get(currentPlayer)) &&
  !currentPlayer.isBust()) {
    return currentPlayer;
  }

  // Find the first player who hasn't stood or bust
  if (currentPlayer == null) {
    for (Player player : players) {
      if (!Action.STAND.equals(playerTurnStatusMap.get(player)) && !
  player.isBust()) {
        currentPlayer = player;
        return currentPlayer;
      }
    }
  }

  // else, find the next player after the current one who hasn't stood
  // or bust
  int currentPlayerIndex = players.indexOf(currentPlayer);
  for (int i = currentPlayerIndex + 1; i < players.size(); i++) {
    Player player = players.get(i) ;
    if (!Action.STAND.equals(playerTurnStatusMap.get(player)) && !
  player.isBust()) {
      if (currentPlayer == dealer) {
        if (!Action.STAND.equals(playerTurnStatusMap.get(dealer)))
        dealerTurn();
        return currentPlayer;
      }
      currentPlayer = player;
      return currentPlayer;
    }
  }

  // If no players are left to act, return null
  return null;
```

```
}

protected void dealerTurn() {
  // Dealer hits if below 17
  while (dealer.getHand().getPossibleValues().last() < 17) {
    Card newDraw = deck.draw();
    dealer.getHand().addCard(newDraw);
  }
  playerTurnStatusMap.put(dealer, Action.STAND);
  checkGameEndCondition();
}

public void startNewRound() {
  deck.reset();
  for (Player player : playerTurnStatusMap.keySet()) {
    player.getHand().clear(); // Clear player's hand
  }
  dealer.getHand().clear(); // Clear dealer's hand
  // Reset all turn statuses to null
  playerTurnStatusMap.replaceAll((p, v) -> null);
  currentPlayer = null; // Reset current player
  currentPhase = GamePhase.STARTED;
}

public void dealInitialCards() {
  if (!GamePhase.BET_PLACED.equals(currentPhase)) {
    throw new IllegalStateException("All players must bet before
  dealing");
  }
  // Deal first card to each real player in order
  for (Player player : players) {
    player.getHand().addCard(deck.draw());
  }
  // Deal first card to dealer
  dealer.getHand().addCard(deck.draw());
  // Deal second card to each real player in order
  for (Player player : players) {
    player.getHand().addCard(deck.draw());
  }
  // Deal second card to dealer
  dealer.getHand().addCard(deck.draw());
  currentPhase = GamePhase.INITIAL_CARD_DRAWN;
}

public void bet(Player player, int bet) {
  if (!GamePhase.STARTED.equals(currentPhase)) {
    throw new IllegalStateException("Bets must be placed at the start
  of the round");
  }
  player.bet(bet);
```

```java
    // Transition to BET_PLACED once all players have bet
    if (players.stream().filter(
    p -> !(p instanceof DealerPlayer)
    ).allMatch(p -> p.getBet() > 0)) {
      currentPhase = GamePhase.BET_PLACED;
    }
  }

  public void hit(Player player) {
    if (Action.STAND.equals(playerTurnStatusMap.get(player))) {
      throw new IllegalStateException("Player has already stood");
    }
    if (player.isBust()) {
      throw new IllegalStateException("Player is already bust");
    }

    Card drawnCard = deck.draw();
    player.getHand().addCard(drawnCard);
    playerTurnStatusMap.put(player, Action.HIT);
  }

  public void stand(Player player) {
    if (Action.STAND.equals(playerTurnStatusMap.get(player))) {
      throw new IllegalStateException("Player has already stood");
    }
    if (player.isBust()) {
      throw new IllegalStateException("Player is already bust");
    }
    playerTurnStatusMap.put(player, Action.STAND);
  }

  // Checks if the game has ended (all players done), then resolves bets
  // by comparing each player's hand to the dealer's.
  private void checkGameEndCondition() {
    boolean allPlayersDone = players.stream()
    .allMatch(p -> Action.STAND.equals(playerTurnStatusMap.get(p)) || p.
    isBust());
    if (!allPlayersDone) {
      return;
    }

    int dealerValue = dealer.getHand().getPossibleValues().last();
    boolean dealerBusts = dealer.isBust();

    for (Player player : players) {
      if (player.isBust()) {
        player.loseBet();
      } else {
        int playerValue = player.getHand().getPossibleValues().last();
        if (dealerBusts || playerValue > dealerValue) {
```

```
                player.payout();
            } else if (playerValue == dealerValue) {
                player.returnBet();
            } else {
                player.loseBet();
            }
        }
    }
    }
    currentPhase = GamePhase.END;
    }

    // getter methods are omitted for brevity
}
```

- Each round begins with `startNewRound()`, which resets the deck, ensuring that players start with a clean slate.
- Once the round starts, players place their bets using the `bet()` method, then `dealInitialCards()` distributes two cards per player, including the dealer. This guarantees a fair and structured start before betting and player actions begin.
- The game progresses through player turns using `getNextEligiblePlayer()`, which selects the next active player who has not yet stood or busted. Once all players have finished their turns, control shifts to the dealer via `dealerTurn()`.

The dealer follows strict, predefined rules:

- The dealer must hit until their total reaches at least 17.
- Once at 17 or higher, the dealer must stand.

Players can take two primary actions during their turn:

- `hit()`: Draws a card and updates the player's hand. If the player exceeds 21, they are marked as bust, eliminating them from further action.
- `stand()`: Locks in the player's hand, preventing further draws.

The `checkGameEndCondition()` method finalizes the round once all players have stood or busted. It compares each player's hand individually against the dealer's:

- If the dealer busts (hand exceeds 21), non-bust players win and receive a payout.
- For non-bust players, if their hand value exceeds the dealer's (but is ≤ 21), they win and are paid out. If it's lower, they lose their bet. In the case of a tie, return the bet to the player.

Now that we've built a working game, let's explore how we can make it more flexible for future changes.

Deep Dive Topic

At this point, you've nailed the core requirements of the Blackjack game. This section will dive deeper into a potential extension to make the design more adaptable.

Decoupling player and dealer decision logic

In the current design, `BlackJackGame` directly controls player actions, calling `hit()` or `stand()` based on predefined conditions in the game logic. Similarly, the dealer's "hit until 17" rule is hardcoded into `dealerTurn()`. This approach tightly couples decision-making with the game class, leaving little room for custom moves. Any rule modification, such as allowing a cautious player to stand at 12 or adjusting the dealer's hit threshold, requires modifying `BlackJackGame`, leading to complex maintenance and potential bugs.

To resolve this, we introduce a decision-making abstraction that shifts control to individual players. This keeps `BlackJackGame` focused on coordinating turns, while each player determines their moves independently.

Step 1: Define a decision-making interface

To give each player control over their moves, we create a `PlayerDecisionLogic` interface with one method, `decideAction(Hand)`, that picks 'Hit' or 'Stand' based on the hand.

```
public interface PlayerDecisionLogic {

  // Decides the next action for a player based on their hand
  Action decideAction(Hand hand);
}
```

Step 2: Tailor decisions for humans and dealers

With the interface in place, we implement two concrete decision classes:

- `RealPlayerDecisionLogic`: This captures a human player's approach, say, hitting if the hand's below 16.
- `DealerDecisionLogic`: This locks in the dealer's rule, hit if under 17.

Here's the code:

```
public class RealPlayerDecisionLogic implements PlayerDecisionLogic {

  @Override
  public Action decideAction(Hand hand) {
    System.out.println("Hand: " + hand.getPossibleValues().last() + ".
    Hit or Stand?");
    return hand.getPossibleValues().last() < 16 ? Action.HIT : Action.
    STAND;
  }
```

```
  }

public class DealerDecisionLogic implements PlayerDecisionLogic {

  @Override
  public Action decideAction(Hand hand) {
    return hand.getPossibleValues().last() < 17 ? Action.HIT : Action.
    STAND;
  }
}
```

Step 3: Integrate decisions into players

We update the Player interface with a `getDecisionLogic()` method, letting each player define its decision style. `RealPlayer` defaults to `RealPlayerDecisionLogic`, while `DealerPlayer` uses `DealerDecisionLogic`:

```
public interface Player {
  // Returns the decision logic for the player
  PlayerDecisionLogic getDecisionLogic();

  // ... other methods …
}

public class RealPlayer implements Player {
  private final PlayerDecisionLogic decisionLogic;

  public RealPlayer(String name, int startBalance) {
    this.name = name;
    this.hand = new Hand();
    this.bet = 0;
    this.balance = startBalance;
    this.decisionLogic = new RealPlayerDecisionLogic();
  }

  // Returns the decision logic for the player
  @Override
  public PlayerDecisionLogic getDecisionLogic() {
    return decisionLogic;
  }
  // ... other methods ...
}

public class DealerPlayer implements Player {
  private final PlayerDecisionLogic decisionLogic;

  public DealerPlayer() {
    this.hand = new Hand();
    this.decisionLogic = new DealerDecisionLogic();
```

```
  }

  // Returns the decision logic for the dealer
  @Override
  public PlayerDecisionLogic getDecisionLogic() {
    return decisionLogic;
  }
  // ... other methods ...
}
```

Step 4: Adjust the game flow

In this step, we refactor the BlackJackGame code to use decision logic for both players and the dealer, streamlining the turn sequence. We introduce the performPlayerAction() method, which queries each player's decision logic (RealPlayerDecisionLogic or Dealer-DecisionLogic) to decide whether to hit or stand. This replaces the hardcoded dealerTurn() method, integrating the dealer into the same flow as the players.

We also add the playNextTurn() method to coordinate turns, relying on getNextEligbilePlayer() to determine who acts next.

Here's the updated code:

```
public class BlackJackGame {

  // ... fields unchanged ...

  // Find the next player who can take an action
  public Player getNextEligiblePlayer() {
    // No current player: find first eligible player from the start
    if (currentPlayer == null) {
      for (Player player : players) {
        if (!Action.STAND.equals(playerTurnStatusMap.get(player)) && !
  player.isBust()) {
          currentPlayer = player;
          return currentPlayer;
        }
      }
      // Instead of calling dealerTurn(), check if the dealer can act
      if (!Action.STAND.equals(playerTurnStatusMap.get(dealer))) {
        currentPlayer = dealer;
        return dealer;
      }
    } else {
      int currentIndex = players.indexOf(currentPlayer);
      for (int i = currentIndex + 1; i < players.size(); i++) {
        Player player = players.get(i);
        if (!Action.STAND.equals(playerTurnStatusMap.get(player)) && !
  player.isBust()) {
```

```
        currentPlayer = player;
        return currentPlayer;
      }
    }
    // If all players are done, check if the dealer can act
    if (currentPlayer != dealer && !Action.STAND.equals(
  playerTurnStatusMap.get(dealer))) {
      currentPlayer = dealer;
      return dealer;
    }
  }
  return null;  // All turns are complete, including the dealer's
}

// Executes the next turn by acting for the next player or dealer.
public void playNextTurn() {
  Player nextPlayer = getNextEligiblePlayer();
  if (nextPlayer != null) {
    performPlayerAction(nextPlayer);
  }
}

// Performs the action decided by the player's decision logic (hit or
  stand).
public void performPlayerAction(Player player) {
  Action action = player.getDecisionLogic().decideAction(player.getHand
  ());
  if (action == Action.HIT) {
    hit(player);
  } else if (action == Action.STAND) {
    stand(player);
  }
}

// ... other methods unchanged, dealerTurn() removed ...
}
```

The getNextEligiblePlayer() method now handles the full turn sequence: it returns the next player who hasn't stood or busted, then the dealer once all players are done, and finally null when the dealer has stood, ending the turns. While dealerTurn() is removed, its logic lives on in DealerDecisionLogic, ensuring the dealer hits until 17 or higher.

This design shifts decision-making to the players, letting BlackJackGame coordinate turns while each player's logic lives separately. If you've heard of the Strategy Pattern, you might notice this follows it, defining a set of decision rules that can swap in and out. Here:

- PlayerDecisionLogic sets the decision contract.
- RealPlayerDecisionLogic and DealerDecisionLogic are the specific behaviors.

- `BlackJackGame` uses them without needing to handle decisions internally.

Note: To learn more about the Strategy Pattern and its common use cases, refer to the **Elevator System** chapter.

Wrap Up

In this chapter, we have built a solid Blackjack game from the ground up, with the key takeaway being how we structured responsibilities across `Card`, `Deck`, `Hand`, `Player`, and `BlackJackGame` into a clear, well-organized design. Each piece does its job, for instance, Card holds the essentials, Deck shuffles and deals, Hand tracks totals, and `BlackJackGame` runs the show. This approach keeps the game logical, easy to follow, and scalable.

We also took things further by decoupling decision-making with `PlayerDecisionLogic`, making it easy to swap strategies for players and the dealer. If you're familiar with the Strategy pattern, you'll recognize how it is applied here, giving the game flexibility without rewrites.

Congratulations on getting this far! Now give yourself a pat on the back. Good job!

12

Shipping Locker System

In this chapter, we will design a Shipping Locker system similar to UPS, FedEx, or Amazon Locker. It offers customers a convenient and secure way to pick up their online orders. The system manages locker availability, assigns incoming packages to appropriate lockers, and ensures a smooth package retrieval process for customers.

To realize this vision of a convenient and secure locker system, let's explore what it needs to do.

Shipping Locker System

Requirements Gathering

The first step in designing a shipping locker system is to clarify the requirements and narrow down the scope. Here is an example of a typical prompt an interviewer might give:

"Imagine you've just received a notification that your online order has been delivered to a shipping locker near you. You head to the locker, enter a secure access code, and instantly, the door pops open, revealing your package. Behind the scenes, the system has already managed locker availability, assigned an appropriately sized compartment, and ensured a seamless pickup experience. Now, let's design a shipping locker system that can do all of this."

Requirements clarification

Here is an example of how a conversation between a candidate and an interviewer might unfold:

Candidate: Does the system support multiple locker sizes?
Interviewer: Yes, the system has lockers of different sizes. The design should ensure packages are assigned to the smallest available locker that fits, optimizing space use.

Candidate: So, what happens when a package gets to the locker, and how does the customer end up picking it up?
Interviewer: When a package arrives, the system finds an open locker that's the right size and assigns it there. Once the package is tucked inside, the customer gets a notification with the locker's location and a unique access code. They just punch in the code to pop the locker open, grab their package, and that frees up the locker for the next delivery.

Candidate: Is there a time limit or any fees for using the locker?
Interviewer: Good question. That's actually a big part of how the system works. We've got a locker policy that gives customers a 'Free Period', a set number of days during which they can use the locker for free. Once that's up, we start charging a daily fee based on the locker's size. And if the package sits there past a 'Maximum Period,' which is also predefined, one of our staff members steps in, pulls it out, and clears the locker for someone else.

Candidate: Since the system tracks locker usage costs through the locker policy, does it handle payments too?
Interviewer: For simplicity's sake, we let an external service take care of the actual payment processing. That's not something the system itself has to worry about.

Requirements

Here are the key functional requirements we've identified.

- The system should keep track of all lockers and support different locker sizes.
- The system should smartly assign lockers by matching package size to the smallest available option that fits, keeping things efficient.

- Customers should be able to pop open their assigned locker with a unique access code.
- The system should monitor storage costs based on the customer's locker policy, factoring in the daily rate tied to that specific locker size.

Below are the non-functional requirements:

- The system should handle a high volume of locker operations per site without performance degradation, accommodating busy locations.
- The system must maintain high availability, ensuring lockers are accessible to customers and staff at all times.

Now that we've outlined the system's needs, let's pinpoint the building blocks to fulfill them.

Identify Core Objects

Before diving into the design, it's important to identify the core objects.

- **Locker:** This class represents an individual locker.
- **Site:** This class represents a locker facility that consists of multiple lockers of various sizes. It is responsible for managing the collection of lockers and organizing them by size.
- **ShippingPackage:** An interface defining the standard for packages, with `BasicShippingPackage` as its concrete implementation, tracking details like order ID, dimensions, and status.
- **Account:** This class represents customers and their associated accounts. Customers own packages stored in lockers, and their accounts store policy information for free and maximum storage periods, along with their current balance.

Design Class Diagram

Now that we know the core objects and their roles, the next step is to create classes and methods that turn the requirements into an easy-to-maintain system. Let's take a closer look.

Locker

The `Locker` class represents a physical storage unit for holding packages. It includes the following attributes:

- **`LockerSize size:`** Represents the size of the locker.
- **`ShippingPackage currentPackage:`** Stores the package currently assigned to the locker.
- **`Date assignmentDate:`** Tracks the date when the package was placed in the locker.

- **String accessCode:** A unique security code required for package retrieval.

Below is the representation of this class.

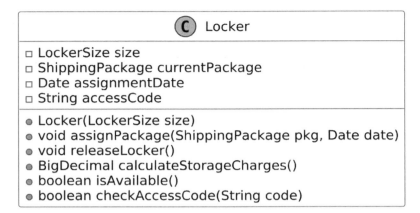

It provides functionalities such as assigning a package to the locker, releasing the locker upon package retrieval, calculating storage charges based on usage duration, determining locker availability, and ensuring secure access through code verification.

> ✂ **Design choice:** The Locker class is designed as a standalone entity to encapsulate the state and behavior of an individual locker, ensuring modularity and ease of maintenance.

LockerSize

The LockerSize enum represents the predefined sizes of lockers available in the system. Each size is associated with specific attributes that define its dimensions and daily usage charge.

- **String sizeName:** A label identifying the locker size (e.g., 'Small,' 'Medium,' 'Large').
- **BigDecimal dailyCharge:** The cost per day for using a locker of a specific size ("Small," "Medium," or "Large").
- **BigDecimal width, height, depth:** The physical dimensions of the locker, determining its capacity to accommodate different package sizes.

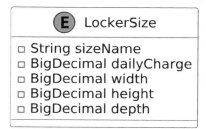

LockerSize

- ☐ String sizeName
- ☐ BigDecimal dailyCharge
- ☐ BigDecimal width
- ☐ BigDecimal height
- ☐ BigDecimal depth

> ⚒ **Design choice:** We use an enum here because locker sizes, such as Small, Medium, and Large, are a fixed set of options that don't change during runtime, ensuring type safety and simplicity.

Site

The `Site` class models a physical location containing a collection of lockers, organized by their size. Key functionalities include:

- **Locker findAvailableLocker(LockerSize size):** This method searches for an empty locker that matches the exact size you need, like "small," "medium," or "large."
- **Locker placePackage(ShippingPackage pkg, Date date):** This method takes a package, finds it a locker that fits, and locks it inside. It also keeps track of when the package was placed there and updates the package's status.

Site

- ☐ Map<LockerSize, Set<Locker>> lockers
- ● Locker findAvailableLocker(LockerSize size)
- ● Locker placePackage(ShippingPackage pkg, Date date)

The lockers at each site are managed using a map-based structure, where the key is a `LockerSize` and the value is a set of lockers for that size. This structure allows quick access to available lockers based on their size.

ShippingPackage

We have modeled `ShippingPackage` as an interface to establish a standard for all package types within the locker system. It defines key methods that any package type must implement to ensure compatibility with locker storage and retrieval processes. The `BasicShippingPackage` class is a concrete implementation of the `ShippingPackage` interface. It represents a standard package intended for storage in a locker.

The `ShippingStatus` enum defines a fixed set of valid states for a package's lifecycle in the locker system, such as PENDING, STORED, and RETRIEVED. This enum ensures that package status updates are consistent and restricted to predefined values, enhancing type safety.

The UML diagram below illustrates this structure.

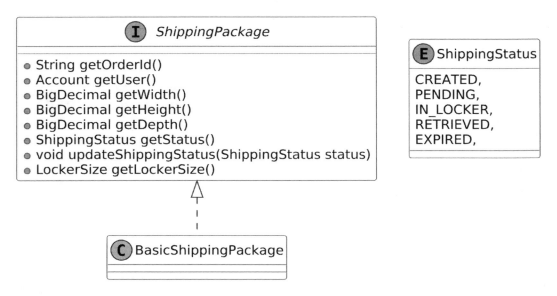

ShippingPackage interface and ShippingStatus enum

> ✂ **Design choice:** Modeling `ShippingPackage` as an interface allows for extensibility, enabling the system to support diverse package types (e.g., fragile or perishable) without modifying core logic.

Account

The `Account` class represents a customer using the locker system. It maintains the customer's balance for locker-related charges and is associated with an `AccountLockerPolicy`, which defines terms for free usage limits and maximum storage duration. This ensures that charges are applied in accordance with the policy.

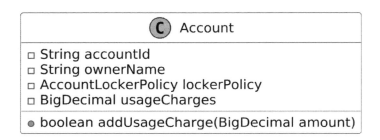

The class provides functionality to add funds to the account.

> ✂ **Design choice:** By associating an `AccountLockerPolicy`, it supports flexible billing rules based on customer policies. This separation of customer and policy data enhances maintainability and allows for personalized locker usage terms.

AccountLockerPolicy

This class defines the rules and policies for locker usage associated with an account. It includes the number of days during which locker usage is free (`freePeriodDays`) and the maximum number of days a package can remain in the locker before it must be cleared (`maximumPeriodDays`). Here is the representation of this class.

NotificationInterface

Defines the contract for sending notifications. It includes a single method, `sendNotification`, which takes a message and an account as parameters.

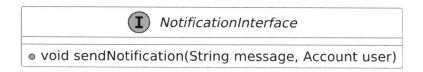

Implementations of this interface manage user notifications, such as alerts for package pickup availability and locker usage fees.

> ♛ **Best practices:** In OOD interviews, external systems like notifications are often represented as interfaces to keep the design flexible and scalable while avoiding unnecessary complexity.

LockerManager

The `LockerManager` class is responsible for managing package storage and retrieval at a specific site, ensuring that packages are assigned to suitable lockers based on size availability. It works with the following components:

- **Site site:** Represents the physical location of the lockers.
- **NotificationInterface notificationService:** Sends notifications to customers when their packages are assigned to a locker or ready for pick-up.
- **Map<String, Account> accounts:** Maintains a mapping of account IDs to user accounts for managing locker usage and charges.
- **Map<String, Locker> accessCodeMap:** Maintains a mapping of access codes to lockers, allowing for quick retrieval during package pick-up.

© LockerManager
□ Site site □ NotificationInterface notificationService □ Map<String, Account> accounts □ Map<String, Locker> accessCodeMap
● Locker assignPackage(ShippingPackage pkg, Date date) ● Locker pickUpPackage(String accessCode)

> ✂ **Design choice:** The LockerManager class is designed as a facade to simplify interactions between core objects, providing a single point of control for package assignment and retrieval.

Complete Class Diagram

Below is the complete class diagram of the shipping locker service:

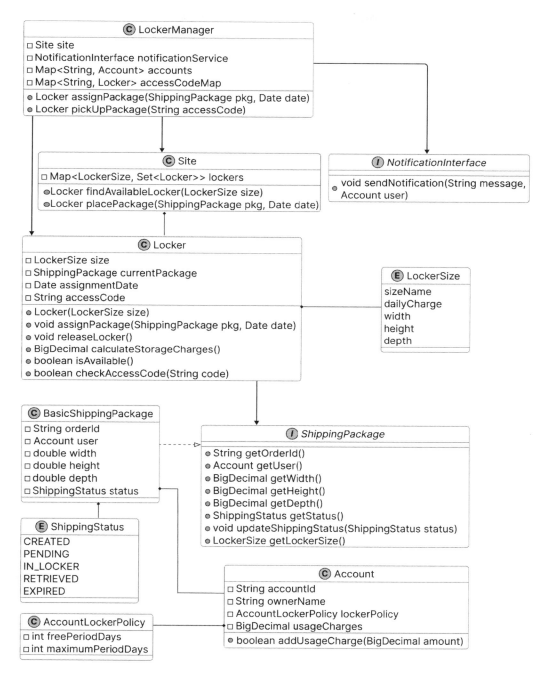

Class Diagram of Locker Service

With the class diagram as our guide, let's bring the system to life through code.

Code - Shipping Locker Service

After completing the class diagram, the interviewer might ask you to implement key components of the shipping locker system. In this section, we'll implement essential classes that handle locker operations, package assignments, and notifications.

Locker and LockerSize

The `Locker` class represents an individual locker unit. Each locker has a fixed size (an instance of `LockerSize`) and maintains details about the currently stored package, including the assignment date and a randomly generated access code for secure retrieval.

This class provides functionalities for:

- Assigning a package to a locker, recording the assignment date, and generating a secure access code.
- Calculating storage charges based on the number of days the package has been stored and the locker's daily rate, according to its size.
- Once the package is picked up, make the locker available for future use.

Below is the implementation of this class.

```java
public class Locker {
  // Size of the locker
  private final LockerSize size;
  // Currently stored package
  private ShippingPackage currentPackage;
  // Date when the current package was assigned
  private Date assignmentDate;
  // Access code for retrieving the package
  private String accessCode;

  public Locker(LockerSize size) {
    this.size = size;
  }

  // Assigns a package to this locker and generates an access code
  public void assignPackage(ShippingPackage pkg, Date date) {
    this.currentPackage = pkg;
    this.assignmentDate = date;
    this.accessCode = generateAccessCode();
  }

  // Releases the locker by removing the current package and its details
  public void releaseLocker() {
    this.currentPackage = null;
    this.assignmentDate = null;
    this.accessCode = null;
```

```java
    }

    // Calculates storage charges based on usage duration and policy
    public BigDecimal calculateStorageCharges() {
        if (currentPackage == null || assignmentDate == null) {
            return BigDecimal.ZERO;
        }

        AccountLockerPolicy policy = currentPackage.getUser().getLockerPolicy
        ();
        long totalDaysUsed = (new Date().getTime() - assignmentDate.getTime()
        ) / (1000 * 60 * 60 * 24);

        // Check if exceeds maximum period
        if (totalDaysUsed > policy.getMaximumPeriodDays()) {
            currentPackage.updateShippingStatus(ShippingStatus.EXPIRED);
            throw new MaximumStoragePeriodExceededException(
            "Package has exceeded maximum allowed storage period of " + policy.
        getMaximumPeriodDays() + " days");
        }

        // Calculate chargeable days (excluding free period)
        long chargeableDays = Math.max(0, totalDaysUsed - policy.
        getFreePeriodDays());
        return size.dailyCharge.multiply(new BigDecimal(chargeableDays));
    }

    // Checks if the locker is available for new packages
    public boolean isAvailable() {
        return currentPackage == null;
    }

    // Verifies if the provided access code matches the locker's code
    public boolean checkAccessCode(String code) {
        return this.accessCode != null && accessCode.equals(code);
    }

    // getter and setter methods are omitted for brevity
}
```

The LockerSize enum defines different locker sizes, each with an associated daily charge rate and physical dimensions (width, height, and depth). These predefined sizes allow the system to categorize lockers and ensure packages are placed in appropriately sized compartments.

```java
public enum LockerSize {
    // Small locker with 10x10x10 dimensions and $5 daily charge
    SMALL("Small", new BigDecimal("5.00"), new BigDecimal("10.00"), new
        BigDecimal("10.00"), new BigDecimal("10.00")),
```

```
    // Medium locker with 20x20x20 dimensions and $10 daily charge
    MEDIUM("Medium", new BigDecimal("10.00"), new BigDecimal("20.00"), new
      BigDecimal("20.00"), new BigDecimal("20.00")),
    // Large locker with 30x30x30 dimensions and $15 daily charge
    LARGE("Large", new BigDecimal("15.00"), new BigDecimal("30.00"), new
      BigDecimal("30.00"), new BigDecimal("30.00"));

    // Name of the locker size
    final String sizeName;
    // Daily charge for using this size locker
    final BigDecimal dailyCharge;
    // Width of the locker in inches
    final BigDecimal width;
    // Height of the locker in inches
    final BigDecimal height;
    // Depth of the locker in inches
    final BigDecimal depth;

    // Creates a new locker size with specified dimensions and charges
    LockerSize(String sizeName, BigDecimal dailyCharge, BigDecimal width,
      BigDecimal height, BigDecimal depth) {
      this.sizeName = sizeName;
      this.dailyCharge = dailyCharge;
      this.width = width;
      this.height = height;
      this.depth = depth;
    }

    // getter methods are omitted for brevity
}
```

Implementation choice: You might have noticed that we have used `BigDecimal` for `dailyC- harge` and dimensions in the `LockerSize` enum to ensure precision in financial calculations, unlike float or double, which could introduce rounding errors.

Site

The `Site` class represents a physical location containing multiple lockers, organized by size for efficient storage management. It maintains a collection of lockers grouped by size, treating lockers of the same size as interchangeable. This means any available locker of a given size can store a package, simplifying locker assignment.

To efficiently manage lockers, the class uses a map-based structure, where:

- Each key is a `LockerSize`, representing a specific locker category ("Small," "Medium," "Large").
- Each value is a `Set<Locker>`, containing all lockers of that size.

This design allows the system to quickly find an available locker and assign packages accordingly.

Here is the implementation of this class.

```java
public class Site {
  // Map of locker sizes to sets of lockers of that size
  final Map<LockerSize, Set<Locker>> lockers = new HashMap<>();

  // Creates a new site with specified number of lockers for each size
  public Site(Map<LockerSize, Integer> lockers) {
    for (Map.Entry<LockerSize, Integer> entry : lockers.entrySet()) {
      Set<Locker> lockerSet = new HashSet<>();
      for (int i = 0; i < entry.getValue(); i++) {
        lockerSet.add(new Locker(entry.getKey()));
      }
      this.lockers.put(entry.getKey(), lockerSet);
    }
  }

  // Finds an available locker of the specified size
  public Locker findAvailableLocker(LockerSize size) {
    for (Locker locker : lockers.get(size)) {
      if (locker.isAvailable()) {
        return locker;
      }
    }
    return null;
  }

  // Places a package in an available locker of appropriate size
  public Locker placePackage(ShippingPackage pkg, Date date) {
    // Determine the smallest locker size that can fit this package
    LockerSize size = pkg.getLockerSize();
    Locker locker = findAvailableLocker(size);
    if (locker != null) {
      locker.assignPackage(pkg, date);
      pkg.updateShippingStatus(ShippingStatus.IN_LOCKER);
      return locker;
    }
    throw new NoLockerAvailableException("No locker of size " + size + "
    is currently available");
  }
}
```

- `findAvailableLocker(LockerSize size)`: Locates and returns an available locker of the specified size.
- `placePackage(ShippingPackage pkg, Date date)`: A convenience method that finds an available locker and assigns the package in one step. If no locker is available,

it returns null.

Implementation choice: While the same result could be achieved by separately calling `findAvailableLocker()` and then manually assigning a package, providing helper methods such as `placePackage()` is beneficial. It provides atomic transaction-like behavior by encapsulating the find-and-assign operations in a single method call, ensuring thread safety and preventing inconsistent states that could occur if these operations were performed separately.

BasicShippingPackage

The `BasicShippingPackage` class represents a standard package within the locker system, implementing the `ShippingPackage` interface. It encapsulates essential package details such as order ID, user account, dimensions (width, height, depth), and shipping status. These attributes allow the system to determine where the package can be stored.

Here is the implementation of this class.

```
public class BasicShippingPackage implements ShippingPackage {
  // Unique identifier for the order
  private final String orderId;
  // User account associated with this package
  private final Account user;
  private final BigDecimal width;
  private final BigDecimal height;
  private final BigDecimal depth;
  // Current status of the package
  private ShippingStatus status;

  // Creates a new shipping package with specified dimensions
  public BasicShippingPackage(String orderId, Account user, BigDecimal
    width, BigDecimal height, BigDecimal depth) {
    this.orderId = orderId;
    this.user = user;
    this.width = width;
    this.height = height;
    this.depth = depth;
    this.status = ShippingStatus.CREATED;
  }

  // Returns the current package status
  @Override
  public ShippingStatus getStatus() {
    return status;
  }

  // Updates the package status
  @Override
  public void updateShippingStatus(ShippingStatus status) {
```

```
    this.status = status;
  }

  // Determines the smallest locker size that can fit this package
  @Override
  public LockerSize getLockerSize() {
    for(LockerSize size : LockerSize.values()) {
      if(size.getWidth().compareTo(width) >= 0 &&
      size.getHeight().compareTo(height) >= 0 &&
      size.getDepth().compareTo(depth) >= 0) {
        return size;
      }
    }
    throw new PackageIncompatibleException("No locker size available for
    the package");
  }

  // getter methods are omitted for brevity
}
```

A key functionality of this class is determining the appropriate locker size for a package. The `getLockerSize()` method evaluates all available locker sizes ("Small," "Medium," "Large") and returns the smallest suitable locker based on the package's dimensions.

Additionally, the `updateShippingStatus()` method allows the locker system to communicate status updates (e.g., when a package is stored or retrieved) to the user.

Account and AccountLockerPolicy

The Account class represents a user's account within the locker system. It stores basic account details, including the `accountId`, `ownerName`, the current usage charges, and the user's lockerPolicy (an instance of `AccountLockerPolicy`), which defines the user-specific rules for locker usage.

The account `usageCharges` is used to track locker usage fees, and funds can be added dynamically using the `addUsageCharge(BigDecimal amount)` method.

```
public class Account {
  private final String accountId;
  private final String ownerName;
  // Policy defining locker usage rules for this account
  private final AccountLockerPolicy lockerPolicy;
  // Total charges accumulated for locker usage
  private BigDecimal usageCharges = new BigDecimal("0.00");

  // Creates a new account with specified details and policy
  public Account(String accountId, String ownerName, AccountLockerPolicy
    lockerPolicy) {
    this.accountId = accountId;
```

```
    this.ownerName = ownerName;
    this.lockerPolicy = lockerPolicy;
  }

  // Adds a charge to the account's total usage charges
  public void addUsageCharge(BigDecimal amount) {
    usageCharges = usageCharges.add(amount);
  }

  // getter methods are omitted for brevity
}
```

The `AccountLockerPolicy` class encapsulates the rules for locker usage. It specifies:

- `freePeriodDays`: The number of days a user can store a package without incurring charges.
- `maximumPeriodDays`: The maximum number of days a package can remain in a locker before further action is required (e.g., additional charges or forced retrieval).

This policy allows customized locker usage limits, ensuring that different users can have varying storage privileges based on their account settings.

Check out the implementation of this class.

```
public class AccountLockerPolicy {
  // Number of days of free storage
  final int freePeriodDays;
  // Maximum number of days a package can be stored
  final int maximumPeriodDays;

  // Creates a new locker policy with specified free and maximum periods
  public AccountLockerPolicy(int freePeriodDays, int maximumPeriodDays) {
    this.freePeriodDays = freePeriodDays;
    this.maximumPeriodDays = maximumPeriodDays;
  }

  // getter methods are omitted for brevity
}
```

LockerManager

The `LockerManager` class acts as a facade for the overall locker system. It serves as the central coordinator for the locker system, coordinating package assignments to lockers, package pick-ups, and locker releases. It interacts with Site, which oversees the locker inventory and handles the actual placement of packages in available lockers. The `NotificationInterface` is responsible for sending user notifications regarding package assignments and pick-ups.

Additionally, it maintains a `Map<String, Account>` to store customer accounts, which are used to track locker usage charges. To ensure secure and efficient package retrieval, it uses a Map<String, Locker> to map access codes to their corresponding lockers.

Below is the implementation of this class.

```java
public class LockerManager {
  // The site being managed
  private final Site site;
  // Service for sending notifications
  private final NotificationInterface notificationService;
  // Map of account IDs to account objects
  private final Map<String, Account> accounts;
  // Map of access codes to lockers
  private final Map<String, Locker> accessCodeMap = new HashMap<>();

  // Creates a new locker manager for a site
  public LockerManager(Site site, Map<String, Account> accounts,
    NotificationInterface notificationService) {
    this.site = site;
    this.accounts = accounts;
    this.notificationService = notificationService;
  }

  // Assigns a package to an available locker
  public Locker assignPackage(ShippingPackage pkg, Date date) {
    Locker locker = site.placePackage(pkg, date);
    if (locker != null) {
      accessCodeMap.put(locker.getAccessCode(), locker);
      notificationService.sendNotification("Package assigned to locker" +
      locker.getAccessCode(), pkg.getUser());
    }
    return locker;
  }

  // Processes package pickup using an access code
  public Locker pickUpPackage(String accessCode) {
    Locker locker = accessCodeMap.get(accessCode);
    if (locker != null && locker.checkAccessCode(accessCode)) {
      try {
        BigDecimal charge = locker.calculateStorageCharges();
        ShippingPackage pkg = locker.getPackage();
        locker.releaseLocker();
        pkg.getUser().addUsageCharge(charge);
        pkg.updateShippingStatus(ShippingStatus.RETRIEVED);
        return locker;
      } catch (MaximumStoragePeriodExceededException e) {
        locker.releaseLocker();
        return locker;
      }
```

```
    }
    return null;
  }

  // getter methods are omitted for brevity
}
```

- assignPackage(ShippingPackage pkg, Date date): Assigns a package to an available locker via site.placePackage().
- pickUpPackage(String accessCode): Retrieves the package if the provided access code matches the stored locker. It then:
  - Calculates charges based on locker usage duration.
  - Updates the user's usage charges.
  - Releases the locker and marks the package as retrieved.

> ♛ **Best practices:** In complex systems, a manager class like LockerManager is commonly used to centralize operations such as package assignment, retrieval, and notifications. However, to maintain a thin manager class, it is essential to delegate low-level operations, such as finding available lockers, storing packages, and enforcing locker policies, to specialized classes like Site and Locker.

Deep Dive Topic

Now that the basic design is complete, the interviewer might ask you some deep dive questions. Let's check out some of these.

Designing an extensible locker creation system

Currently, lockers are created directly based on predefined sizes, which makes the system rigid and difficult to extend. For example, if we need to introduce a new locker size (e.g., XLARGE) or a specialized locker type (e.g., temperature-controlled lockers), we would have to modify multiple parts of the codebase where lockers are instantiated manually. This increases maintenance overhead and reduces flexibility.

To address this, we can use the Factory design pattern to centralize the creation logic for different types of lockers, making the system more modular and extensible.

Note: To learn more about the Factory Pattern and its common use cases, refer to the **Further Reading** section at the end of this chapter.

Here is the code for the LockerFactory class.

```
class LockerFactory {
```

```
    // Creates a new locker of the specified size
    public static Locker createLocker(LockerSize size) {
      return switch (size) {
        case SMALL -> new Locker(LockerSize.SMALL);
        case MEDIUM -> new Locker(LockerSize.MEDIUM);
        case LARGE -> new Locker(LockerSize.LARGE);
        case XLARGE -> new Locker(LockerSize.XLARGE);
      };
    }
}
```

Here's how a `LockerFactory` class enhances the locker system:

- **Centralized object creation:** The `LockerFactory` encapsulates the locker instanti-ation process, so any changes to locker creation (e.g., adding new sizes or types) are localized to this class.

- **Extensibility:** If we need to add new locker sizes or types in the future, the factory class can be easily updated, without modifying core business logic in other parts of the system.

- **Improved readability and maintainability:** Using a factory method to create lock-ers allows us to separate locker creation from locker usage logic, aligning with the Single Responsibility Principle.

Decoupling event handling with an event-driven approach

Currently, the `LockerManager` directly invokes `NotificationInterface.sendNotifica-tion()` to notify customers when key events occur, such as package assignment or locker expiration. While this approach works, it tightly couples `LockerManager` with the no-tification system, meaning any changes to how notifications are sent require modifying `LockerManager` itself.

How can we improve the system design to make event handling more flexible and scalable?

To decouple event handling from `LockerManager`, we can use an event-driven approach where multiple components can subscribe to and respond to system events dynamically. Instead of directly calling `sendNotification()`, `LockerManager` will broadcast events to registered observers, ensuring a more modular and extensible system.

By implementing the Observer pattern, we can send notifications to customers or admin-istrative staff when certain events occur, such as when a package is delivered or a locker exceeds its maximum usage period.

Note: To learn more about the Observer Pattern and its common use cases, refer to the **Elevator System** chapter.

Instead of hardcoding the notification logic in the `LockerManager`, the locker system can maintain a list of observers. These observers can be various notification services (e.g., email, SMS) or other systems (e.g., analytics, metrics). When a key event occurs, the LockerManager can notify all registered observers, allowing the system to be easily extended without modifying the core logic.

Below is the implementation of the relevant interface and classes for the observer pattern.

- **Subject:** LockerManagerChange, which maintains a list of observers and notifies them of state changes, such as package assignments.

```
class LockerManagerChange {
  // List of observers that will be notified of locker events
  private final List<LockerEventObserver> observers = new ArrayList<>();

  public void addObserver(LockerEventObserver observer) {
    observers.add(observer);
  }

  public void removeObserver(LockerEventObserver observer) {
    observers.remove(observer);
  }

  private void notifyObservers(String message, Account account) {
    for (LockerEventObserver observer : observers) {
      observer.update(message, account);
    }
  }

  // Assigns a package to an available locker and notifies observers.
  public void assignPackage(ShippingPackage pkg) {
    Locker locker = assignLockerToPackage(pkg);
    if (locker != null) {
      notifyObservers("Package assigned to locker", pkg.getUser());
    }
  }

  private Locker assignLockerToPackage(ShippingPackage pkg) {
    return null;
  }
}
```

- **Observer:** The LockerEventObserver interface, which defines the update() method that observers must implement to handle notifications.

```
// Interface for objects that need to be notified of locker events
public interface LockerEventObserver {
  // Updates the observer with a message and the affected account
  void update(String message, Account account);
}
```

- **Concrete Observers:** Classes like `EmailNotification`, which implement `LockerEventObserver` to send email alerts for specific events, enabling flexible and extensible event handling.

```
// Implementation of LockerEventObserver that sends email notifications
class EmailNotification implements LockerEventObserver {
  // Updates the observer with a message and sends it to the account
  owner
  public void update(String message, Account account) {
    System.out.println("Email sent to " + account.getOwnerName() + ": " +
    message);
  }
}
```

Wrap Up

In this chapter, we designed a Shipping Locker System. We began by clarifying requirements through a structured Q&A discussion, similar to an interviewer-candidate exchange. From there, we identified core objects and developed a class diagram to represent the system's structure. We implemented the key components of the locker service, bringing the design to life.

In the deep dive section, we explored advanced topics, including how the Factory Pattern simplifies locker instantiation for future scalability and how the Observer Pattern decouples event handling, enabling flexible notifications.

Congratulations on getting this far! Now give yourself a pat on the back. Good job!

Further Reading: Factory Design Pattern

This section gives a quick overview of the design patterns used in this chapter. It's helpful if you're new to these patterns or need a refresher to better understand the design choices.

Factory design pattern

The Factory Method Pattern is a creational design pattern that provides an interface for creating instances of a class but allows subclasses to alter the type of objects that will be created.

In the shipping locker system, we use the Factory pattern through the `LockerFactory` class to centralize locker creation, enabling easy addition of new locker sizes (e.g., XLARGE) without modifying existing code. To illustrate the Factory pattern in another domain, the following example uses an e-commerce payment system.

Problem

Imagine building an e-commerce payment system that initially supports only credit card payments, with logic tied to a `CreditCardPayment` class. As demand grows for new payment options like digital wallets or cryptocurrency, adding them requires altering multiple parts of the tightly coupled codebase, increasing maintenance effort, and reducing flexibility.

Solution

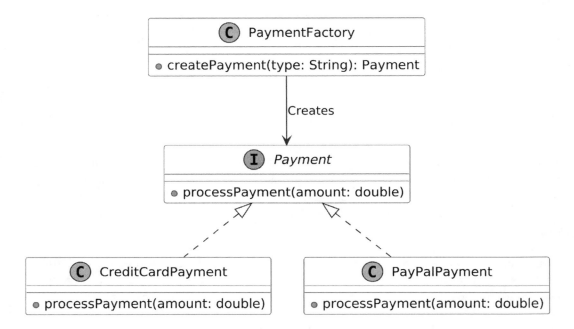

Factory design pattern

The Factory Method pattern addresses this by replacing direct object creation (using the new operator) with a factory method that encapsulates instantiation. This allows new payment types to be added via subclasses without changing existing code, decoupling payment processing from the main system for better scalability and maintainability.

When to use

The factory design pattern is particularly useful in the following scenarios:

- Use the Factory Method when the specific types and dependencies of objects required by your code are unknown in advance.
- Use the Factory Method to allow users of your library or framework to extend its internal components without modifying existing code.
- Use the Factory Method to optimize resource utilization by reusing existing objects rather than creating new instances each time.

13

Automated Teller Machine (ATM) System

In this chapter, we will explore the object-oriented design of an ATM system. The primary purpose of an ATM is to automate banking tasks for users, allowing them to check balances, withdraw cash, and transfer funds. This design aims to make these operations seamless by designing classes that model key components, such as the ATM machine, bank accounts, hardware interfaces, and transaction states.

Automated Teller Machine (ATM)

Let's gather the specific requirements through a simulated interview scenario.

Requirements Gathering

Here is an example of a typical prompt an interviewer might give:

"Picture yourself approaching an ATM on a busy afternoon to manage your banking needs. You insert your card, enter your PIN, and then choose from options such as checking your balance, withdrawing cash, or depositing funds. Within seconds, the system verifies your credentials and processes your request. Behind the scenes, the ATM coordinates with the bank, manages account transactions, and interacts with hardware like the card reader and cash dispenser. Now, let's design an ATM system that handles these operations smoothly and reliably."

Requirements clarification

The first step in designing the ATM system is to understand precisely what the interviewer wants you to design. Here is an example of how a conversation between a candidate and an interviewer might unfold:

Candidate: For user interactions, I think the ATM should have a card reader to process debit cards, a keypad for entering the PIN and selecting options, a screen to display instructions and menus, a cash dispenser for withdrawals, and a deposit slot for accepting cash. Does this cover the main components, or are there additional ones I should consider?
Interviewer: That's a solid list.

Candidate: I envision the ATM guiding users through a clear flow: the user inserts their card, enters a PIN for authentication, and then sees a menu with options like checking balance, withdrawing cash, or depositing funds. After completing a task, the ATM offers the choice to continue or exit, ejecting the card at the end. Does this flow align with your vision, or should I adjust any steps?
Interviewer: Your flow is accurate. It starts with card insertion, PIN entry, and a menu for tasks. After each task, the user can continue or exit, with the card ejected at the end.

Candidate: For authentication, I assume the ATM validates the card and PIN combination. If either is invalid, it displays an error.
Interviewer: Yes, the ATM validates the card and PIN, showing an error for invalid inputs. Including a limit of three PIN attempts before locking the card is a good security measure. Let's keep that in scope.

Candidate: Regarding accounts, I propose that the ATM supports multiple accounts per user, such as Checking and Savings, linked to their card. Users can select an account for transactions. Does this match your requirements?
Interviewer: That's correct. The ATM should support Checking and Savings accounts, with users able to select one for transactions. No additional account types are needed for now.

Candidate: For transactions, I think the ATM should handle Withdraw and Deposit operations. For example, withdrawals check for sufficient funds, and deposits update the balance. Should we include other transactions like transfers, or focus on these two?

Interviewer: Let's focus on Withdraw and Deposit for simplicity. Transfers are out of scope for now. Ensure withdrawals validate funds and deposits process cash accurately.

Candidate: To handle errors, I suggest the ATM displays clear messages for issues like insufficient funds, invalid PINs, or hardware failures.

Interviewer: I agree that clear error messages are essential.

Requirements

Based on the requirements gathering dialogue, the following functional requirements are identified for the ATM system:

- Authenticate users via a debit card and PIN.
- Support multiple accounts per user, including Checking and Savings account types, with the ability to select an account for transactions.
- The machine should include a Card Reader, Keypad, Screen, Cash Dispenser, Deposit Slot, and an optional Printer for receipts.
- Support Withdraw and Deposit transactions, ensuring withdrawals validate sufficient funds and deposits update the account balance.
- Handle exceptions, such as insufficient funds or incorrect inputs, by displaying clear error messages and retaining the card after repeated invalid attempts.

Below are the non-functional requirements:

- The ATM must protect user data with strong security measures and retain cards after repeated invalid PIN attempts to ensure user trust.
- The ATM must operate reliably, minimizing disruptions and safely ejecting cards during failures to maintain user confidence.

Use Case Diagram

In the ATM system, a use case diagram illustrates how customers interact with the system to perform banking tasks, clarifying essential actions such as card insertion, PIN entry with up to three attempts, account selection, transaction processing, and error handling.

Below is the use case diagram of the ATM system.

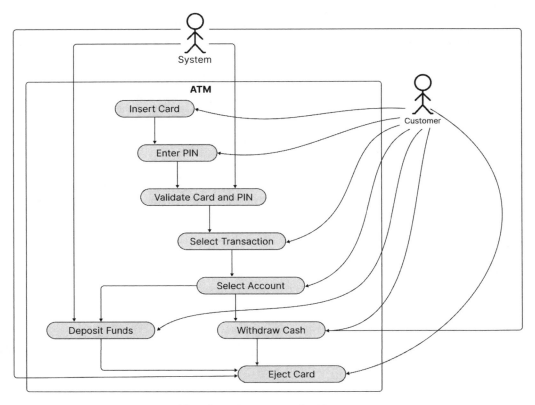

Use Case Diagram of ATM

The **Customer** actor has the following main use cases:

- **Insert Card:** The customer initiates a session by inserting their card into the ATM.
- **Enter PIN:** After inserting the card, the customer then enters their PIN for authentication.
- **Select Transaction:** The customer chooses a transaction type, such as withdrawing cash or depositing funds, from the menu.
- **Select Account:** The customer selects an account (e.g., Checking or Savings) for the transaction.
- **Withdraw Cash:** The customer requests a cash withdrawal and specifies the desired amount.
- **Deposit Funds:** The customer deposits cash into the ATM.
- **Eject Card:** The customer requests card ejection (e.g., by canceling or ending the session), the ATM ejects the card, and the session terminates.

The **System** actor's use cases are listed below. Note that actors may not always be human.

- **Validate Card and PIN:** The system verifies the customer's card and PIN to grant access to banking options.

- **Withdraw Cash:** The system processes the withdrawal request, confirms sufficient funds, and dispenses cash.
- **Deposit Funds:** The system accepts the deposited cash and updates the customer's account balance accordingly.
- **Eject Card:** The ATM ejects the card, and the session ends.

Identify Core Objects

To design a modular and maintainable ATM system, we identify core objects that encapsulate distinct responsibilities, aligning with the functional requirements and user flow. These objects model the system's key entities and interactions, ensuring clear separation of concerns and extensibility.

Bank: Stores and manages accounts.

Account: Represents a customer's bank account. Manages a customer's account details, including balance, account number, card number, PIN (hashed for security), and account type (Checking or Savings).

ATMMachine: Acts as the main coordinator, managing user interaction and connecting with hardware elements like the card reader, keypad, screen, cash dispenser, and deposit slot.

> ✂ **Design choice:** We consolidate hardware access and management within the `ATMMachine` object to ensure consistent behavior across components, enabling a seamless user flow from card insertion to transaction completion.

Transaction: Manages financial transactions like cash withdrawals and deposits, including validation checks (e.g., sufficient balance for withdrawals) and transaction execution.

Design Class Diagram

With the core objects and their roles defined, we now design their classes, attributes, and methods to construct a modular and extensible ATM system that meets the specified requirements.

Account

This class represents a customer's bank account as a distinct entity within the ATM system, encapsulating the essential data and operations needed to support user authentication and financial transactions.

The `Account` class manages critical information, including the account balance, account number, associated card number, and PIN, while using an `AccountType` enum to distinguish between account types like Checking and Saving. It enables authentication by validating the PIN and supports transactions by updating the balance for withdrawals and deposits, ensuring the account's state reflects the user's financial activities accurately and efficiently.

Below are representations of those classes.

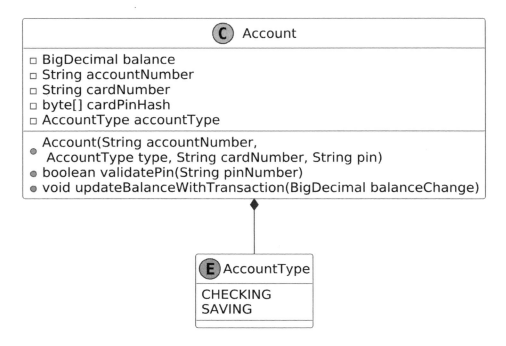

Account class and AccountType enum

> ✂ **Design choice:** Rather than maintaining a transaction ledger for auditability and deriving the balance from it, as is typical in real-world banking, we simplify the system by directly updating the account balance during each transaction. This approach prioritizes the ATM's core functionality and effective scope management.

Bank

In object-oriented design questions, systems are usually self-contained and don't use real databases or web service API calls. The Bank class is designed to be a separate component that handles the main data and operations needed for the ATM to work.

The Bank class stores Account objects and links them to cards for fast retrieval, enabling efficient card and PIN validation for authentication, account access for transactions, and funds availability checks for withdrawals.

To ensure flexibility and scalability, we define a BankInterface to decouple the Bank implementation from the ATM. This allows the local Bank object to be easily replaced with a networked implementation, such as an API client adapter, if the system were to be extended for production use, without modifying the ATM's core logic.

The UML diagram below illustrates this structure.

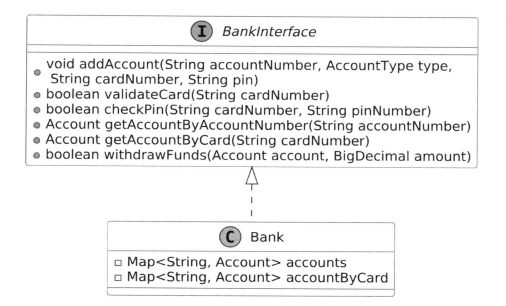

BankInterface interface and concrete class

> ⚙️ **Alternative approach:** We could integrate the Bank's functionality directly into the ATMMachine. However, this would tightly couple account management with the ATM's operations, reducing modularity and making it harder to adapt the system for networked banking or other extensions in the future.

Transaction

The purpose of designing the Transaction class is to provide a unified framework for handling financial operations in the ATM system, enabling the system to process withdrawals and deposits consistently and reliably.

The Transaction class, as an interface, defines a contract for all transaction types, supported by a TransactionType enum that specifies Withdraw and Deposit operations. It validates transactions, such as checking funds for withdrawals, and updates the account balance, using concrete classes like WithdrawTransaction and DepositTransaction for reliable processing.

> ✂ **Design choice:** By abstracting Transaction as a separate object, we can represent different transaction types (e.g., Withdraw, Deposit) with shared behavior, making it easier to introduce new types in the future without modifying the core logic.

The UML diagram below illustrates this structure.

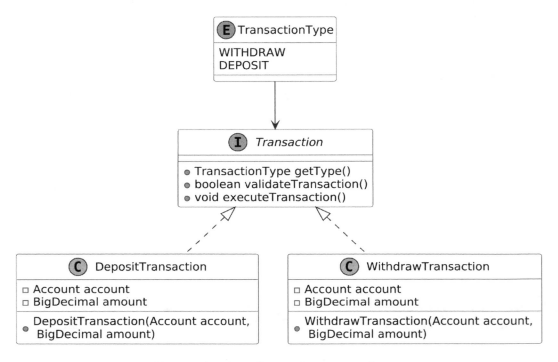

Transaction interface and concrete classes

ATMState

The purpose of designing the `ATMState` interface is to provide a framework for handling the distinct stages of the ATM's interaction process, ensuring the `ATMMachine` can manage each user step systematically.

The `ATMState` interface defines the operations for each stage of the ATM's flow, such as card insertion, PIN entry, transaction selection, and cash handling. Concrete state classes like `IdleState`, `PinEntryState`, `TransactionSelectionState`, `WithdrawAmountEntryState`, and `DepositCollectionState` implement the specific behavior for each stage.

The following diagram shows the class hierarchy of `ATMState` and its concrete states:

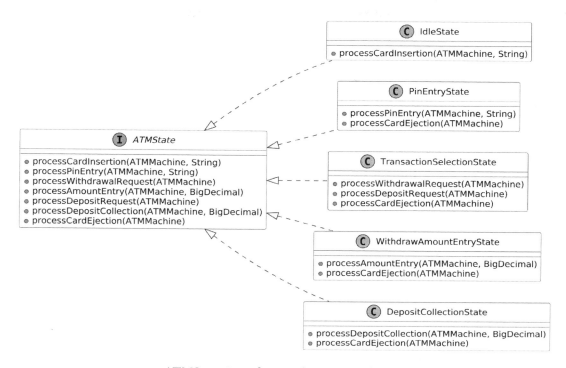

ATMState interface and concrete classes

The following state transition diagram visualizes this design.

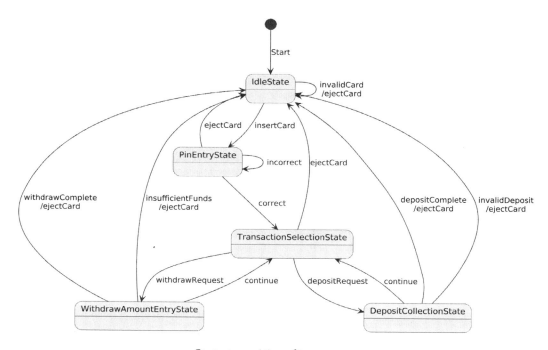

State transition diagram

- `IdleState:` Awaits card insertion, transitions to PinEntryState on valid card.

- `PinEntryState:` Processes PIN entry, transitions to `TransactionSelectionState` on valid PIN.

- `TransactionSelectionState:` Processes transaction selection, transitions to `WithdrawAmountEntryState` or `DepositCollectionState`.

- `WithdrawAmountEntryState:` Handles withdrawal amount entry, executes transaction, returns to `TransactionSelectionState` or `IdleState`.

- `DepositCollectionState:` Processes deposit amount, executes transaction, returns to `TransactionSelectionState` or `IdleState`.

Note: To learn more about the State pattern and its everyday use cases, refer to the **Vending Machine** chapter of the book.

Hardware component interfaces

The purpose of designing the hardware component interfaces is to provide a set of interfaces that handle user interactions and physical operations within the ATM system, ensuring the `ATMMachine` can operate independently of specific hardware implementations.

The hardware components, including `CardProcessor`, `Keypad`, `Display`, `CashDispenser`, and `DepositBox`, define the operations needed for interacting with the user and managing physical tasks, such as reading cards, accepting PIN entries, displaying messages, dispensing cash, and collecting deposits. They enable the `ATMMachine` to perform these tasks through well-defined interfaces, ensuring flexibility and ease of testing with simulated implementations.

CardProcessor

The `CardProcessor` interface enables the `ATMMachine` to read a card during insertion and release it after the user's session, managing card-related operations for starting and ending transactions.

Keypad

The `Keypad` interface captures user inputs such as PINs, transaction choices, and amounts.

DepositBox

The `DepositBox` interface collects the deposited amount during a deposit transaction, enabling the `ATMMachine` to handle cash deposits from users.

CashDispenser

The `CashDispenser` interface delivers the requested cash to the user during a withdrawal transaction.

Display

The `Display` interface shows messages and prompts to guide the user.

The following diagram shows the hardware component interfaces and their relationship with the ATMMachine:

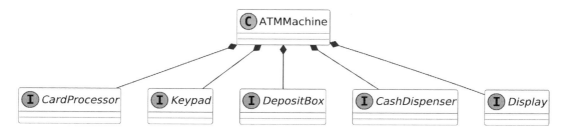

Hardware component interfaces

ATMMachine

The ATMMachine class acts as a facade for the ATM system, orchestrating user interactions, coordinating hardware components while relying on a Bank instance to access Account data and process Transactions. It uses the ATMState class to manage the sequence of steps in a user's session, ensuring a clear and reliable experience from card insertion to session end.

Below is the representation of this class.

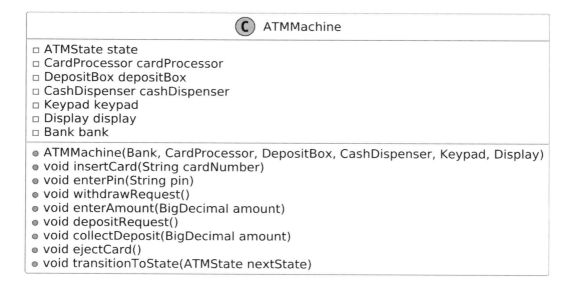

> ✂ **Design Choice:** We employ the State pattern with `ATMState` classes to man-
> age the ATM's sequential workflow, such as transitioning from card insertion to
> PIN entry, ensuring each stage is encapsulated and clearly defined. Additionally,
> we use interface-based hardware components (e.g., `CardProcessor`, `Keypad`) to
> abstract physical interactions. This separation of concerns enhances modularity,
> simplifies maintenance, and enables testing with mock hardware implementations.

With all classes defined, let's review how they fit together in the complete class diagram.

Complete Class Diagram

Take a moment to review the complete class structure and the relationships between them.
The detailed methods and attributes are skipped to make the diagram more readable.

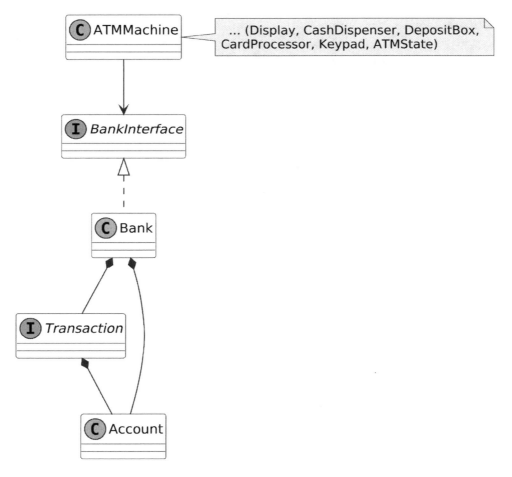

Summarized Class Diagram of ATM System

Code - ATM System

In this section, we will implement the core functionalities of the ATM System, focusing on key areas such as defining different account types and transactions, managing accounts and banking operations, handling user interactions through hardware components, and implementing the ATM's interaction flow using a state machine.

Account

The `Account` class represents a bank account in our ATM system, encapsulating core banking attributes like balance, account number, card details, and account type. It maintains security through PIN hashing and is designed with a mix of immutable (`accountNumber`, `cardNumber`, `accountType`, and `cardPinHash`) and mutable (`balance`) fields. This ensures account identity remains constant while allowing balance updates for deposits and withdrawals.

Tied to this, the AccountType enum defines the type of account a customer can hold, currently supporting `CHECKING` and `SAVING` types. This simple enum design enables type-safe account categorization while allowing for future expansion of account types.

Below is the code implementation of the `Account` class and `AccountType` enum:

```
// Represents a bank account with balance, card details, and PIN security
public class Account {

  private BigDecimal balance;
  private final String accountNumber;
  private final String cardNumber;
  private final byte[] cardPinHash;
  private final AccountType accountType;

  // Creates a new account with initial zero balance and hashed PIN
  public Account(final String accountNumber,
  final AccountType type,
  final String cardNumber,
  final String pin) {
    this.accountNumber = accountNumber;
    this.accountType = type;
    this.cardNumber = cardNumber;
    this.cardPinHash = calculateMd5(pin);  // PIN is hashed for security
    this.balance = BigDecimal.ZERO;
  }

  // Validates the entered PIN against stored hash
  public boolean validatePin(String pinNumber) {
    byte[] entryPinHash = calculateMd5(pinNumber);
    return Arrays.equals(cardPinHash, entryPinHash);
  }
```

```
  // Updates account balance by adding the specified amount
  public void updateBalanceWithTransaction(final BigDecimal balanceChange
    ) {
    this.balance = this.balance.add(balanceChange);
  }

  // getter methods omitted for brevity

}

// Defines the type of bank account
public enum AccountType {
  // Regular checking account for daily transactions
  CHECKING,
  // Interest-bearing savings account
  SAVING
}
```

- The `validatePin` method ensures secure authentication by comparing the hashed input PIN with the stored hash.
- The `updateBalanceWithTransaction` handles both deposits and withdrawals through a single method that adds the transaction amount (positive for deposits, negative for withdrawals) to the current balance.

Implementation choice: We have used `BigDecimal` for balance to ensure precise financial calculations, while the immutable fields for account identity (`accountNumber`, `cardNumber`) maintain data consistency throughout the account's lifecycle.

Bank

The `BankInterface` defines the contract for banking operations in the ATM system. Its concrete implementation, the Bank class, provides a local implementation to manage accounts and handle operations like card validation and fund withdrawals. This separation allows the system to remain flexible, supporting potential future extensions such as replacing the Bank with a networked implementation.

Here's how it's structured:

```
public interface BankInterface {
  void addAccount(String accountNumber, AccountType type, String
    cardNumber, String pin);

  boolean validateCard(String cardNumber);
  boolean checkPin(String cardNumber, String pinNumber);
  Account getAccountByAccountNumber(String accountNumber);
  Account getAccountByCard(String cardNumber);
  boolean withdrawFunds(Account account, BigDecimal amount);
}
```

```java
// Manages bank accounts and provides banking operations like validation
    and transactions
public class Bank implements BankInterface {
  private final Map<String, Account> accounts = new HashMap<>();
  private final Map<String, Account> accountByCard = new HashMap<>();

  // Creates a new account and stores it in both account and card maps
  @Override
  public void addAccount(final String accountNumber,
  final AccountType type,
  final String cardNumber,
  final String pin) {
    final Account newAccount = new Account(accountNumber, type,
    cardNumber, pin);
    accounts.put(newAccount.getAccountNumber(), newAccount);
    accountByCard.put(newAccount.getCardNumber(), newAccount);
  }

  // Checks if a card number exists in the bank's records
  @Override
  public boolean validateCard(final String cardNumber) {
    return getAccountByCard(cardNumber) != null;
  }

  // Verifies if the provided PIN matches the card's stored PIN
  @Override
  public boolean checkPin(String cardNumber, String pinNumber) {
    Account account = getAccountByCard(cardNumber);
    if (account != null) {
      return account.validatePin(pinNumber);
    }
    return false;
  }

  // Retrieves account by account number
  @Override
  public Account getAccountByAccountNumber(String accountNumber) {
    return accounts.get(accountNumber);
  }

  // Retrieves account by card number
  @Override
  public Account getAccountByCard(String cardNumber) {
    return accountByCard.get(cardNumber);
  }

  // Attempts to withdraw specified amount from account if sufficient
    funds exist
  @Override
```

```
  public boolean withdrawFunds(Account account, BigDecimal amount) {
    if (account.getBalance().compareTo(amount) >= 0) {
      account.updateBalanceWithTransaction(amount.negate());
      return true;
    }
    return false;
  }
}
```

The Bank class implements efficient account management through:

Two HashMaps for $O(1)$ lookup time:

- accounts: Maps account numbers to Account objects
- accountByCard: Maps card numbers to Account objects for quick access by card number during authentication and transactions.

Account operations:

- addAccount: Creates new accounts.
- validateCard: Checks if the card number is associated with an account, used during card insertion.
- checkPin: Verifies the PIN for the given card, enabling user authentication.
- withdrawFunds: Processes withdrawals with balance checks.

Implementation choice: We chose HashMap for both accounts (mapping account numbers to Account objects) and accountByCard (mapping card numbers to Account objects) because it provides average-case O(1) time complexity for lookups, ensuring fast performance for real-time operations like card validation and account retrieval during a user session.

Transaction

The Transaction interface establishes a consistent framework for handling all financial transactions within the ATM system. It ensures that different transaction types, such as withdrawals and deposits, adhere to a uniform process for validation and execution. The WithdrawTransaction and DepositTransaction classes implement this interface to manage their respective operations. This abstraction promotes extensibility, making it easy to introduce new transaction types, like transfers, without altering existing code.

Here is the implementation of the interface and its concrete classes.

```
public interface Transaction {

  TransactionType getType();
  boolean validateTransaction();
```

```java
    void executeTransaction();
}

// Handles the withdrawal transaction process for removing funds from an
    account
public class WithdrawTransaction implements Transaction {
  Account account;
  BigDecimal amount;

  // Returns the transaction type as WITHDRAW
  @Override
  public TransactionType getType() {
    return TransactionType.WITHDRAW;
  }

  // Validates if the account has sufficient funds for withdrawal
  @Override
  public boolean validateTransaction() {
    assert account != null;
    return account.getBalance().compareTo(amount) > 0;
  }

  // Creates a new withdrawal transaction, throws exception if validation
    fails
  public WithdrawTransaction(Account account, BigDecimal amount) {
    if (!validateTransaction()) {
      throw new IllegalStateException("Cannot complete withdrawal:
    Insufficient funds in account");
    }
    this.account = account;
    this.amount = amount;
  }

  // Executes the withdrawal by subtracting the amount from account
    balance
  @Override
  public void executeTransaction() {
    account.updateBalanceWithTransaction(amount.negate());
  }
}


// Handles the deposit transaction process for adding funds to an account
public class DepositTransaction implements Transaction {
  final Account account;
  final BigDecimal amount;

  // Returns the transaction type as DEPOSIT
  @Override
  public TransactionType getType() {
```

```
    return TransactionType.DEPOSIT;
}

// Deposit transactions are always valid
@Override
public boolean validateTransaction() {
  return true;
}

public DepositTransaction(Account account, BigDecimal amount) {
  this.account = account;
  this.amount = amount;
}

// Executes the deposit by adding the amount to the account balance
@Override
public void executeTransaction() {
  account.updateBalanceWithTransaction(amount);
}
}
```

The Transaction interface includes essential methods to manage transactions:

- getType(): Returns the transaction type (e.g., WITHDRAW or DEPOSIT).
- validateTransaction(): Validates the transaction's feasibility, such as checking funds availability for withdrawals.
- executeTransaction(): Executes transaction by updating the account balance.

ATMState

The ATMState abstract class forms the foundation of our ATM's state machine, ensuring that each stage of the user flow, from card insertion to transaction completion, follows a consistent process. Its seven concrete implementations manage distinct stages, enabling the ATMMachine to execute the user flow by transitioning between states as the user progresses through their session.

The ATMState interface includes essential methods to manage each stage:

- processCardInsertion(String cardNumber): Handles card insertion, used at the start of a session.
- processCardEjection(): Handles card ejection, which is used to end a session.
- processPinEntry(String pinNumber): Processes PIN entry for authentication.
- processWithdrawalRequest(): Initiates a withdrawal transaction.
- processDepositRequest(): Initiates a deposit transaction.
- processAmountEntry(BigDecimal amount): Processes the amount for withdrawals.

- processDepositCollection(BigDecimal amount): Processes the amount for deposits.

Below is the implementation for the ATMState interface, showing its default behavior, followed by implementations of IdleState and WithdrawAmountEntryState:

```
public class ATMState {
  // Displays an invalid action message on the ATM screen
  private static void renderDefaultAction(ATMMachine atmMachine) {
    atmMachine.getDisplay().showMessage("Invalid action, please try again
    .");
  }

  // Default implementation for card insertion
  public void processCardInsertion(ATMMachine atmMachine, String
    cardNumber) {
    renderDefaultAction(atmMachine);
  }

  // Default implementation for card ejection
  public void processCardEjection(ATMMachine atmMachine) {
    renderDefaultAction(atmMachine);
  }

  // Default implementation for PIN entry
  public void processPinEntry(ATMMachine atmMachine, String pin) {
    renderDefaultAction(atmMachine);
  }

  // Default implementation for withdrawal request
  public void processWithdrawalRequest(ATMMachine atmMachine) {
    renderDefaultAction(atmMachine);
  }

  // Default implementation for deposit request
  public void processDepositRequest(ATMMachine atmMachine){
    renderDefaultAction(atmMachine);
  }

  // Default implementation for amount entry
  public void processAmountEntry(ATMMachine atmMachine, BigDecimal amount
    ) {
    renderDefaultAction(atmMachine);
  }

  // Default implementation for deposit collection
  public void processDepositCollection(ATMMachine atmMachine, BigDecimal
    amount) {
    renderDefaultAction(atmMachine);
  }
```

```
}
```

The `IdleState` waits for the user to insert a card and start the session, supporting only card insertion. If the card is valid, it transitions to `PinEntryState`. Otherwise, it displays an error.

```java
public class IdleState extends ATMState {
  /**
   * This method is called when a card is inserted into the ATM.
   * This transitions the ATM to the PinEntryState if the card is valid.
   */
  @Override
  public void processCardInsertion(ATMMachine atmMachine, String
    cardNumber) {
    if (atmMachine.getBankInterface().validateCard(cardNumber)) {
      atmMachine.getDisplay().showMessage("Please enter your PIN");
      atmMachine.transitionToState(new PinEntryState());
    } else {
      atmMachine.getDisplay().showMessage("Invalid card. Please try again
    .");
    }
  }
}
```

The `EnterWithdrawalAmountState` manages the step where the user enters a withdrawal amount, coordinating with the `ATMMachine` to execute the withdrawal via the Bank, using a `WithdrawTransaction` to validate funds and update the account balance.

```java
public class WithdrawAmountEntryState extends ATMState {
  // Handles card ejection by canceling transaction and returning to idle
    state
  @Override
  public void processCardEjection(ATMMachine atmMachine) {
    atmMachine.getDisplay().showMessage("Transaction cancelled, card
    ejected");
    atmMachine.transitionToState(new IdleState());
  }

  // Processes withdrawal request by checking balance and dispensing cash
    if sufficient funds
  @Override
  public void processAmountEntry(ATMMachine atmMachine, BigDecimal amount
    ) {
    String cardNumber = atmMachine.getCardProcessor().getCardNumber();
    Account account = atmMachine.getBankInterface().getAccountByCard(
    cardNumber);
    boolean isSuccess = atmMachine.getBankInterface().withdrawFunds(
    account, amount);
```

```
    if (isSuccess) {
      atmMachine.getCashDispenser().dispenseCash(amount);
      atmMachine.getDisplay().showMessage("Please take your cash.");
    } else {
      atmMachine.getDisplay().showMessage("Insufficient funds, please try
    again.");
    }
    atmMachine.transitionToState(new TransactionSelectionState());
  }
}
```

For brevity, we have omitted the code for the PinEntryState, TransactionSelectionState, and DepositCollectionState classes. The complete code for all state classes is available in the accompanying materials of this book.

ATMMachine

The ATMMachine class acts as the central controller of the ATM system, applying the Facade pattern to offer a simplified interface to the underlying complexities. It manages the ATM's hardware components, delegates state-specific behavior to corresponding ATMState classes such as IdleState and DepositCollectionState, and utilizes the BankInterface to perform banking operations.

Here is the implementation of this class.

```
// Main ATM machine class that manages the state and hardware components
    of the ATM
public class ATMMachine {
  private ATMState state;

  private final CardProcessor cardProcessor;
  private final DepositBox depositBox;
  private final CashDispenser cashDispenser;
  private final Keypad keypad;
  private final Display display;

  private final Bank bank;

  // Initializes ATM with all required hardware components and bank
    interface
  public ATMMachine(Bank bank, CardProcessor cardProcessor, DepositBox
    depositBox, CashDispenser cashDispenser, Keypad keypad, Display
    display) {
    this.bank = bank;
    this.cardProcessor = cardProcessor;
    this.depositBox = depositBox;
    this.cashDispenser = cashDispenser;
    this.keypad = keypad;
    this.display = display;
```

```java
    this.state = new IdleState();
  }

  // Forwards card insertion to current state for processing
  public void insertCard(String cardNumber) {
    state.processCardInsertion(this, cardNumber);
  }

  // Forwards card ejection to current state for processing
  public void ejectCard() {
    state.processCardEjection(this);
  }

  // Forwards PIN entry to current state for validation
  public void enterPin(String pin) {
    state.processPinEntry(this, pin);
  }

  // Forwards withdrawal request to current state for processing
  public void withdrawRequest() {
    state.processWithdrawalRequest(this);
  }

  // Forwards deposit request to current state for processing
  public void depositRequest() {
    state.processDepositRequest(this);
  }

  // Forwards amount entry to current state for processing
  public void enterAmount(BigDecimal amount) {
    state.processAmountEntry(this, amount);
  }

  // Forwards deposit collection to current state for processing
  public void collectDeposit(BigDecimal amount) {
    state.processDepositCollection(this, amount);
  }

  // Returns the display component for showing messages
  public Display getDisplay() {
    return display;
  }

  // Returns the cash dispenser component for handling withdrawals
  public CashDispenser getCashDispenser() {
    return cashDispenser;
  }

  // Returns the bank interface for account operations
  public BankInterface getBankInterface() {
```

```java
    return bank;
  }

  // Returns the card processor component for handling card operations
  public CardProcessor getCardProcessor() {
    return cardProcessor;
  }

  // Returns the keypad component for user input
  public Keypad getKeypad() {
    return keypad;
  }

  // Updates the current state of the ATM
  public void transitionToState(ATMState nextState) {
    this.state = nextState;
  }

  // Returns the current state of the ATM
  public ATMState getCurrentState() {
    return state;
  }

  // Returns the deposit box component for handling deposits
  public DepositBox getDepositBox() {
    return depositBox;
  }
}
```

Hardware management:

- The `ATMMachine` class manages all hardware components, including the card processor, cash dispenser, deposit box, keypad, and display, to enable user interactions.
- It provides access to these hardware components through getter methods like `getCard-Processor` and `getDisplay` for use by state classes.

State management:

- The `ATMMachine` class maintains the current state of the ATM using a state field to track the active stage of the user flow.
- It provides state transition functionality through the `setState` method, allowing the ATM to move between stages like `IdleState` and `PinEntryState`.

Wrap Up

With the ATM system fully implemented, it's time to step back and consider what we've achieved. This chapter began by gathering requirements through a structured dialogue, then progressed to defining core objects like accounts and transactions, designing their class structure, and coding the essential components, including the state machine and hardware interactions.

The system's maintainability and extensibility are ensured by the clear division of responsibilities among the classes: Account and Bank manage account data and banking operations, Transaction handles financial operations, `ATMState` and its state classes (`IdleState`, `PinEntryState`, etc.) manage the user flow stages, hardware interfaces (`Keypad`, `CardProcessor`, etc.) handle user interactions, and `ATMMachine` orchestrates the entire flow as a facade. Our choices, such as using the state pattern with `ATMState` and separating hardware interactions into interfaces, improve modularity and allow future extensions, like adding new transaction types or hardware components.

Congratulations on getting this far! Now give yourself a pat on the back. Good job!

14

Restaurant Management System

In this chapter, we will explore the design of a Restaurant Management System. The goal is to create classes that represent the system's essential components, such as menus, reservations, and tables. We will develop a system that supports critical functions like booking reservations, managing orders, and assigning tables, ensuring the design is both straightforward and flexible for future enhancements.

Restaurant reservation

Requirements Gathering

The first step in designing a Restaurant Management System is to clarify the requirements and define the scope. Here's an example of a typical prompt an interviewer might present:

"Picture yourself planning a dinner outing on a Friday night. You call the restaurant to reserve a table for your group, check available times, and secure a spot. When you arrive, the staff assigns your party to the reserved table, takes your order, and later presents the bill. Behind the scenes, the system is smoothly handling table reservations, tracking orders, and calculating costs. Now, let's design a Restaurant Management System that manages all of this."

Requirements clarification

Here is an example of how a conversation between a candidate and an interviewer might unfold:

Candidate: Let's start by setting the scope. I assume the system manages reservations, menu, order tracking, and payments. For now, I focus on reservations and order management. Does that work?
Interviewer: That's a reasonable starting point

Candidate: Does the system allow customers to make and manage their reservations?
Interviewer: Yes, customers can book tables for a future date and time based on availability.

Candidate: How does the system determine if a table is available for a reservation?
Interviewer: It checks for a table that fits the party size and is free at the requested time. Each reservation reserves a table for exactly one hour, so it's available if no other booking overlaps with that hour.

Candidate: Does the system let customers cancel a reservation after making it?
Interviewer: Yes, customers can cancel reservations.

Candidate: When a party with a reservation arrives, do they automatically get their reserved table?
Interviewer: Yes, they do. They arrive with their name, and the system uses it to find their reservation, which already has a table assigned to it.

Candidate: What happens when a walk-in party arrives for dine-in without prior reservation?
Interviewer: The system should assign walk-in parties to tables based on current availability and their party size.

Candidate: Does the system allow orders to be altered or removed after they're placed?
Interviewer: Yes, you can remove items or adjust their quantities.

Candidate: Does the system track the status of orders?
Interviewer: Yes, it keeps track of their progress.

Candidate: Are there rules for splitting the bill at checkout?
Interviewer: For now, just present a single total bill amount.

Requirements

Based on the questions and answers, we can now list the functional requirements for our restaurant management system.

Reservations

- Customers can book tables for a future date and time based on availability.
- Each reservation reserves a table for exactly one hour.
- The system checks if a table is free at the requested time with no overlapping bookings.
- The system assigns a table to a reservation, and customers get it when they arrive using their name.
- Customers can cancel reservations.

Walk-in seating

- The system assigns walk-in parties to tables based on current availability and party size.

Order management

- The system allows orders to be altered or removed after they're placed.
- The system tracks the progress of orders.

Billing

- The system presents a single total bill amount at checkout.

Below are the non-functional requirements:

- The system should handle increased traffic during busy periods (e.g., weekend evenings) without performance degradation, supporting concurrent users seamlessly.

With these requirements, we are ready to model the objects for the core system.

Identify Core Objects

Let's identify the core objects of the restaurant management system.

- **Menu:** Represents the restaurant's menu, storing a collection of available items for ordering.
- **MenuItem:** This object models an individual item on the menu, encapsulating details such as its name and price. Each MenuItem is a building block of the Menu, used when staff place orders for a table.
- **Layout:** This object represents the restaurant's physical arrangement, organizing all tables efficiently to support quick and effective assignment for both walk-ins and reser-

vations.

- **Table:** This object models an individual table in the restaurant, holding details such as its capacity, current reservations, and active orders.

- **Reservation:** This object represents a single reservation, storing details like the party name, party size, and reserved time, along with the assigned table.

- **ReservationManager:** This object oversees all restaurant reservations, managing their creation, lookup, and cancellation to ensure accurate and efficient booking. It checks table availability for free time slots and works with Layout to assign tables, keeping reservations well-scheduled and tracked.

- **Restaurant:** This acts as a facade, providing a central interface to manage the system's key functionalities: reservations, table assignments, orders, and bill calculations. We keep its logic lightweight by delegating tasks like scheduling reservations to **Reservat-ionManager**, assigning tables to Layout, and managing orders to Table, ensuring it coordinates actions without performing the underlying operations itself.

Design Class Diagram

You're set to dive into the heart of the object-oriented design interview: crafting classes and interfaces, shaping data and state through attributes, wrapping logic in methods, and linking your classes with clear relationships.

Below, we detail each class, its purpose, and its responsibilities, ensuring a clear separation of concerns.

Menu

The Menu class represents the restaurant's menu, storing menu items in a map with names as keys to quickly retrieve them for ordering. It separates menu data from the Restaurant and Table classes, enabling Table to order items by holding a collection of **MenuItem** objects that list all available choices.

Below is the representation of this class.

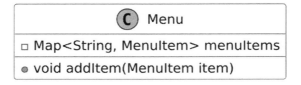

MenuItem

The **MenuItem** defines each item on the menu, holding its name, description, price, and category for use in orders. The Menu class uses these items to provide the list of choices, and the Table class records them as ordered items for order management and updates. The

Category enum assigns each item a type, such as main course, appetizer, or dessert, to group them on the menu.

The UML diagram below illustrates this structure.

MenuItem class and Category enum

Table

The Table class models restaurant tables. Some of the attributes, like capacity and tableId, rarely change. But other attributes, like reservations and orderedItems, associated with the table represent current-state data that changes over time.

Its purpose is to oversee a table's current use, tying into the Layout class for availability checks and the OrderItem class to handle what's being served. It includes methods to add or remove orders, tally up bills, and check availability at specific times.

Here is the representation of this class.

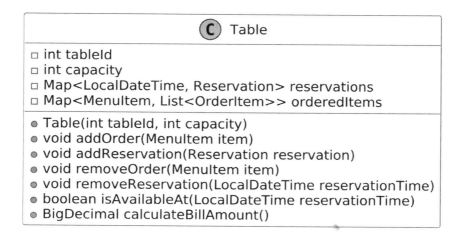

Layout

The Layout class oversees all restaurant tables, organizing them by ID and capacity to pinpoint the right one for each booking. Its purpose is to streamline table assignments, working with ReservationManager to match parties to available tables and relying on Table to confirm free slots. It handles this by finding a table that fits the party size and is available at the requested time, keeping the process efficient.

> ✂ **Design choice:** We isolate table organization in the Layout class to optimize assignment efficiency and separate it from menu and order logic managed by the Menu and Table classes. Alternatively, integrating table assignment into the Restaurant class could simplify the design but would overburden its facade role, mixing high-level coordination with low-level table management.

Below is the representation of the Layout class.

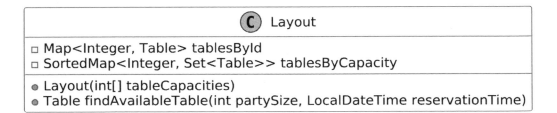

OrderItem

The OrderItem class represents each item a customer orders, linking it to a specific MenuItem to provide details like price for the Table class. Its purpose is to track the status of ordered items, allowing the Table class to calculate costs accurately and add or remove items as requested. The class is created when customers place orders, using the Status enum, set to values like pending or delivered, to indicate the item's current state.

The UML diagram below illustrates this structure.

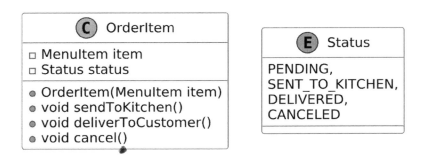

OrderItem class and Status enum

ReservationManager

The ReservationManager class handles reservation scheduling by finding available times, creating reservations, and processing cancellations. It stores all Reservation objects and uses a reference to the Layout class to manage table assignments. This reference enables the class to verify table availability and assign suitable tables for each reservation based on party size and time.

Below is the representation of this class.

Reservation

The Reservation class represents a single booking managed by the ReservationManager class, storing the party name, number of people, reservation time, and assigned table. It serves to hold all details of a reservation, enabling the ReservationManager class to schedule and cancel bookings effectively.

The class is contained within ReservationManager as one of its entries, maintaining a structured and accessible set of reservation data.

Restaurant

The Restaurant class serves as the primary interface and facade for the restaurant management system. It coordinates core user-facing operations, such as managing reservations, assigning tables, processing orders, and handling checkout.

It simplifies access to these features by delegating tasks to other classes:

- The class relies on ReservationManager to schedule and cancel reservations.

- The class uses Layout through `ReservationManager` to identify available tables for assignments.
- The class depends on Menu to supply items for orders.
- The class directs order and billing actions to the Table for processing.

This delegation keeps the Restaurant class focused and manageable, organizing the system into distinct components that ensure clarity and ease of maintenance through a structured use of composition.

> **Design choice:** We structure the Restaurant as a facade to unify system operations, delegating tasks to maintain a clean interface and modularity. We can design the Restaurant class as a central controller managing all logic internally, but that would increase its complexity and reduce scalability by centralizing responsibilities.

Below is the representation of this class.

Ⓒ Restaurant

□ String name
□ Menu menu
□ Layout layout
□ ReservationManager reservationManager

● LocalDateTime[] findAvailableTimeSlots(
  LocalDateTime rangeStart, LocalDateTime rangeEnd, int partySize)
● Reservation createScheduledReservation(String partyName,
  int partySize, LocalDateTime time)
● Reservation createWalkInReservation(String partyName, int partySize)
● void removeReservation(String partyName, int partySize,
  LocalDateTime reservationTime)
● void orderItem(Table table, MenuItem item, int quantity)
● void cancelItem(Table table, MenuItem item, int quantity)
● BigDecimal calculateTableBill(Table table)

Next, we'll connect these objects in a class diagram to visualize their relationships.

Complete Class Diagram

Below is the complete class diagram of our restaurant management system:

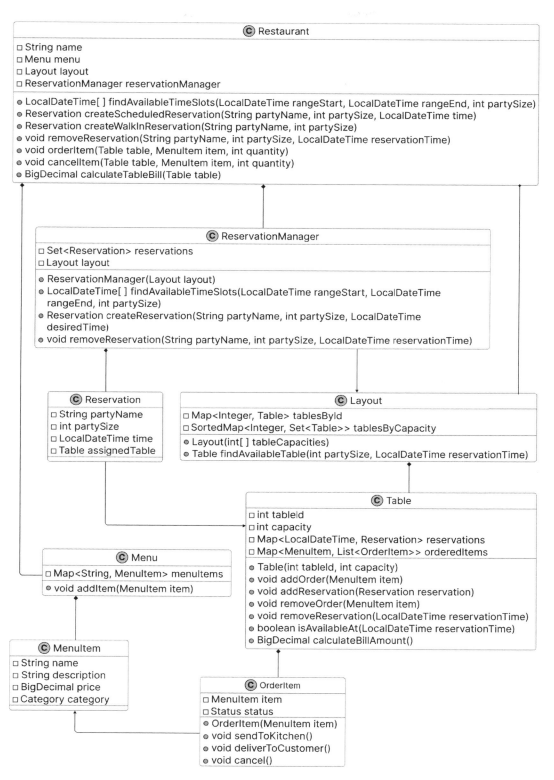

Class Diagram of Restaurant Management System

With this structure in place, let's move on to implement the code that brings this design to life.

Code - Restaurant Management System

In this section, we'll implement the core functionalities of the Restaurant Management System, focusing on key areas such as managing menu items, scheduling and canceling reservations, assigning tables for bookings and walk-ins, and processing orders with billing through a table-based system.

Menu

The Menu class manages the restaurant's menu by storing MenuItem objects in a HashMap, using each item's name as the key to enable fast retrieval for order processing. It provides methods to add an item with addItem, retrieve a specific item using getItem, and access the full menu through getMenuItems as a read-only view.

Implementation choice: We selected HashMap to store MenuItem objects for its quick lookup performance through key-based access, ensuring efficient retrieval for the Table class during order processing, whereas a List alternative, while simpler for storage, requires a linear search that slows access time.

The definition of the Menu class is given below.

```
public class Menu {
  private final Map<String, MenuItem> menuItems = new HashMap<>();

  // Adds a new item to the menu
  public void addItem(MenuItem item) {
    menuItems.put(item.getName(), item);
  }

  public MenuItem getItem(String name) {
    return menuItems.get(name);
  }

  public Map<String, MenuItem> getMenuItems() {
    return Collections.unmodifiableMap(menuItems);
  }
}
```

With the Menu defined, let's detail its individual items in MenuItem.

MenuItem

The MenuItem class represents an individual item on the menu, storing its name, description, price, and category as private final fields to ensure immutability. This class uses BigDecimal for the price field instead of a floating-point type like float or double. BigDecimal is better suited for financial data, as it provides precise control over decimal values and helps avoid rounding errors or precision issues that can arise with floating-point calculations.

```java
// Represents a single item available on the restaurant menu
public class MenuItem {
  private final String name;
  private final String description;
  private final BigDecimal price;
  private final Category category;

  public MenuItem(String name, String description, BigDecimal price,
    Category category) {
    this.name = name;
    this.description = description;
    this.price = price;
    this.category = category;
  }

  // Enumeration of possible menu item categories
  public enum Category {
    MAIN,
    APPETIZER,
    DESSERT
  }

  // getter methods are omitted for brevity
}
```

Having established the menu's contents, let's model the restaurant's tables with `Table`.

Table

The `Table` class represents a restaurant table, storing its fixed properties, such as `tableId` and `capacity`, while maintaining its bookings and orders by updating reservations and `orderedItems`. Its purpose is to manage a table's reservations and orders, using Layout to confirm available time slots and `OrderItem` to provide price and status details.

Below is the implementation of this class.

```java
// Represents a table in the restaurant with its properties and current
    state
public class Table {
  // immutable properties
  private final int tableId;
  private final int capacity;

  // current state
  private final Map<LocalDateTime, Reservation> reservations = new
    HashMap<>();
  private final Map<MenuItem, List<OrderItem>> orderedItems = new HashMap
```

```java
      <>();

  public Table(int tableId, int capacity) {
    this.tableId = tableId;
    this.capacity = capacity;
  }

  // Calculates the total bill amount for all ordered items at this table
  public BigDecimal calculateBillAmount() {
    return orderedItems.values().stream()
    .flatMap(List::stream)
    .map(OrderItem::getItem)
    .map(MenuItem::getPrice)
    .reduce(BigDecimal.ZERO, BigDecimal::add);
  }

  // Adds multiple orders of the same menu item to the table
  public void addOrder(MenuItem item, int quantity) {
    for (int i = 0; i < quantity; i++) {
      addOrder(item);
    }
  }

  // Adds a single menu item to the table's order
  public void addOrder(MenuItem item) {
    List<OrderItem> orderItems = orderedItems.get(item);
    if (orderItems == null) {
      orderItems = new ArrayList<>();
      orderedItems.put(item, orderItems);
      orderItems.add(new OrderItem(item));
    } else {
      orderItems.add(new OrderItem(item));
    }
  }

  // Removes a menu item from the table's order
  public void removeOrder(MenuItem item) {
    List<OrderItem> orderItems = orderedItems.get(item);
    if (orderItems != null) {
      orderItems.remove(0);
      if (orderItems.isEmpty()) {
        orderedItems.remove(item);
      }
    }
  }

  // Checks if the table is available at a specific time
  public boolean isAvailableAt(LocalDateTime reservationTime) {
    return !reservations.containsKey(reservationTime);
  }
```

```
  // Adds a reservation to this table
  public void addReservation(Reservation reservation) {
    reservations.put(reservation.getTime(), reservation);
  }

  // Removes a reservation from this table for a specific time
  public void removeReservation(LocalDateTime reservationTime) {
    reservations.remove(reservationTime);
  }

  // getter methods are omitted for brevity
}
```

The class uses a Map with reservation times as keys to store reservations. This setup enables quick availability checks through the isAvailableAt method. It also uses a separate Map with MenuItem keys to manage orderedItems. This structure supports the addOrder method to include items, the removeOrder method to remove them, and the calculateBillAmount method for billing.

With tables in place, let's organize them efficiently using Layout.

Layout

The Layout class represents the seating arrangement of the entire restaurant, managing all tables to support efficient assignments for reservations and walk-ins. It organizes tables using two indexing methods:

- **Tables by ID:** Stored in a Map (tablesById) with each table's ID as the key. This method allows fast retrieval of a table by its unique identifier during operations.
- **Tables by capacity:** Stored in a SortedMap (tablesByCapacity) where each capacity level maps to a set of tables with that capacity. This method enables the findAvailableTable method to locate the smallest available table that fits a party's size quickly.

Below is the implementation of this class.

```
// Manages the collection of tables in the restaurant and their
    arrangement
public class Layout {
  private final Map<Integer, Table> tablesById = new HashMap<>();
  // Groups tables by their capacity for efficient table assignment,
    sorted from smallest to largest capacity
  private final SortedMap<Integer, Set<Table>> tablesByCapacity = new
    TreeMap<>();

  public Layout(List<Integer> tableCapacities) {
    for (int i = 0; i < tableCapacities.size(); i++) {
      int capacity = tableCapacities.get(i);
```

```
      Table table = new Table(i, capacity);
      tablesById.put(i, table);
      tablesByCapacity.computeIfAbsent(capacity, k -> new HashSet<>()).
    add(table);
    }
  }

  // Finds the smallest available table that can accommodate a party of
    the given size at the given time
  public Table findAvailableTable(int partySize, LocalDateTime
    reservationTime) {
    for (Set<Table> tables : tablesByCapacity.tailMap(partySize).values()
    ) {
      for (Table table : tables) {
        if (table.isAvailableAt(reservationTime)) {
          return table;
        }
      }
    }
    return null;
  }
}
```

Implementation choice: We chose SortedMap structures for tablesByCapacity. This structure provides sorted key access that supports efficient range searches by capacity. This efficiency is crucial for the findAvailableTable method to match tables to party sizes. A basic Map lacks sorting capability. It would require additional logic to identify the smallest suitable table, making it less efficient.

Now that tables are arranged, let's manage individual order items with OrderItem.

OrderItem

The OrderItem class defines each item ordered by a customer, storing a reference to a specific MenuItem and maintaining its current status to track its state during order processing.

The class includes methods to update the order's state:

- **sendToKitchen** changes the status from PENDING to SENT_TO_KITCHEN
- **deliverToCustomer** updates it from SENT_TO_KITCHEN to DELIVERED
- **cancel** sets it to CANCELED if not yet delivered

```
// Represents a food item ordered by a customer with its current status
    in the order process
public class OrderItem {
  private final MenuItem item;
  private Status status = Status.PENDING;
```

```java
  public OrderItem(MenuItem item) {
    this.item = item;
  }

  // Updates the status to indicate the item has been sent to the kitchen
  public void sendToKitchen() {
    if (status == Status.PENDING) status = Status.SENT_TO_KITCHEN;
  }

  // Updates the status to indicate the item has been delivered to the
    customer
  public void deliverToCustomer() {
    if (status == Status.SENT_TO_KITCHEN) status = Status.DELIVERED;
  }

  // Updates the status to indicate the item has been canceled
  public void cancel() {
    if (status == Status.PENDING || status == Status.SENT_TO_KITCHEN) {
      status = Status.CANCELED;
      System.out.println(item.getName() + " has been canceled.");
    }
  }

  // getter methods are omitted for brevity
}
```

With orders tracked, let's oversee reservations through `ReservationManager`.

ReservationManager

The `ReservationManager` class oversees all reservations in the restaurant, managing their scheduling, creation, and cancellation to ensure tables are assigned accurately. It serves as a central coordinator, connecting to the Layout class to locate available tables and storing Reservation objects to maintain booking details.

Here is the implementation of this class.

```java
// Manages all reservations for the restaurant and handles table
   assignments
public class ReservationManager {
  private final Layout layout;
  private final Set<Reservation> reservations = new HashSet<>();

  // Constructor that takes the restaurant's table layout
  public ReservationManager(Layout layout) {
    this.layout = layout;
  }

  // Finds potential time slots for a reservation within the given time
    range and party size
```

```java
public LocalDateTime[] findAvailableTimeSlots(LocalDateTime rangeStart,
    LocalDateTime rangeEnd, int partySize) {
  // checking every hour in the time range
  LocalDateTime current = rangeStart;
  List<LocalDateTime> possibleReservations = new ArrayList<>();
  while (!current.isAfter(rangeEnd)) {
    Table availableTable = layout.findAvailableTable(partySize, current
);
    if (availableTable != null) {
      possibleReservations.add(current);
    }
    current = current.plusHours(1);
  }
  return possibleReservations.toArray(new LocalDateTime[0]);
}

// Creates a reservation for a specific time, party size and name
public Reservation createReservation(String partyName, int partySize,
  LocalDateTime desiredTime) {
  desiredTime = desiredTime.truncatedTo(ChronoUnit.HOURS);
  Table table = layout.findAvailableTable(partySize, desiredTime);
  Reservation reservation = new Reservation(partyName, partySize,
  desiredTime, table);
  table.addReservation(reservation);
  reservations.add(reservation);
  return reservation;
}

// Removes an existing reservation
public void removeReservation(String partyName, int partySize,
  LocalDateTime reservationTime) {
  // Find matching reservation before removing it
  for (Reservation reservation : new HashSet<>(reservations)) {
    if (reservation.getTime().equals(reservationTime) &&
    reservation.getPartySize() == partySize &&
    reservation.getPartyName().equals(partyName)) {
      // Clear the reservation from the table first
      Table table = reservation.getAssignedTable();
      table.removeReservation(reservationTime);
      // Then remove from the reservation collection
      reservations.remove(reservation);
      return;
    }
  }
}

// getter methods are omitted for brevity
}
```

- **findAvailableTimeSlots:** This method identifies available reservation times within a specified range. It examines each hour in the range, assuming a one-hour duration per reservation.

- **createReservation:** This method creates a reservation for a given time, party size, and party name. It uses Layout.findAvailableTable to confirm a table's availability. If a table is found, it generates a new Reservation object, adds it to the reservations set, and updates the table's booking status.

- **removeReservation:** This method cancels a reservation based on its time, party size, and party name. It searches the reservations set to locate the matching entry, removes it, and clears the table's booking if found.

Implementation choice: We chose a Set to store Reservation objects because its unique entry enforcement prevents duplicate bookings, aligning with the need to manage reservations accurately. An alternative could use a List, which allows simpler iteration but risks duplicates unless additional checks are added, or a Map with time-based keys, which could speed up lookups but complicate removal by requiring keys that combine multiple fields, like time, party size, and name, less suited for the system's focus on reservation uniqueness.

Next, let's define the reservation entries with Reservation.

Reservation

The Reservation class is a simple, immutable entity class that stores essential reservation details, including the party name, number of people, reservation time, and assigned table. It serves as the foundational unit for the ReservationManager class, holding the data needed to manage bookings effectively.

```
// Represents a reservation made at the restaurant for a specific party,
    time and table
public class Reservation {
  private final String partyName;
  private final int partySize;
  private final LocalDateTime time;
  private final Table assignedTable;

  public Reservation(String partyName, int partySize, LocalDateTime time,
    Table assignedTable) {
    this.partyName = partyName;
    this.partySize = partySize;
    this.time = time;
    this.assignedTable = assignedTable;
  }

  // getter methods are omitted for brevity
}
```

Finally, let's unify these components in the Restaurant.

Restaurant

The `Restaurant` class acts as the central interface for the restaurant management system, offering methods to book reservations, seat walk-in parties, place orders, and compute bills. It follows the facade design pattern to unify these features, delegating reservation and walk-in seating tasks to `ReservationManager`, which uses Layout to find available tables, order placement, and billing to Table, which uses Menu to access items.

Below is the implementation of this class.

```java
// Main restaurant class that manages reservations, orders, and tables
public class Restaurant {
  private final String name;
  private final Menu menu;
  private final Layout layout;
  private final ReservationManager reservationManager;

  public Restaurant(String name, Menu menu, Layout layout) {
    this.name = name;
    this.menu = menu;
    this.layout = layout;
    this.reservationManager = new ReservationManager(layout);
  }

  // Finds possible reservation times within a time range for a party of
    specified size
  public LocalDateTime[] findAvailableTimeSlots(LocalDateTime rangeStart,
    LocalDateTime rangeEnd, int partySize) {
    return reservationManager.findAvailableTimeSlots(rangeStart, rangeEnd
    , partySize);
  }

  // Creates a reservation for a party at the specified time
  public Reservation createScheduledReservation(String partyName, int
    partySize, LocalDateTime time) {
    return reservationManager.createReservation(partyName, partySize,
    time);
  }

  // Removes an existing reservation
  public void removeReservation(String partyName, int partySize,
    LocalDateTime reservationTime) {
    reservationManager.removeReservation(partyName, partySize,
    reservationTime);
  }

  // Creates a reservation for a party without prior reservation
  public Reservation createWalkInReservation(String partyName, int
    partySize) {
    return reservationManager.createReservation(partyName, partySize,
```

```
    LocalDateTime.now());
  }

  // Adds an item to a table's order
  public void orderItem(Table table, MenuItem item) {
    table.addOrder(item);
  }

  // Removes an item from a table's order
  public void cancelItem(Table table, MenuItem item) {
    table.removeOrder(item);
  }

  // Calculates the bill amount for a table
  public BigDecimal calculateTableBill(Table table) {
    return table.calculateBillAmount();
  }

  // getter methods are omitted for brevity
}
```

- **Reservation methods:** The Restaurant class includes findAvailableTimeSlots to list available times, createScheduledReservation to book reservations, and removeReservation to cancel them, each delegating to ReservationManager for scheduling and management.

- **Walk-in seating:** The createWalkInReservation method assigns tables to walk-in parties, delegating to ReservationManager, which uses Layout to locate available tables.

- **Order management:** The orderItem method adds items to a table's order, and cancelItem removes them, both delegating to Table methods addOrder and removeOrder for order processing.

- **Checkout:** The calculateTableBill method computes a table's total cost, delegating to Table.calculateBillAmount for billing calculations.

Implementation choice: We designed the Restaurant as a facade without its data structures. It delegates all operations to Menu, Layout, ReservationManager, and Table. This approach maintains a lightweight structure that simplifies system access. An alternative could have Restaurant store reservations or orders internally using a Map or List. That design would increase complexity and reduce modularity by centralizing responsibilities.

Having built the core system, let's explore an enhancement in the deep dive to extend its capabilities.

Deep Dive Topics

In this section, we'll explore an enhancement to the Restaurant Management System by improving order handling during peak times. We'll focus on adding a centralized order queue tracking mechanism to streamline kitchen coordination, ensure scalability, and maintain consistency with the system's modular design.

Order queue tracking

Consider a high-traffic scenario, such as a busy Friday evening at the restaurant, where a significant volume of orders is received, staff work diligently to communicate these to the kitchen, and cancellations accumulate. In the existing system, the `Table` class directly governs the status of `OrderItem` instances (e.g., through methods like `sendToKitchen()` and `deliverToCustomer()`). However, this decentralized structure lacks a cohesive overview of order progression across all tables. Consequently, staff face challenges in prioritizing time-sensitive orders, monitoring kitchen delays, or verifying cancellations without individually inspecting each table's state. This approach introduces risks of inconsistency and undermines effective coordination during periods of elevated demand.

To address these limitations, we propose an enhancement by introducing a centralized `OrderManager` class responsible for queuing and processing order-related actions. Let's take a closer look.

Implementation steps:

To implement this enhancement effectively, we'll follow these steps:

Step 1: Define a command interface for order actions: The staff needs a consistent way to issue actions like sending an order to the kitchen or canceling it, improving reliability over direct calls. We define an interface called `OrderCommand` with a single method, `execute()`, which concrete classes will implement to perform their tasks.

Here's the code for the `OrderCommand` interface:

```
public interface OrderCommand {
  void execute();
}
```

Step 2: Implement concrete command classes: To give staff a flexible way to manage distinct order actions and prepare them for centralized queuing, we build specific classes for each task, unlike the original system, where Table directly updated `OrderItem` statuses.

- The `SendToKitchenCommand` class takes an `OrderItem` and, when executed, calls `sendToKitchen()` to update its status to `SENT_TO_KITCHEN`.
- The `DeliverCommand` class uses `deliverToCustomer()` to change the `OrderItem`'s status to `DELIVERED`, signaling completion.

- The `CancelCommand` class invokes `cancel()` to set the status to CANCELED if the item hasn't been delivered, marking it as voided.

Here's the code for the action classes:

```java
// Command that handles sending order items to the Kitchen
public class SendToKitchenCommand implements OrderCommand {
  private final OrderItem orderItem;

  public SendToKitchenCommand(OrderItem orderItem) {
    this.orderItem = orderItem;
  }

  @Override
  public void execute() {
    orderItem.sendToKitchen();
    System.out.println(orderItem.getItem().getName() + " has been sent to
    kitchen.");
  }
}

// Command that handles delivery of order items
public class DeliverCommand implements OrderCommand {
  private final OrderItem orderItem;

  public DeliverCommand(OrderItem orderItem) {
    this.orderItem = orderItem;
  }

  @Override
  public void execute() {
    orderItem.deliverToCustomer();
  }
}

// Command that handles cancellations of order items
public class CancelCommand implements OrderCommand {
  private final OrderItem orderItem;

  public CancelCommand(OrderItem orderItem) {
    this.orderItem = orderItem;
  }

  @Override
  public void execute() {
    orderItem.cancel();
  }
}
```

Step 3: Introduce the OrderManager class: To handle these actions efficiently, we introduce an OrderManager class. This class maintains a list of OrderCommand objects, allowing us to add commands with addCommand() as orders are placed. The executeCommands() method processes all queued commands in sequence and clears the list afterward, ensuring orders are managed in an organized way without directly altering the Table's OrderItems.

Here's the code for the OrderManager class:

```java
public class OrderManager {
  private final List<OrderCommand> commandQueue = new ArrayList<>();

  // Adds a command to the queue for later execution
  public void addCommand(OrderCommand command) {
    commandQueue.add(command);
  }

  // Executes all commands in the queue and clears it
  public void executeCommands() {
    for (OrderCommand command : commandQueue) {
      command.execute();
    }
    commandQueue.clear();
  }
}
```

Step 4: Integrate with the Restaurant class: To connect this system to staff actions, we update the Restaurant class to use OrderManager for order handling. When staff place an order, orderItem adds it to the table and queues a SendToKitchenCommand to send it to the kitchen. Similarly, cancelItem and deliverItem queue their respective commands, ensuring all actions flow through the centralized system for consistent tracking and execution.

Here's the essential code for integrating OrderManager into the Restaurant:

```java
public class Restaurant {
  // ... fields unchanged ...
  private final OrderManager orderManager;

  public Restaurant(String name, Menu menu, Layout layout) {
    // ... fields unchanged ...
    this.orderManager = new OrderManager();
  }

  // Adds an item to a table's order and sends it to the kitchen
  public void orderItem(Table table, MenuItem item) {
    table.addOrder(item);
    // Get the last added order item
    List<OrderItem> orderItems = table.getOrderedItems().get(item);
    if (orderItems != null && !orderItems.isEmpty()) {
      OrderItem lastOrder = orderItems.get(orderItems.size() - 1);
```

```
    OrderCommand sendToKitchen = new SendToKitchenCommand(lastOrder);
    orderManager.addCommand(sendToKitchen);
    orderManager.executeCommands();
  }
}

// Removes an item from a table's order and cancels it
public void cancelItem(Table table, MenuItem item) {
  List<OrderItem> orderItems = table.getOrderedItems().get(item);
  if (orderItems != null && !orderItems.isEmpty()) {
    OrderItem lastOrder = orderItems.get(orderItems.size() - 1);
    OrderCommand cancelOrder = new CancelCommand(lastOrder);
    orderManager.addCommand(cancelOrder);
    orderManager.executeCommands();
    table.removeOrder(item);
  }
}

// Delivers an item to the customer
public void deliverItem(Table table, MenuItem item) {
  List<OrderItem> orderItems = table.getOrderedItems().get(item);
  if (orderItems != null && !orderItems.isEmpty()) {
    OrderItem lastOrder = orderItems.get(orderItems.size() - 1);
    OrderCommand deliverOrder = new DeliverCommand(lastOrder);
    orderManager.addCommand(deliverOrder);
    orderManager.executeCommands();
  }
}

// ... other methods unchanged ...
}
```

What we've just implemented follows a well-known software design pattern called the **Command Pattern**.

> 📖 **Definition:** The Command is a behavioral design pattern that encapsulates a request as an independent object, containing all the details needed to carry it out. This encapsulation allows you to treat requests as parameters for methods, delay or schedule their execution.

In this pattern:

- **Command:** The OrderCommand interface and its implementations (SendToKitchenCommand, DeliverCommand, CancelCommand) define each action as an object, executed via execute().
- **Invoker:** The OrderManager class queues these command objects and triggers their

execution, decoupling the Table from direct state changes.

- **Receiver:** The `OrderItem` class, with its existing `Status` enum and methods like `sendToKitchen`, receives and processes the commands, updating its state to reflect actions like preparation or delivery.

The UML diagram below illustrates this structure.

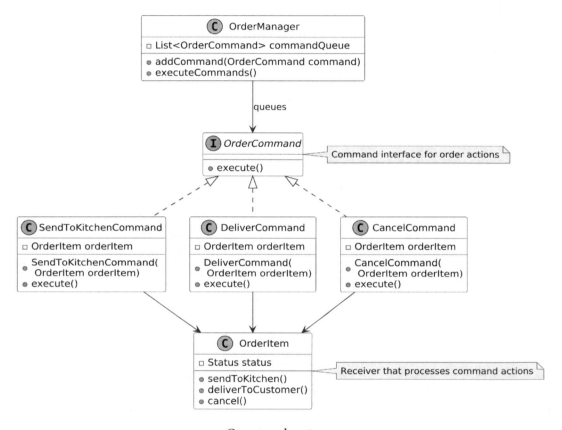

Command pattern

With our restaurant management system designed and implemented, let's wrap up with key takeaways.

Wrap Up

In this chapter, we gathered requirements for the Restaurant Management System through a series of detailed questions and answers. We then identified the core objects involved, designed the class structure, and implemented the key components of the system.

A key takeaway from this design is the importance of modularity and adherence to the single responsibility principle. Each component, such as the Menu, `ReservationManager`, Layout, and Table classes, manages a distinct responsibility, ensuring the system remains maintainable and adaptable for future enhancements.

Our design choices, such as delegating operations in the Restaurant to act as a facade or using immutable `MenuItem` objects, prioritize flexibility and consistency. An alternative, like implementing reservation and order logic directly in the Restaurant class, may simplify the design but could increase complexity and reduce scalability by centralizing responsibilities. In an interview, revisiting these decisions and explaining their rationale demonstrates your ability to think critically about system design.

Congratulations on getting this far! Now give yourself a pat on the back. Good job!

Afterword

Congratulations! You've completed this interview guide, gaining crucial skills and knowledge to design complex systems. Not everyone has the discipline or persistence to achieve what you've accomplished. Take a moment to recognize your efforts—your dedication will pay off.

Securing your dream role in this fast-evolving field is a journey that requires continuous learning and practice. The more you refine your skills, the more confident you'll become. Keep practicing, and best of luck on your path ahead!

Thank you for purchasing and reading this book. It's readers like you who make our work meaningful. We sincerely hope you found value in these pages.

If you have any comments or questions about the book, feel free to reach out to us at oodbook@bytebytego.com. And if you come across any errors, please let us know so we can improve future editions. Thank you!

Made in the USA
Monee, IL
24 June 2025

19934928R00171